Sue Dengate is a psychology graduate and former high school teacher. As a result of her own children's experiences, she became a food intolerance counsellor with an interest in the effects of foods on children's behaviour, learning and health. In 2001 she completed a 'supermarket tour' around the world, checking food additive use in fifteen countries. Her research concerning behavioural effects of a common bread preservative was published in a medical journal in 2002. Her books *Fed Up*, *Fed Up with Asthma* and *The Failsafe Cookbook* are bestsellers. She and her husband, a food technologist and former research scientist, run the Food Intolerance Network through the website www.fedupwithfoodadditives.info.

GW00535926

Also by Sue Dengate

Fed Up
The Failsafe Cookbook
Fed Up with Asthma

Fed Up
with
ADHD

**How food affects children
and what you can do
about it**

Sue Dengate

RANDOM HOUSE AUSTRALIA

Author's note: *Always read labels: ingredients change!*
For Product Updates go to www.fedupwithfoodadditives.info.

Random House Australia Pty Ltd
20 Alfred Street, Milsons Point, NSW 2061
http://www.randomhouse.com.au

Sydney   New York   Toronto
London   Auckland   Johannesburg

First published by Random House Australia 2004

National Library of Australia
Cataloguing-in-Publication Entry

Dengate, Sue.
Fed up with ADHD.

Bibliography.
Includes index.

ISBN 1 74051 230 8.

1. Attention-deficit hyperactivity disorder – Diet therapy.
2. Attention-deficit hyperactivity disorder – Nutritional
aspects. 3. Food additives – Health aspects. I. Title.
II. Title : Fed up with Attention Deficit Hyperactivity Disorder.

641.5631

Cover photograph by www.comstock.com
Cover design by Darian Causby/Highway 51
Illustrations by Joanne Van Os
Typeset in 11/13 pt Times by Midland Typesetters, Maryborough, Victoria
Printed and bound by Griffin Press, Netley, South Australia

10 9 8 7 6 5 4 3 2 1

Acknowledgements

It's ten years since the publication of my first book about the magic answer for our daughter's ADHD. In response to an avalanche of reader mail, I agreed to update *Different Kids* and I am deeply indebted to my family, especially Rebecca, Matthew, Howard, Arran and Emma for their courage in continuing to share their personal stories to help others.

To the thousands of readers who have shared their tears, triumphs, laughter, questions, recipes and blunders, my heartfelt thanks. I couldn't have done this without you. Special mention goes to Linda Beck, Christine Black, Sue Black, Ingrid Boyle, Susan Bull, Andrea Collins, Moya Connell, Annette Cowie, Sharon Delpol, Robin Fisher, Caroline Francis, Brigid Goodman, Julie Guilfoyle, Megan Gunn, Deborah Halliwell, Dani Hewton, Nicole Howard, Bronwyn Howland, Brenda Hunting, Ann Hurman, Elaine Keely, Carmel Kuhr, Karyn Longford, Janice Marsh, Karen Martin, Jane Moore, Kate Penrose, Tracy Percival, Diane Pracy, Caroline Robertson, Jenny Saal, Jenny Savige, Birgit Setiawan, Andra Somerville, Eleanor Staude, Melita Stevens, Stephanie Stevens, Samantha Tinsley, Bernard and Marie Trudgett, Margie Turner, Erica Waite, Diane Wilson, Jan Wockner, Annette Wyley and members of the failsafe email discussion groups.

And finally, thanks to Joanne Van Os for her cartoons and the team at Random House, especially Roberta Ivers, Lydia Papandrea and Jane Alexander, for their patience and dedication.

Contents

Introduction

Over the last forty years, an increasing number of mothers have discovered that their children don't bring them the joy they expect. Instead, their children are demanding or defiant, forgetful or anxious, irritable or restless. Perhaps they aren't doing well at school, or are difficult to live with. They're all different, but they share one characteristic – they make life hard for their parents and teachers.

At first, experts told us it was our fault. If we couldn't control our children, it was because we weren't firm enough. We just needed to learn better behaviour management. Then they told us that our children had been born with a chemical imbalance in their brain which must be treated with medication. They were encouraged by drug companies which spend millions of dollars a day promoting their products to doctors.

'What about food?' some parents asked. There are hundreds of additives in our food and thousands of chemicals in our air, soil and water which weren't there forty years ago. Funded by the giant food industry, a few experts in the 1970s carried out some studies and concluded that children's behaviour wasn't affected by foods. Those who disagreed were ignored.

The US Food and Drug Administration (FDA) is the world's most powerful food authority. In a booklet co-sponsored by the food industry, the FDA says that food colours don't affect children's behaviour. Independent scientists disagree. There is now overwhelming evidence of the effects of foods on children's behaviour and anyone who says otherwise is out of date.

In 2002, research with Isle of Wight preschoolers found that children could be affected by colours and preservatives whether they had ADHD or not, that avoiding additives could be as effective as some forms of ADHD medication and it was estimated that the prevalence of ADHD might be reduced from 15 to 6 per cent by removing certain additives from the diet. In the following year, when additive-free food was provided for an entire primary school class for two weeks, nearly 60 per cent of the children improved.

Most people talk about diet versus medication for behaviour problems, but the question should really be: *which diet?* There are as many diets as there are allergy clinics. Some are much better than others. This book is about my search: it took me eleven years to find the most effective – and best researched – diet in the world from an allergy clinic in Sydney. I call it the FAILSAFE diet because that's what the diet is: Free of Additives and Low in Salicylates, Amines and Flavour Enhancers.

I had never heard of salicylates but for most children with behaviour problems, salicylates are at least as important as food additives. Salicylates are natural pesticides produced by plants to protect themselves against insects and diseases. We all know that artificial pesticides can affect people, but it is harder to understand that natural pesticides can affect some people too.

Salicylates are in most plant foods such as fruits and vegetables. A group of food chemicals called amines also occur in some fruit and vegetables as well as protein foods such as cheese. Amines may be associated with impulsive and aggressive behaviours in some children. Foods we consider healthy may not necessarily be the best for our children.

Then there are the additives which have crept in to our foods: preservatives, colours or flavour enhancers in foods as basic as our bread and butter. Whether you feed your family junk food or healthy food, you might unknowingly be fuelling your child's behaviour and learning problems. People think they will know if their children are affected by food chemicals because they will see obvious reactions, but that's not what happens. Parents rarely see the connection.

In the US, nearly one child in five is estimated to have developmental, behavioural or learning disabilities such ADHD (attention deficit hyperactivity disorder), developmental co-ordination disorder (DCD), oppositional defiant disorder (ODD), conduct disorder (CD), Asperger's disorder, Tourette's disorder, autism, autistic spectrum disorder (ASD), pervasive developmental disorder (PDD), anxiety, depression or bipolar disorder. Some children don't have any diagnosed disorders, but they can be moody or defiant.

Many of the symptoms of food intolerance overlap with the symptoms of the disorders above. It is possible to have food intolerance by itself or in association with other conditions.

If your child's behaviour is related to food intolerance, then the failsafe diet will take care of the food-related symptoms but you may need other programs such as behaviour management, special education, and motor sensory programs. Parents report that these programs are much more effective once the diet has kicked in.

FOOD INTOLERANCE AND BEHAVIOUR

The quiet ones
· Inattention, forgetfulness, unexplained tiredness, difficulty concentrating · anxiety, depression, panic attacks.
May be diagnosed with inattentive ADHD.

The restless ones
· Irritability · restlessness · inattention · difficulty settling to sleep, restless legs, night waking, night terrors.
May be diagnosed with hyperactive ADHD.

The defiant ones
· Losing temper · arguing with adults · refusing requests and defying rules · deliberately annoying others · blaming others · touchy and easily annoyed · angry and resentful · spiteful and vindictive.
May be diagnosed with oppositional defiant disorder (ODD).

Other symptoms of food intolerance include low muscle tone in muscles associated with coordination, handwriting, reading, speech, bladder and bowel control and ailments such as headaches, rashes and asthma.

It makes sense to get rid of the problems caused by foods before deciding which management strategies or medication to use for the symptoms that are left – if any.

Part of this story appeared in my first book, *Different Kids*, which was about my search for the magic answer to my daughter's problems. Thousands of families found it was their magic answer too, and you can read some of their stories on my website www.fedupwithfoodadditives.info, like this report from a teacher about her Asperger's son:

> 'He is thinking more clearly, acting more rationally, is more cooperative, is more confident socially and generally just a nicer kid to be around. I wish the parents of the students at my work were fully informed of the benefits that the failsafe diet can have both for the child and on family life.'

Many readers wrote to ask me 'How is your daughter now?' This book tells the story of how our children and others with behaviour and learning problems have been helped to become motivated and happy young adults, despite authorities who continue to deny and ignore the harmful effects of food chemicals.

Australia has the third highest use of food additives – and ADHD medication – in the world, after the USA and Canada, and the use of additives continues to increase. During my quest two more additives have quietly become widespread throughout our food supply, with devastating results for some consumers. Parents who want to protect their children from the harmful effects of food chemicals must do it themselves. To find out how, please read on . . .

part one

The Story

1 Rebecca 0–2

My first baby, Rebecca, was born in Christchurch, New Zealand, in 1982. When she was four days old I overheard a nurse saying, 'Come and have a look at Mrs Dengate's baby, she's a real peach,' and I glowed with pride. Two nurses bent over the crib.

'She looks like a two-year-old, the way she sleeps,' mused one. It was true. Rebecca had none of the clenched-fist tension of other newborns. She lay sprawled in what I thought at the time was a relaxed posture, but know now was an indication of low muscle tone.

I also noticed that the top fold of one of Rebecca's ears appeared to be stuck down. It was barely noticeable unless you looked closely. I had worried about possible birth defects since a camping trip in early pregnancy when I ate a freshly caught fish before finding a dumped herbicide container in the water upstream. Some versions of this herbicide were used as defoliants in the Vietnam War, so a tiny ear malformation seemed nothing compared to what I had feared.

These were to be the first of many clues which would be misinterpreted and rationalised. We had no idea then that it would take eleven gruelling years for us to find out what was affecting our beautiful daughter.

The six-week siege

'It's a six-week siege,' our friends had told us, about looking after a new baby. 'After that you start getting into a routine.' Six weeks turned into eight, then ten, and I started to feel mystified about the easy babies described in the baby book. In fact, we ended up feeling that our siege lasted for years, but in those first four months, things were desperate. There were always heaps of unfolded washing, unmade beds and piles of washing up. I was always exhausted. My husband Howard worked a full day as a research scientist then came home to a mess and started cooking and cleaning up.

Rebecca spent a lot of time crying. We carried her around and waited for her to become the settled baby promised by our child-care book. Our doctor prescribed a drug, now considered not safe, to help with colic.

A friend advised me to watch what I ate. I just loved the sweet New Zealand cherries, apricots and plums. 'I'm not going to stop eating fruit at the beginning of the summer fruit season,' I protested, but trial and error showed that fruit obviously did affect Rebecca. Since we paid for each lapse with a couple of hours of inconsolable screaming, I was motivated to stick to my limited diet and by the time Rebecca was four months old I found I had a more settled baby if I avoided some vegetables and all fruit except bananas.

Howard had hay fever, so we knew we were considered to be an allergy-risk family. I considered myself free of allergies and

Behaviour problems are linked to food intolerance not food allergy		
	Food allergy	**Food intolerance**
How many?	rare	common
Family history	asthma, eczema, hay fever	migraine, irritable bowel, behaviour
Symptoms	itching, swelling, rash, breathing difficulties, diarrhoea	wide range – includes the above, same as allergy, and more (see p. 155)
Timing	within 30 minutes	can be delayed up to three days, effects can last for hours, days or weeks
Which foods?	usually only one or two, most commonly in Australia: milk, soy, egg, peanut, fish	a wide range of foods, for example, salicylates in fruits, vegetables, herbs, flavours
Identification	often obvious	very difficult
Diagnosis	laboratory tests, skin prick test	elimination diet

was surprised when I developed hay fever that year for the first time. I knew very little about allergies and had never heard of food intolerance.

'Keep breastfeeding,' the breastfeeding counsellor told me. 'She's likely to develop more problems if switched to formula.'

'All babies sleep, don't they?'

Food related sleep disturbance can vary from difficulty falling asleep or frequent night waking to night terrors or sleepwalking. Of course, we didn't know what we were dealing with, and I had thought that sleep came naturally to babies, but even when she was obviously exhausted Rebecca would not drop off to sleep. I have always been the sort of person who falls asleep when my head hits the pillow, and I need a good night's sleep to function. Exhausted by the infectious hepatitis I developed when Rebecca was seven weeks old, I followed the rule of *sleep when your baby sleeps*. I would feed Rebecca to sleep then fall into a deep sleep myself, only to be woken by her cries half an hour later. At night she woke often and was becoming less rather than more settled.

Before our marriage I had spent three years backpacking around the world. The highlight of my travels was the seven months I spent in the mountains of Nepal, trekking more than 2,000 kilometres, mostly alone. During these treks I often stayed with families in one-roomed huts, unthinkingly observing the mothers breastfeeding, carrying and sleeping with their babies. I was an only child of older parents, so the mothers in Nepal provided me with my first role models. 'I can't remember the mothers in Nepal having these problems,' I thought. 'The babies were always carried around. They slept with their mothers, and the whole family went to bed soon after dark, so they weren't left alone.'

Survival

Howard had always had difficulty getting to sleep and getting back to sleep when woken. 'Rebecca must have inherited this difficulty sleeping,' we thought, so we worked out a system which would enable us to survive. I would feed Rebecca to sleep on a double mattress in her room, start the night off with Howard, then move to Rebecca's bed at the next waking. If she didn't fall asleep at the breast I would spend hours rocking her stroller across a ridge in the kitchen floor, singing grimly.

Rebecca's wakefulness was worsened by teething. 'We didn't know our daughter had her first tooth until we heard it clinking on the spoon,' a young doctor friend commented. By contrast, Rebecca started teething early and we were plagued by sleepless nights and daytime grumpiness for each tooth. My friend was more sympathetic after her third child experienced teething problems but how could she be expected to know what I was dealing with? My child was difficult in every major area of child rearing. I always felt there was something wrong with my skills as a mother. I found myself constantly trying to explain why Rebecca was so fussy or difficult, and often felt inadequate and embarrassed that she wasn't easier, like other children.

Controlled crying

By the time Rebecca was nine months, she was waking at least five times every night. Our doctor suggested teething gel and paracetamol. We also tried controlled crying. It was very traumatic for all of us, and it didn't work. Rebecca had far more stamina for screaming than we had for listening and I doubt if she would ever have fallen asleep exhausted.

In desperation I went to my doctor again. He prescribed some medicine. 'It's a mild sedative,' he explained. We looked forward to having a good night's sleep at last. The medicine had the reverse effect. Rebecca spent the next four hours leaping around, laughing and generally having a great time. This was from eleven at night until three in the morning. Other mothers of food intolerant children have experienced the same paradoxical effects of medicines intended to help children to sleep. I felt we had turned to medicine as a last resort and it had failed us utterly. I interpreted this to mean that our doctor had nothing more to offer us and felt alone and desperate.

In her first winter, Rebecca had a number of colds which led to ear infections. This, too, is a classic symptom of food intolerance, although I didn't know that. On one occasion, when Rebecca was ten months old, I gave her some paracetamol and took her into a warm bath with me. Afterwards, I lay her on my bed briefly while I dressed. When I turned around she was lying motionless on the bed, eyes closed.

Panicking, we called the duty doctor. He quickly examined her. 'This child is asleep,' he said, perplexed. Howard and I looked at each other. So far she had never fallen asleep without such a huge effort that the possibility hadn't crossed our minds. The doctor obviously thought we were very peculiar. He didn't know Rebecca. We laugh about it now, saying, 'The only time she fell asleep on her own we called the doctor.' But living with a child who couldn't go to sleep was no joke.

Howard's children

One day I was talking about our sleeping problems in a mothers' group and a mother said, 'That's interesting. I only know of one other family who have found controlled crying didn't work.' She mentioned the name of the family. I was astonished. She was talking about biological children of Howard's living in another city.

Before our marriage, Howard had been approached by friends who shared his university background and love of the outdoors. Desperate to have children, the husband's infertility meant that their only option was donor insemination. Like many other couples they objected to an anonymous donor. Howard had agreed to father two children for them and to keep this secret. 'I told them I didn't like the idea of secrecy,' he explained to me, 'but they insisted they didn't want the children to know.' After our marriage we retained our friendship with the family for a while, but were advised by a marriage counsellor to break the connection for the children's sake. 'Children can pick up on hidden emotions,' she said. 'They will sense there is something going on and won't be able to work out what it is. They'll be confused.' So Howard's donated children were growing up unknown to us.

I told Howard what I had heard at the playgroup: 'One of

those children must have a sleeping problem just like Rebecca's.' We were to remember this many years later.

The entertainer

When Rebecca was awake she needed constant attention. We decided that this was because she was bright, as she always seemed alert and welcomed new playthings, but I found I could get very little done during the day unless I carried her everywhere, so she spent most of the time in a frontpack and from six months in a backpack. Although the backpack was physically easier for me, by this time I had to be doing something reasonably interesting or energetic to keep her from complaining.

The best way to keep Rebecca happy was to give her undivided attention. She would be charming and delightful. Left to her own devices she would find adventure, which soon involved gigantic messes like emptying drawer contents, or unsafe practices like crawling down our stairs. If confined, she would be restless and grizzly.

By the time Rebecca was six months old I had realised that if I stayed at home with my baby, she would drive me mad. The only way I could cope with her was to keep her busy. 'She needs lots of stimulation,' I told Howard, and spent my time providing it. We had a campervan, and I would spend my days going from one diversion to the next. When Rebecca fell asleep I would park in a quiet place and sleep too. It is hard to find places to entertain a young baby in a cold climate, but I went to everything on offer – mothers' groups, playgroups and visits with friends.

'How do other mothers have time for a cup of tea and a chat?' I thought. I often felt lonely because I was always too busy looking after my daughter.

Into everything

Once Rebecca attained mobility at about nine months I had to watch her every minute in an unconfined space or she would disappear. At the doctor's surgery other children investigated the toybox while Rebecca headed for the stairs, down the hall, into the doctors' rooms. I spent the whole time entertaining or retrieving her. At playgroup I wondered if I was overprotecting her, but if I wasn't there constantly she would be out the door or trying something too big and dangerous for her, ending up in frustration, tears or a squabble. Setting her up at something safe like playdough would last about two minutes, unless I played with her.

'Isn't she cute,' everyone said.

'I love the way she gets into everything,' one mother told me, after I had spent a meeting continually jumping up to prevent Rebecca from reaching the gas heater beside the guest speaker. The other children spent the meeting sitting at their mothers' feet, playing quietly.

When the weather was fine I spent hours walking along the riverbanks not far from our home, feeding the ducks and going to the Botanic Gardens. It was a good way to keep Rebecca happy and entertained, to keep constantly on the move, but I took a long time to recover from the hepatitis I had caught at Rebecca's birth and would usually be exhausted the next day.

The libraries in Christchurch had safe areas with beanbags and toys for babies and I spent many hours with Rebecca every day reading books because it gave me a chance to sit down. Even by six weeks I had found that if I read aloud Rebecca seemed soothed, presumably by the sound of my voice, so right from the beginning I started 'reading' to her, as it was something I could do lying down. By the time she was nine months, I was reading her at least twenty books a day. I had discovered that this was one of the most relaxing ways for me to entertain her.

In the car

Travelling in the car presented a problem. We had tried to keep up our habit of going to the mountains every second weekend and on holidays. If Rebecca was awake, I had to play with her to keep her interested. When she moved into a baby car seat, she sat in the front between us, and I always had a tray and a changing selection of toys plus books and snacks to entertain her, otherwise she squirmed and cried endlessly. Rattles and teething rings became blocks and puzzles as she grew. Occasionally she would have a brief sleep. A long trip was hard work and required frequent stops. By the end of her first year, we knew every playground between our house and the Mount Cook National Park.

Some friends recommended their method of leaving home at 5 p.m., eating an evening meal after an hour, then letting the toddler sleep the rest of the way. We tried it once. Rebecca was still awake at 11 p.m., exclaiming in wonder at the street lights when we passed through towns.

'My child isn't hyperactive'

When Rebecca was nearly one, I left her with my closest friend Robin for a few hours. Unlike me, Robin is an organised person. When I called to collect Rebecca she was looking rather hassled. 'We've been making muesli,' she said.

'I don't know how you do it,' I exclaimed. 'I've given up trying to do anything in the kitchen with Rebecca, because she makes mess far faster than I can cope with it. The place ends up a shambles.'

'She needs a lot more attention than Rosemary,' Robin agreed. I could guess what had happened. Robin would have installed the girls on chairs while she fetched the rolled oats, dried fruit, nuts and seeds. Robin's daughter Rosemary would watch the proceedings with interest and pour a cupful of ingredients into the mixture when asked whereas Rebecca, if she wasn't watched every minute, would grab handfuls of whatever she could reach and empty it into the sink, on the benches, the floor, everywhere except the appropriate container, losing interest and wandering off to create havoc in another room half-way through. She created so much work it wasn't worth the effort of including her.

Soon after this we had a visit from a bachelor friend who also knew Robin and had not seen us since Rebecca's birth. The place was clean because I had finally admitted I couldn't cope and had hired a cleaner, and for once Rebecca was asleep. Looking around our tidy lounge room he noticed one small box of toys in the corner. 'It's easy to see you have a baby now,' he chuckled. Howard and I exchanged looks. If he had arrived on a normal day there would have been toys all over the floor, piles of unfolded washing on the table, and Rebecca would have interrupted every sentence.

'I hear you've got a hyperactive daughter,' he continued. Affronted, I answered with the words that I hear now so often from so many mothers, 'Oh, no, she's not really *hyperactive.*' When I look back I try to think what motivated me to say that.

'I know what a hyperactive child is,' I thought. 'It's a little boy who runs around a lot, makes a lot of noise, is disobedient, unpleasant, aggressive, and generally to be avoided. My child isn't like that.'

Hyperactivity, now called ADHD, was so new in Australia and New Zealand that I didn't know much about it except what the name implied. Mothers often assume their children are not hyperactive because they can be attentive in a one-to-one situation, and the common idea of a hyperactive child is one who never stops.

IN THE BEGINNING

'In my general paediatric practice in Jackson, Tennessee (population 50,000) in the 1950s, my partners and I were "the only game in town". There were no other full-time paediatricians and only a rare family practitioner. Yet we only saw an occasional hyperactive kid . . . In the 1970s, I saw so many hyperactive children that I kept records . . .'

Dr William G Crook (see p. 242).

My British child-rearing book was silent on the subject. Spurred on by our friend's comments, I found an American child-rearing book which described how many ADHD children started off as fussy babies. 'Perhaps this *is* it,' I thought.

The author observed that mothers react to these babies in one of two ways: immersion mothers raise the child themselves, and are constantly attentive to the child's needs; escape mothers return to work and often leave the child with others. He recommended immersion mothering. 'That's what I'm doing,' I thought, and then he went on to talk about consulting psychologists for behaviour modification and pediatricians for medication. 'My child isn't as bad as that,' I decided. The book also advised avoiding highly processed foods.

'I knew nothing about additives'

Fast food wasn't common in New Zealand then. Most people still cooked for themselves. Howard and I were eating a mainly vegetarian, natural, wholemeal, low-sugar diet high in fruit and vegetables. We bought very few processed foods, although while pregnant I had started eating a vegetable relish on my sandwiches. It never occurred to me that it might contain an artificial food colouring called tartrazine. I knew nothing about food additives.

It would be eight years before a group of Australian researchers showed that tartrazine could cause irritability, restlessness, inattention and sleep disturbance in children – exactly the problems I was dealing with every day. Another group would show that salicylates in fruits and vegetables could cause the same problems. These food chemicals can pass through breastmilk and affect babies.

At the time, however, I was determined to be unruffled about food, which seems rather ironic now. When Rebecca was first introduced to solid foods, she ate well but as her range of foods widened, she became more fussy and unreliable about eating meals.

I shall never forget the first children's Christmas party at the playgroup we attended. A trestle table had been set up with a tablecloth and party foods. Rebecca was thirteen months old and it was the first time she had ever come across party food or sweets. The other children ate and then moved away to play. Rebecca remained at the table, alone, for the whole two hours, stuffing herself with all these new treats. She was obviously having a wonderful time and everyone said, 'Isn't she cute?', but I was embarrassed. Why was my child making such a pig of herself?

I decided it must be because I had been denying her sweet foods, so we started eating ice-cream for dessert. This was a disaster. It seemed to establish a craving in her and all she did was whine and fuss endlessly for more, so I stopped buying it. By now she was not eating at all well, still breastfeeding and showing no signs of stopping, but I was determined not to let food become a battlefield so I more or less ignored it.

The three Rs

We led a haphazard sort of life. Howard was easily bored by routine and preferred spontaneity. Because we were always tired, we always slept as long as we could until Rebecca woke us, with the result that he worked different hours every day, we ate meals at odd times, and frequently went out on the spur of the moment.

Howard and I share a passionate love for the bush, mountains, wilderness and getting away from it all. We started hiking again, with Rebecca in the backpack, and often went for day walks or camping for the weekend in the mountains, sleeping in the van, the tent or a hikers' hut. Over the Christmas break we took Rebecca on a three-day hike among the golden grasslands, beech forests and snowcapped mountains that would become famous in the *Lord of the Rings* movies.

She loved the constant change, riding high in the backpack, new places to explore and the undivided attention of two adults. Like Howard, Rebecca thrived on variety, never wanting to stop, always wanting to do more. Looking back I can see that our life would have been much easier if I had established a firm routine early on. The spontaneity was fun and exciting but management of eating and sleeping would have been easier. *Routine*, *regularity*, and *repetition* are the best way to raise difficult children. We had none of those.

A move

When Rebecca was just over one year old we decided to move to a house that was easier to live in. This was the first of many moves inspired by the need to find an easier place to live with a difficult child. Still constantly exhausted, we wanted a house that was quiet, so we could sleep – Rebecca permitting – and a yard that was flat, so we could drive our car up to the house. We had had enough of lugging bundles up and down steps. So we said goodbye to our beautiful view of the Southern Alps and moved into an old house on nearly half a hectare of land bordered by ancient poplars. Here we established a sort of suburban 'good life'. Howard, with his boundless energy, cleared away old fallen trees and planted rhododendron gardens, a pine forest, fruit trees and a vegetable garden. It was always easier being outside with Rebecca, and now that there was no danger of her falling off a terrace we had more freedom.

I continued to take Rebecca on many outings but I was beginning to notice that she was quite different from her little friends in a playground. She spent her time dashing from one piece of equipment to the next but was reluctant to spend much time on each. My parents commented that they thought she was timid on the swings. Timid was not a word I would ever have applied to Rebecca, but I agreed that her attitude was unusual.

All this time I was taking Rebecca for her regular checks to the child health nurse. Rebecca was learning to walk and run. I couldn't pinpoint any specific worries about her coordination. I had already assumed that, like her father, she would be poor at ball games. The child health nurse never seemed to notice anything unusual. 'Any problems?' the nurse would ask me.

'She seems to have a lot of pain with teething,' I'd say, or 'She wakes a lot at night.'

It was impossible for me to give a verbal picture of exactly why Rebecca was such hard work. She didn't do anything particularly different from other children, just more of it, or less of it, or at the wrong times. She was meeting all her developmental milestones such as sitting, crawling and walking at the right times. The few times I did try to explain to other people that I was scarcely coping, I was greeted by scepticism and ended up feeling foolish. The problem behaviours seemed so trivial when I talked about them, although it was the total sum which made life so difficult. I felt as if it was my fault I found it so hard to cope. Rebecca was a charming little girl if I gave her my undivided attention all the time. There just wasn't time to do anything else.

The hard-work holiday

Howard and I were discovering that holidays were hard work unless we had some help with Rebecca. A neighbouring school-girl named Donna had started babysitting for us, and now she started coming with us on weekends away to the mountains. The three of us would take it in turns to give our undivided attention to Rebecca. It also helped us to have my parents come from Australia to share the load.

When Rebecca was eighteen months old we went on a three-week trip with them to the Cook Islands. My parents doted on Rebecca, who was their only grandchild. They were more than happy to devote large amounts of time to her, which was what Rebecca enjoyed most. She spent hours walking on stepping stones around the hotel pool holding a grandparent's hand.

One American tourists asked my mother, 'Is that your grand-daughter? She's a doll, a real doll.' It was continual comments like this which made me think, 'She must be all right. How can there be anything wrong with this child?' Yet sometimes Rebecca was so restless and demanding that I needed all my self-control to avoid losing my temper.

My only goal was a good night's sleep. Like any other parents, we loved our adorable little daughter with all our hearts and thought she was the most beautiful and intelligent child in the world. Although I could barely cope with caring for her, we had not accepted that there could be anything really 'wrong' with our sweet little girl. None of the experts – the doctor, the breastfeeding counsellor, the child health nurse, the authors of parenting books – had been able to help us understand or manage our problems with Rebecca. I feel sad that, with the knowledge I have now, we could have enjoyed a calm and settled child during those first two years.

2 Beyond the terrible twos

When we moved back to Australia because of Howard's new job, Rebecca was nearly two and a half. We had survived the fussy baby and impulsive toddler stages and were launched into the terrible twos, a stage when most children are learning to say 'no'. By the time we were established in a rented house in Wagga Wagga in south-western NSW, I was finding her very difficult.

In an attempt to meet people, I went to every parents' group I could find and was lucky enough to make friends at playgroup straight away. The first breastfeeding association meeting I attended was quite crowded and Rebecca was overwhelmed by all the people. She refused to join the other children playing in the playroom but wouldn't keep still in the room where the mothers were having a discussion. Eventually she disappeared for a while.

'Have you seen your daughter?' one of the mothers asked me with a smile. People still thought she was cute. She had opened a packet of chocolate biscuits on the morning tea table and had taken one bite out of each biscuit. If she stayed with me she was noisy and restless but she refused to stay in the playroom without me. The only way to keep her out of mischief was to play with her in the playroom, although I wanted to be with the mothers. A counsellor found me there and had a sympathetic welcoming chat, for which I was grateful although I was really gritting my teeth and wanting to strangle my daughter.

I tried several more meetings. 'It's no good. I can't go if I have to take Rebecca,' I decided. We still had playgroup, the park, the library and friends.

One day an article on hyperactivity appeared in a parents' magazine. I read and re-read it and discussed it with Howard. 'She hasn't got all those symptoms and she's not like that all the time.' We were always confused by how charming and delightful Rebecca could be at her best.

The never-ending party

I was finding that what children ate in Australia was quite different from what we fed Rebecca in New Zealand. Here, every day seemed like a party: sweets, cakes, ice-creams and processed snack foods were constantly available. Rebecca's diet had suddenly changed. 'She's eating very badly,' I fretted.

'Don't worry,' Howard reassured me. 'Children burn up so much energy at that age, they can tolerate more fat and sugar than adults.' This was a view backed up by a popular Australian pediatrician who dismissed the idea that hyperactive children might react to food additives. So I ignored Rebecca's poor diet.

First mention of salicylates

One new friend kept telling me about her nephew who was on a diet low in salicylates. I had never heard of salicylates. In retrospect I can see she was observing my child's behaviour and trying to get the message across. I was totally unreceptive. When my friend told me that most fruits contain salicylates I was horrified. Life without fruit was unimaginable. 'I'm glad we don't have to worry about that,' I told her.

I couldn't have been more wrong, but it would take me another eight years to find that out. Rebecca was now three; it was 1985, and Australian research about salicylates had just been published. But it takes many years for the results of research to find their way into doctors' surgeries.

FROM THE MEDICAL JOURNALS

'This is the most comprehensive set of data on food salicylates yet published . . .'

Swain AR and others, 'Salicylates in foods', *J American Dietetic Association* 1985;85(8):950–960.

'Of 86 children who experienced improvement, nearly three-quarters reacted to double-blind challenge with salicylates . . .'

Swain AR and others, 'Salicylates, oligoantigenic diets and behaviour', *Lancet* 1985;ii:41–42.

Meanwhile, I was finding Rebecca's behaviour impossible and there were so many areas of conflict that I tried to concentrate on a few and reduce the battlefield. She refused to get dressed, so I took her out in her pyjamas. It didn't seem to bother her. She refused to have her hair washed, so I had it cut very short, which was a battle, and left it unwashed for a month. She was an expert at getting her clothes dirty in no time at all. I think children should be encouraged to play creatively and not have to worry about their clothes, but Rebecca had paint all over every item of clothing she owned. Getting her to change was so much trouble that I didn't bother.

We bought a television for the first time. Rebecca would not even watch *Playschool* unless I sat with her. 'Perhaps it's because she's not in the habit of watching television,' I thought.

'Creativity'

I found an Early Childhood Education student to replace our Christchurch babysitter. 'I have minded lots of kids and your little girl is the brightest two-year-old I've ever met. She's so creative. Look at this,' she said, and showed me a drawing Rebecca had done and pointed out why it was so advanced in terms of child development. We had always thought that Rebecca was very bright, articulate and creative. It was good to hear it from someone who was in a position to make comparisons.

After that, when Rebecca preferred to paint herself or the furniture rather than paper, I put it down to 'creativity'. At playgroups I was finding that if all the children were doing something one way, Rebecca was bound to do it differently, and she never joined in the group activities.

Rebecca's curly hair was often admired by strangers. The frequent compliments we received about her appearance helped me to feel good about my daughter at times when I was struggling to enjoy her.

I was now pregnant again which was making me very tired and I started enforcing a quiet time after lunch. I knew Rebecca would never sleep but she had to play by herself for at least half an hour, which she learned to do, especially if she could spend the time drawing.

Choosing isolation

Howard likes to live in unconventional houses with space for a garden, privacy, a view and quiet. For affordable houses that comply with this list, there's always a catch: the first was built on the side of an absurdly steep hill, the second had noisy neighbours. For our third, the catch was distance. We fell in love with a house on over a hectare of land, surrounded by farmland, 20 kilometres out of Wagga Wagga.

'How am I going to cope with living a half-hour drive from shops, friends and playgroup?' I worried.

'I worry about that, too,' Howard answered. 'Especially if we get another baby who doesn't sleep and you're always tired.'

'We couldn't possibly get a worse sleeper than Rebecca,' I replied, optimistic to the last.

Howard got to work at our new house, putting in a watering system, establishing an orchard, a vegetable garden and building a henhouse.

After we settled in Howard said, 'I'd like to start going away every second weekend again, the way we did in New Zealand. That's the part of my life that I enjoy most.' We liked camping with Rebecca because she always went to sleep better in the tent, perhaps from the fresh air and all the exercise, and she liked us all to be together. A few times we had tried a caravan and she drove me mad in about ten minutes. It was my idea of hell, to be confined in a small space with her.

A Christmas surprise

Our son Arran was born three weeks early at 9 a.m. on Christmas morning. Despite having newborn jaundice, Arran was a healthy baby and the pediatrician commented on his unusually good muscle tone. I had more trouble establishing breastfeeding with him than I'd had with Rebecca and when we got home he would throw up frequently and noisily. Mothers often have problems breastfeeding food intolerant babies. Changing what the mother eats can make a big difference although health professionals are only just starting to realise that.

Finally I learned always to feed Arran lying down, and only one side at a time. It was impossible to feed him while reading to a squirming three-year-old, so Rebecca was banished to another room, armed with textas and paper, while Arran fed. These were good times for her. She did a lot of creative work by herself. I had hoped Arran would settle down after he started on solids but he seemed to get worse.

'How will she manage school?'

To give myself a break, I tried Rebecca at a preschool class for three-year-olds. She didn't enjoy it and I had to stay with her for a long time to help her to settle in to each session. After a few weeks the teacher asked me to leave her behind even though she was screaming. When I returned she was still screaming and the teacher said, 'I've never had a child do that before. They always settle down after the mother goes.' I gave up. 'We'll try again next year,' I said.

Meanwhile, friends were starting to make comments about Rebecca's behaviour. She was not as compliant as their children and played well in a one-to-one situation but not in a group. 'How is she going to get on at school?' one friend asked me. I was worried too, but rationalising as usual, I explained that I thought Rebecca was more creative than most children and needed artistic freedom. In a way, I was right. Children with behaviour problems can usually survive happily in an unstructured situation. Often they come to grief only when they are expected to conform to rigid rules in the classroom.

We continued to go away on weekends, waking to snow several times before Arran was six months. At first we carried one child each in a backpack, later towing them in a home-made sled. In bad weather we took turns at cross-country skiing and minding the children in the campervan. These were my favourite times, alone in the softly falling snow and fading light.

'Where do you get the energy?' our friends used to say. Howard was the driving force. He believes life is too short to waste a minute. I share his passion for the bush and remote places but needed more quiet times. I couldn't keep up with his and Rebecca's pace and always needed more sleep, but it was easier to go camping with Rebecca than to stay at home.

The lull before the storm

During the summer holidays, when Arran turned one and Rebecca was just four, we camped on the south coast of NSW near a lagoon set in sand dunes. We were pleased to have managed a relaxing holiday by ourselves and were unduly optimistic about the coming year.

During this holiday we began a blitz on saying 'please' and 'thank you'. It would take us about three years of persistent effort to get Rebecca to say these reliably. Arran learned in about three weeks. This summarises for me the size of the problem we were up against. Expecting Rebecca to acquire common social skills through observation was unrealistic, including basic skills such as washing of hands and waiting in turn. I estimated that if I needed to remind Arran about something several hundred times, for Rebecca it would take several thousand times. This represented a drastic increase in the parenting workload which could have been avoided. She learned eventually, but why bother? It would have been easier to change what she ate.

When Rebecca started preschool at the age of four, I joined the local breastfeeding association as a trainee counsellor. After struggling though several levels of assignments, I gave up, having learned a great deal about telephone counselling which would help me later. I was envious that other women seemed to have so much more time and energy than I did, as I was always exhausted and found caring for my children very demanding.

Hard times

From the winter of Rebecca's fourth year to the end of first term at preschool in her fifth year turned out to be the hardest time in my life. The terrible twos had turned into the terrible threes and now the terrible fours. Despite a superb teacher, preschool was not the success that we had hoped for. Rebecca was with her little friends but didn't take to it the way they did – she had good days and bad days for no reason I could see.

She was frequently demanding. I still found it hard to get her to do anything I wanted. I thought of her as being 'no-ey'. She was always restless, a fussy eater, had difficulty sleeping and couldn't entertain herself. Nothing was ever enough for her, she always wanted more, whether it was attention, games with parents, toys or treats, and I often heard myself saying to her, 'Don't be so *difficult*, Rebecca.'

Although I could happily spend days at home with Arran, I still found I had to take Rebecca on outings or arrange for friends to play. The mothers of her two closest friends and I had formed a threesome and this was hard on Rebecca: she could play reasonably with one other child but if there were three children she would always be the one left out. I felt constantly hurt by her disappointment. I clung to my belief that she was bright and creative, but one of my friends was openly sceptical about Rebecca's ability to manage at school.

At about thirteen months Arran had stopped gaining weight and the clinic sister was worried about him. He'd had constant diarrhoea since a gastric bug at ten months and was waking about ten times a night so I was always tired. I slept with him on the double mattress on the floor and Rebecca slept in the same room. She still had difficulty getting to sleep and often woke at night, so I felt as if I was working day and night. I had heard of sleep deprivation being used as a form of torture and felt that this was what I was going through. I was always desperately tired and each day was a struggle for survival. For many years, every time I saw the first star of the evening, I made the same wish: 'Please let me have a good night's sleep.' But I never did.

Asthma

During that winter Howard, Rebecca and I were all diagnosed with asthma. We all had puffers, and Rebecca would get alarming exercise asthma when we went skiing or did any exercise. I was unhappy at the thought of having an asthmatic child who was becoming increasingly reliant on medication, but there didn't seem to be any alternative and it was not important compared to our problems with Rebecca's behaviour.

At the preschool the children were encouraged to bring cakes to share on their birthday, which meant that there was a birthday cake nearly every week. One Thursday someone brought a cake decorated with bright orange icing and I will never forget the long weekend that followed. We were confined to the house by bleak weather. Rebecca became progressively noisy, restless, rude and aggressive until I felt as if I was living with a wild animal. I wished I could chain her to a tree in the orchard and walk away.

'She just needs a good smack'

We were finding that we would get into a spiral of negativity with Rebecca, an escalating war of hostility and criticism, which could go on for weeks. 'She won't take "no" for an answer,' I fumed. Howard and I had previously decided to avoid smacking as a punishment because it teaches children how to win arguments by physical force. It was hard in a crisis to think of some other way of handling an outburst and tempting to do what so many people recommended: 'She just needs a good smack.'

We were finding that our decision was often severely tested by Rebecca's outrageously disobedient behaviour but the few times we lost our temper and smacked her made things worse. We would feel wc had lost contact with our daughter and she would become even more hostile and aggressive.

Backing off

The only way out of it was to back off, to stop the criticism, find something to praise, and to be positive. This was a frustrating and almost impossible task when she was behaving like a little monster. It was like tip-toeing around a volcano. 'I feel as if I'm biting my tongue until it bleeds,' said Howard. But it was the only way to restore some kind of family harmony.

'You are so good at backing off. I don't know how you can do it,' my mother said. 'My instinct is to get in there and lay down the law, but you're right. That doesn't work. It only makes things worse.'

Years later, I found that experts agreed. An authoritarian approach, especially smacking, with oppositionally defiant children does make them worse and is likely to lead to aggression, violence, crime and drug abuse. It is really important to use a calm approach but much easier to change what they eat.

Howard's job involved business trips and social functions which he was obliged to attend. I handled the business trips very badly. Without an adult to share the load, I was exhausted and uptight by the time he returned, which was to a messy house and a wife who was hoarse from screaming. The socialising was even worse. I felt that as his wife I ought to accompany him, remember everyone's names and make interesting conversation. Instead, I was far too tired to go out at night. If I did make the effort, I felt under-confident and inadequate due to extreme sleep deprivation. I had gained a lot of weight, found shopping with the children impossible, had few 'going-out' clothes and felt very unattractive.

About this time, Arran had a record night of about twenty-five wakings. He suffered from chronic diarrhoea and was starting to look like a failure-to-thrive baby. The long years of broken nights, insufficient sleep and Rebecca's draining behaviour problems were wearing me down.

EFFECTS OF FATIGUE

'The stress of combat and lack of sleep affect soldiers so badly that after a week they perform worse than if they were drunk or sedated, according to a US Army study . . . "Their performance was actually worse than if they were legally drunk".'

Sabo E, 'Soldiers "drunk" with fatigue', *New Scientist*, 12/4/2003, 9.

I was so tired all the time I found the long drive home from town very difficult. The road seemed to get longer in front of me. I felt as if I was hallucinating from exhaustion and worried about running off the road. Sometimes I felt that deliberately driving into a tree might be an easy way to put an end to my problems. Howard was concerned about my safety. He confided his fears to our doctor who gave me a lecture about depression and wanted to prescribe tricyclic antidepressants for me.

'The only problem is that they will make you tired,' he said.

I couldn't imagine being any more exhausted than I was, and wondered how he thought I was going to cope with the children. I refused to take medication but agreed to go to counselling. Howard and I had a few sessions together while a friend minded the children. We quickly realised that we needed time together without the children and determined to make a bigger effort to find a babysitter.

Buying an isolated house in the country had been a big mistake in terms of support for me. One of our neighbours commented, 'Things go in cycles in the country. You've moved in at the wrong time. Everyone around here has teenagers.' Most of these were away at university or boarding school, but we eventually found some twins who were happy to come and mind our children.

Once or twice a week they would come for a few hours. I was too tired to want to get dressed up and drive into town, so we would walk and chat on the quiet country roads and hill tops around our valley. These times became very special. I particularly enjoyed evening walks through the open countryside, the silence, the huge star-spangled sky spread out above us and scattered farmhouse lights in the distance.

Food colouring

The clinic sister was my saviour during this difficult time, listening sympathetically when I took Arran to be weighed. Eventually, she suggested I see a community dietitian, as I was beginning to feel that some of our problems may be food-related. Here I had some luck. I saw a dietitian who had worked with the Royal Prince Alfred Hospital (RPAH) Allergy Unit in Sydney.

'What does Arran have to eat?' she asked. I told her. Most of it was all right. She wasn't happy about the processed fish fingers which both children enjoyed and when I got to orange-flavoured breakfast drink, she looked at me in horror.

'You'll have to cut that out,' she said. Since Arran, like Rebecca, seemed sensitive to oranges, I had been giving the children the same packaged drink we used to take hiking. This seems inconceivable to me now as the drink contains tartrazine yellow food colouring. I still didn't understand the effects of food additives.

I thought if my children were affected by food additives, I would notice an obvious reaction, but the truth is, parents usually don't. The effects just seemed to be part of their normal behaviour. When I removed food colours and some preservatives from Arran's diet he started sleeping through the night straight away, although he still had diarrhoea.

FROM THE MEDICAL JOURNALS

'The younger children had constant crying, tantrums, irritability, restlessness and severe sleep disturbance, and were described as "disruptive", "easily distracted and excited", "high as a kite" and "out of control". Their parents were exhausted through lack of sleep and the constant demands of their children, who were unable to be comforted or controlled. The older children were described as "irritable", "aimlessly active", "lacking self-control", "whiney and unhappy", and "like a bear with a sore head".'

Rowe KS and Rowe KJ, 'Synthetic food coloring and behavior', *J Pediatrics* 1994;125:691–698.

In retrospect, I wish the dietitian had explained more to me about the effects of food intolerance and how to use the RPAH elimination diet, in case avoiding additives wasn't enough. Unlike the other health professionals I saw, she had all the information I needed. She just didn't give it to me. It didn't occur to me that Arran's health problems and Rebecca's behaviour problems could have the same cause so I didn't talk about Rebecca and I don't think the dietitian realised just how bad our situation was.

I stopped giving the children food colouring, but when I bought bread at a shop on the way home, Rebecca would ask, 'What can I have?' and I'd buy her an ice-cream. She was less restless but she still seemed moody, unpredictable and intellectually dull. Her face was usually exceptionally pale, sometimes with the dark shadows under her eyes which doctors call 'allergic shiners'.

Confused, and by now wondering if Rebecca could possibly be intellectually handicapped, I approached her preschool teacher: 'Tell me, is she bright or not?'

'I honestly don't know,' replied her teacher thoughtfully. 'Sometimes I think she is. She likes craft. She always has lots of ideas and everything she does looks good,' she said, pointing to some of Rebecca's work on the wall. 'She has good days and bad days,' she continued. 'But we see some fairly bizarre behaviour, like hiding in the lockers, or painting with all the paint brushes at once.'

More about salicylates

A friend gave me a book describing the Feingold diet. First published in the 1970s, Dr Feingold's book, *Why Your Child is Hyperactive*, was the first to bring the effects of food additives and salicylates to the notice of the general public in the US.

Although not as effective as the diet we use now, it did help many families. I had only heard of salicylates before from my friend at playgroup. 'Maybe I should find out about these,' I thought. There was a list of salicylate-containing foods, including fruits, vegetables, drinks, condiments, nuts, seeds and confectionery. I couldn't imagine avoiding so many foods.

The paragraph which caught my eye stated that if a child reacts to one food colouring they almost certainly react to some other food chemicals as well.

FROM THE MEDICAL JOURNALS

'In 1973, Dr Ben Feingold postulated that dietary chemicals such as salicylates and colours could cause hyperactivity . . . However, the original Feingold diet failed to adequately exclude natural salicylates, amines and glutamates which may provoke adverse reactions in some sensitive individuals . . .'

Clarke L and others, 'The dietary management of food allergy and food intolerance in children and adults', *Australian Journal of Nutrition and Dietetics* 1996;53(3):89–98.

Over the next few weeks I removed obvious artificial colours, flavours, preservatives and a few salicylates – not enough to make any difference – from our diet and cut down a lot on sugar. Rebecca, now five, was much calmer and more cooperative. We had visited her new school, and her attitude was positive. I thought we were in reasonable shape for starting her at school the next year but I couldn't have been more wrong. We were about to launch Rebecca into an environment full of all the things she hated most, including noise, crowds, rules and rigid expectations.

'Schooldays are the best days of your life – not'

Nothing prepared me for the violence of Rebecca's reaction to school. She hated it. Those first ten weeks were a nightmare for me. Rebecca was angry with me all the time. She fought against going to school, cried, and when I went to pick her up after school she would run away. I talked to the teacher, who was perplexed, and had no complaints about her in class. 'If anything, she's too quiet. She just sits there and doesn't do anything. She never joins in.'

Friends who drove past the school would report, 'I saw your daughter in the playground today. She was sitting alone.' Sometimes they reported she was crying. I was distressed by my little daughter's plight and often returned to the car in tears after dropping her off at school.

I went back to see the preschool teacher to see if Rebecca should return to preschool. I didn't know where else to turn. She tried it for a day. 'No, she's outgrown preschool,' the teacher decided, and suggested, 'Have you noticed how she shuts down completely when she's feeling overloaded?'

I visited small private schools and put our name on a waiting list. I received plenty of advice such as 'Pour yourself a stiff gin,' and 'She'll get used to it.' The only mother who seemed to understand confided to me that her teenage son had always hated school. He later committed suicide. I share her grief.

I visited the school counsellor who obviously thought I was a neurotic mother. 'The teacher doesn't have any complaints?' she kept asking. She recommended a health department counsellor.

As an afterthought she mentioned that some mothers with children like this had found a certain chiropractor helpful.

Some behaviour management

The health department counsellor saw me once. 'You'll have to leave the children in the waiting room. The receptionist will be there,' he insisted. For the whole interview I worried about my restless five-year-old and just-two-year-old being expected to sit quietly for an hour. Afterwards I found my children playing unsupervised on the top level of a two storey concrete stairwell.

I felt as if the counsellor didn't really understand, but he gave me some useful general guidelines for disciplining children. 'These are my three rules,' he said and wrote on a card:

- Be firm • Be consistent • Be positive

These may seem obvious, but it's easy to forget rules at the front line of the battle. However, in the time I spent with him, I could have watched the *1–2–3 Magic* video in which actors play scenarios that mothers can remember and use while under fire.

The *1–2–3 Magic* program is designed to stop parents getting hooked in to endless arguments.

Child:	Can I have a cookie?
Mother:	It's nearly time for dinner, you can have a stick of celery.
Child:	But I want a cookie.
Mother:	That's one.
Child:	It's not fair, everyone else gets what they want.
Mother:	That's two.
Child:	I hate you!
Mother: (calmly)	That's three. Take five.

'Take five' means five minutes of time out. *1–2–3 Magic* is available as a video or book (see p. 253) which explains how to implement the program. If you cannot get it to work, either you are not doing it properly, or your child is affected by food. For severely oppositional children in off-diet mode, you can use the system in reverse, that is, count silently to yourself then remove yourself for time out.

1–2–3 Magic still wouldn't have worked for us – we needed diet to do that – but it would have been a giant step in the right direction.

The counsellor also suggested a reward system, giving Rebecca a star for each good behaviour such as getting dressed for school. When she had ten stars on her chart she could exchange them for a small toy. This system worked so well that we used it for years, exchanging the stars for credit points, and constantly changing the required behaviours and rewards.

Everyone I saw helped me in some way, but there was no single magic treatment – or at least, there was, but no one could tell me about it.

Chiropractic

Not knowing what to expect, I visited the chiropractor recommended by the school counsellor. He explained applied kinesiology to me. It involved what he called muscle-testing to aid diagnosis and he demonstrated by asking me to hold my arm up while he pushed against it under different conditions. Despite my scepticism I had to admit it seemed to work.

There were also gentle spinal adjustments and some exercises to do every day. We thought this was strange but we noticed Rebecca's coordination and concentration improving. Years later I found they were the standard cross-crawl exercises used by physiotherapists where the opposite arm and leg are raised simultaneously, rather like marching lying down. When I was a schoolgirl we used to march around the playground to music. Perhaps it actually helped us to concentrate better.

The chiropractor also did some food tests on Rebecca using muscle-testing. 'You should eliminate artificial additives, milk and sugar from her diet completely,' he said. At that time, many people believed that sugar caused children's behaviour problems. Studies have since shown that this does not happen. Children who appear to react to sugar are generally reacting to other food chemicals such as additives and salicylates.

> **FROM THE MEDICAL JOURNALS**
> 'The meta-analytic synthesis of the studies to date found that sugar does not affect the behavior or cognitive performance of children.'
> Wolraich M and others, 'The effect of sugar on behavior or cognition in children', *Journal of the American Medical Association* 1995;274(20): 1617–1621.

Despite doubts about the chiropractor's unscientific-looking tests, I eliminated milk and the strawberry yoghurt Rebecca had been eating every day which was her main source of sugar. We had already removed the most obvious artificial additives. The results were dramatic. She settled down immediately.

By this time, Rebecca was in a different class at school. Some of the children in the class were taking readers home but she was making no progress with reading and writing. At the end of the week, the teacher sought me out. 'She's reading,' she said. 'I can't believe it, it's happened so quickly.' Later she confided to me, 'I think Rebecca is one of the brightest in the class, although she's not showing it in achievement.'

We were delighted with the change in Rebecca's behaviour. Within a few days she had changed from being aggressive and negative into a happy little girl, very eager to please. We congratulated ourselves on how lovely she was and started enjoying life again. It didn't occur to me to do challenges to confirm which food chemicals were affecting Rebecca. We decided that sugar was one of her problems but we had just blamed the wrong suspect. I didn't realise that salicylates in the strawberry yoghurt were more likely to be the culprit than sugar.

More salicylate denial

With Rebecca happy at school I was able to enjoy Arran more. He had settled down completely with the change of diet and was a companionable child, so different from Rebecca at that age. I could spend days at home with him, never feeling the need to go out for extra stimulation. We fed the chickens together, put out the compost, made boats on the dam, collected mushrooms and picked fruit and vegetables. I loved the life and resented having to drive into town.

One weekend we went to visit some good friends in a nearby city and I noticed that their five-year-old son, whom I normally regarded as rather demanding, was unusually agreeable. For morning tea there was a pink iced bun, which my children were not allowed to eat. I watched their son eat the pink icing and, right under my eyes, he became restless and demanding.

'When we came in he was behaving very well, but I've noticed he's changed since we had morning tea. Do you think he could have the same problem as Rebecca?' I asked his mother.

My friend was remarkably receptive. 'I've been wondering about that,' she admitted, and described how the preschool teacher had referred him to the school nurse for an assessment. The nurse had commented, 'He doesn't concentrate very well, does he?' It was true. He wasn't concentrating, and couldn't finish the test, despite excellent concentration at home.

By the end of our visit my friend had bought a copy of Dr Feingold's classic book, which is still a good read despite the outdated diet. Her son was already on the diet although he was not a hyperactive child. In many ways he was the opposite of Rebecca – a sedentary, good sleeper who was reading fluently before he entered preschool. But his messy handwriting, poor social skills, intermittent concentration problems and inappropriate temper outbursts improved on the diet. 'He seems to be most affected by salicylates, just as the book says,' his mother commented.

'Thank goodness that's not a problem for us,' I answered. 'I'd hate to have to cut out fruit, although I have noticed that Rebecca gets aggressive if she eats a lot of almonds, so I suppose that's salicylates. I think she has a mild intolerance.' How I wish I had paid more attention. Dietary management so far had improved all of Rebecca's behaviours except sleeping. Here was someone telling me the answer to our problems but I still wasn't listening.

Like most people, I didn't want to hear about salicylates.

I still thought that if your child was sensitive to certain foods, then you would see an obvious reaction soon after eating. I couldn't understand that when children eat food chemicals many times a day, as with salicylates, the result is good days and bad days which come and go for no obvious reason. The concept of trying an elimination diet in which all additives and salicylate-containing foods are avoided, then reintroduced one group at a time, was still far beyond me.

Insomnia rules, OK?

We had made friends with a couple in town who shared our love of the mountains. We did several weekend trips with them, and were invited to parties at their house. They would always say, 'You can put the children to sleep in our room.'

I would disappear obediently into the master bedroom and try to put our children to sleep. Sometimes it would work with Arran. Rebecca was terrified both of the dark and of being left alone. Eventually, I would reappear with her and spend the evening entertaining her. Our host was always puzzled. He would recall his children, who now lived with his first wife. 'We always took our kids out with us,' he'd say, 'but they'd go to sleep, and we wouldn't have to bother about them.' When I think back, I realise how remarkably tolerant our friends were. At a housewarming party to celebrate renovations, Rebecca tipped a plate of fried rice over the new carpet within five minutes of our arrival. I don't know why they invited us again.

On another occasion we were invited to dinner with two other families. There were seven children altogether. The idea was that the children would watch a video and go to sleep in their sleeping bags, while the adults made intelligent conversation. All the other children went to sleep. Rebecca came in every ten minutes.

'I can't get to sleep,' she'd say. 'Can I bring my sleeping bag in here, Mummy?' she asked quietly. I finally gave in. 'Only if you agree to keep quiet.' She lay on the floor and tossed and turned for hours, never once interrupting us and eventually crawling into her pillow case and falling asleep.

'I think you were brave agreeing to let her come in with us,' one of the other mothers commented later. 'It turned out to be the right thing to do. I don't think I could have made that decision.'

I appreciated her support, but it made me realise how different our experience of child-rearing was from other people's. I felt it must be my fault Rebecca couldn't get to sleep. It was hard to have a social life as I always ended up feeling as if I had been looking after children for most of the night. I could never look forward to having a few hours at night after the children were asleep to call my own. By the time Rebecca got to sleep I was exhausted and ready for bed too. Her sleeping problems meant that we rarely went out as a couple, instead preferring to have family-oriented outings.

'Nutritionally it's excellent'

Howard's parents came to visit us. Three men in Howard's family, on both sides, had had early heart attacks, so Howard's mother was worried for her sons. Each year she would give me a Pritikin cookbook, which I would read, always deciding 'that's too extreme'.

The Pritikin lifestyle involves removing all processed foods, sugar and added fats and oils from the diet. It limits intake of protein foods like meat and dairy products and requires moderate amounts of regular exercise and relaxation. There have been many cases of remarkable improvements in chronic diseases, especially heart disease, among its adherents. In New Zealand, Donna, our babysitter and her family had been following the Pritikin lifestyle since her father, a slim, non-smoking jogger, died of a heart attack in his fifties.

This time Howard's mother gave me a Pritikin book which was aimed at athletes. As I read it I realised that the mental image I had of myself as a fit, athletic mountain-climber was badly out of date. I was now a blimp who did very little exercise. I asked the community dietitian what she thought of Pritikin's diet: 'Nutritionally it's excellent,' she said, 'but socially it's a disaster.'

Since we had already removed many additives and sugar from our diet we were more than halfway there. All we had to do was avoid fats and oils and limit quantities of protein foods. Although Pritikin permits low-fat dairy foods we had to avoid milk because of our intolerances.

I decided to give the Pritikin lifestyle a go. I thought we could eat Pritikin at home and fall off the wagon when we went out, not realising that we wouldn't feel like falling off the wagon after a few months. Howard was very sceptical at first, although he was keen to lose a bit of weight.

Hidden additives

I emptied our remaining processed food onto the compost heap and kept reading. I was surprised at the fat content of foods. Our diet was already low-fat, I thought, but I was quite wrong. I also realised there were many hidden additives we had so far failed to avoid.

The Pritikin lifestyle involves relaxation and exercise as well. Both meditators before our marriage, we had kept meditating whenever possible through our times of crisis. Now I started rolling out of bed in the dark and jogging down the country road beside the house. The frost crunched under my feet and as I reached each gum tree a flock of galahs would rise in unison with a great flapping noise. Soon this was the part of the day I enjoyed most.

There were some interesting consequences. Howard and I lost weight, for me 15 kilograms in six months, and both of us ended up with exceptionally good cholesterol and blood pressure levels. The premenstrual tension which had bothered me for years vanished. Howard found that he was able to concentrate better. Best of all, our asthma symptoms improved and were no longer a problem. Sulphite preservatives (220–228) in dried fruit and many other foods are the additives most commonly associated with asthma. As with other additives, we had never taken them seriously because we had never seen a reaction.

A bun with pink icing

One day Howard came home after going to an important meeting in a nearby town. 'I was hungry and had no food with me so I stopped at a country bakery,' he said. 'All I could buy was a bun with pink icing. When I got to the meeting I knew I was fidgeting. Everyone was looking at me, but I couldn't stop and I was very embarrassed.' For the first time we realised that Howard too needed to watch additives.

By now Rebecca was being invited to birthday parties by other children at school. I was in a group of mothers who were running healthy birthday parties. The children were offered sandwiches, fruit and home-made birthday cake but the emphasis was on games rather than food. Instead of lollies for prizes there were little trinkets. There was none of that over-excited behaviour that is usually associated with parties, and the children had a good time.

The hypoglycemic sidetrack

That summer we went camping on the south coast of NSW. We had a lovely holiday with Donna, our wonderful New Zealand babysitter, exploring the empty golden beaches and even managing a scuba dive. During this holiday an old friend who now lives in Italy came to visit. She was openly scornful of Rebecca's behaviour and clearly thought it was all due to poor parenting.

'What is all this talk about hyperactivity?' our friend demanded, in her usual outspoken manner. 'My sister talked about it too. She says her son has it. That's ridiculous. They can't all have it. None of the children in Italy have it. I've never heard of it.'

What our friend said was true. Many years later, when we visited Italy, I found that most Italians don't like food additives and rarely use them – and compared to other Western countries, Italian children have low incidences of dyslexia, ADHD and asthma.

One morning we all arranged to go on a long bushwalk. After a short distance Rebecca stopped. 'I'm too tired,' she said and lay down on the track.

'Nonsense. A child of that age should be able to walk this distance,' said our friend. She clearly thought we were being too easy on Rebecca. I had noticed food would get her moving and I gave her some dried fruit. After another ten minutes she was up again but quite white-faced and shaky. Howard helped her back to camp.

Episodes like this were to occur sporadically, usually associated with exercise. A friend suggested hypoglycemia and the symptoms did seem to fit. I talked to our doctor, who described hypoglycemia as an American fad and reassured me that Rebecca did not have diabetes. We adopted the principles of the diet anyway, feeding Rebecca every couple of hours, especially on waking and before going to sleep and avoiding refined foods and sugar. This seemed to help and so we embarked on what turned out to be the wrong track for the next six years.

A scuba-diving weekend

We felt as if we were getting somewhere with Rebecca, so what happened next came as a shock. Since our scuba dive at Christmas I had said to Howard, 'It's time I did a diving course. I can't go with you on boat dives unless I have a qualification.' I had started diving long ago, before scuba courses were commercially available. Howard had done his course after we were married so he could join me.

Exactly twenty years after I started diving I joined a scuba class in Wagga Wagga. The sea dives were to be completed in a weekend on the coast and as I was still breastfeeding Arran, Howard would come too and mind the children.

We left on the Friday afternoon, stopping at a small café for hamburgers which seemed quite plain and safe. Arriving late at night, we rented a cabin in a camping ground. Rebecca slept badly, waking frequently. 'What's wrong with Rebecca?' I asked Howard on Saturday morning. 'She's standing on a rubbish bin in the playground shouting nonsense.' She appeared to be uncooperative and out of touch. During the day her aggressive behaviour increased. She was refusing to eat anything other than a whole-wheat breakfast cereal and a soy milk powder which we hadn't tried before. Howard minded her while I did my dives in strong winds and rough seas. 'I'm finding her very difficult to look after,' he reported.

That night the only way we could get Rebecca to sleep was to lie on the double bed with her. She lay on her back, so tense she was vibrating slightly, opening her eyes about every fifteen minutes and demanding reassurance. Howard and I took two hour shifts during the night.

In the morning the aggression and abuse continued. Howard and I sat on the edge of the bed with our arms around each other, exhausted and despairing. Then we heard Rebecca helping herself to the soy milk powder. The thought struck us both at the same time. 'It's the soy milk!' We grabbed the packet from her and threw it into the rubbish bin outside. Rebecca was like an addict denied her fix. She screamed and raged but started improving.

With hindsight I wonder if we had fallen into the trap of suspecting the last food eaten as the culprit. Rebecca subsequently did not react to that soy milk but eventually we found she would react to whole wheat in large quantities. She may have been reacting to a build up of the whole wheat or experiencing a reaction to the take-away meal on the Friday night, or extra salicylates we didn't even consider, or a combination of all three. We were right about one thing: our daughter reacted to foods. But which ones?

I felt that Rebecca was the only child in the world who reacted to food in this way, and there was no one to whom I could turn for help.

'She'll grow out of it'

Rebecca, aged six, was now in her second year at school. The teacher had identified a problem with fine motor control. I was surprised because she loved drawing, had always done so much of it and, as her preschool teacher said, her work looked good. But her handwriting was terrible and she hated colouring in. She reversed a lot of letters, sometimes to the extent of writing a whole line of mirror writing. In reading she constantly confused words like 'saw' and 'was'.

The teachers said, 'Don't worry, she'll grow out of it.' This is a standard line, which all mothers of these children have heard. It goes in the collection along with 'There's nothing wrong with your child', 'Would you like a prescription for some anti-depressants' and, later on, 'Could do better if he tried'. Some people suggest it means the child will grow out of the current problem and into a worse one.

I came across an advertisement for educational kinesiology which specifically mentioned reversals. Following our success with applied kinesiology I decided to give it a go. Again, muscle testing was a feature. Rebecca was given some exercises to do called Brain-gym. Some were similar to the cross-crawl exercises she had done before, but quicker and more fun.

The complete set took about two minutes. We continued these nearly every morning for about eighteen months. You could see a reduction in the number of reversals in her work on the days she did Brain-gym and she was more focused, although the effect wore off during the day.

'I can see the difference in her work,' her teacher said. 'What are the exercises? I have some other children who could use that.'

Another move

Howard was feeling increasingly frustrated by the lack of scope in his job and by the difficulties I was experiencing living in such an isolated place. He was offered a position in charge of plant industries in the Northern Territory which included horticulture, crops and weed control. The position was located in Darwin.

As we prepared to leave our beautiful rural retreat Rebecca was six and a half and Arran was three and a half. In the four years we had lived in Wagga Wagga, we had come a long way in our understanding of our daughter. We had accepted that Rebecca was hyperactive and that she responded well to dietary treatment. We thought we had it all sorted out. Happy with her progress at school and enjoying her company at home, except for her sleeping problem, we were again feeling unwarranted optimistism about the future.

Asthma answer revealed

We made our way slowly to Darwin, visiting relatives and detouring via the Great Barrier Reef for some scuba diving. In one outback town we stopped for a local brand of 'pure' fruit ice-creams. Within minutes we were all coughing and struggling for breath. After we recovered, we realised that one mystery had been solved for us. Sulphite preservatives are the additives most likely to affect asthmatics and can be used in high doses to preserve fruit pulp. We had just experienced our first classic sulphite reaction.

Like us, most asthmatics are unaware of their sensitivity because frequent small amounts of sulphites – in such foods as dried fruit, muesli bars and sausages – can cause irritable airways with no obvious symptoms which results in asthma during exposure to certain triggers. Between us, our triggers had included exercise, rye grass, cold air, viruses and hairspray. When we avoided sulphites, exposure to those triggers no longer resulted in asthma and it took a very large dose of sulphites while on an additive-free diet to demonstrate a reaction.

I was very surprised. I had known that sulphites were related to asthma but thought they didn't affect us because we never suffered asthma directly after eating dried apricots. Yet all we had to do to avoid chronic asthma was to avoid these additives. Although our doctor told us asthma was not related to food, since then we have avoided sulphites. Arran is the only one who has experienced a few mild episodes of asthma – while walking past a mountain of sulphur on a wharf and showering in sulphurous bore water – and none of us has ever needed a puffer again.

3 School and learning delays

Driving the 5,000 kilometres to Darwin took us six weeks. This trip was the sort of life that Howard and Rebecca thrived on, constantly moving, with new and interesting places to be explored every day. Howard always claimed he could spend his whole life travelling like this, if only he could find a way to make a living from it.

After Wagga Wagga, Darwin was a tropical paradise. I was enchanted by the unexpectedly azure sea, palm trees and Asian style markets.

We rented an elevated house with louvres, ceiling fans and large rainforest garden. It was a run-down survivor of Cyclone Tracy but had a swimming pool which was perfect for entertaining Rebecca. She could splash around on an air mattress and wear herself out without too much effort on my part.

Struggling to keep Rebecca diverted without friends, I joined the toy library. Unable to amuse herself, a bored Rebecca was a dangerous Rebecca who was likely to annoy her brother for fun. Over the years the toy library turned out to be more help than anything else offered by the community. Novelty was an important part of the attraction for Rebecca. Toys didn't have to be new and expensive, just different. I soon learned to try everything.

Assessments for Rebecca

At the new school I explained Rebecca's problem briefly to the teacher.

'Rebecca does appear to be deaf sometimes,' she commented. 'Have you had her hearing checked?' The test showed perfect hearing. We would find later that 'Seems not to listen' is a symptom of ADHD.

Coordination

I felt that Rebecca may have some minor coordination problems and was surprised when an assessment discovered delays in two areas, 'vestibular' and 'proprioceptive' functions. This meant that her brain was not properly processing messages about the position and movement of her body. The physiotherapist explained that she compensated by relying on her vision, and when deprived of sight, her delays became obvious.

'This problem is very subtle,' the physiotherapist explained. 'It's hard for mothers to recognise.' Essentially, Rebecca didn't feel where she was in space and relied on visual cues. When deprived of these by closing her eyes, in the dark or walking backwards, she panicked. Her fear of the dark was a minor problem compared to her inability to get to sleep but we were much more sympathetic about having a night-light after hearing this. I felt good having a report which showed there was *something* wrong with my child. Until now, I had felt that no one believed me.

Along with a twice weekly motor sensory class, the physiotherapist suggested Rebecca try sleeping in a hammock. The rocking motion was supposed to help with vestibular dysfunction. 'Only for six months,' he warned. 'Any longer might compromise her posture.' I bought a second-hand, free-standing hammock and Rebecca slept well, waking happily on the first morning. For her, this was unusual. She normally woke in tears as a baby and like a bear with a sore head when older.

'Looks as if it's doing something for her,' Howard commented. We persevered with the hammock and the cheerfulness on waking persisted. Motor sensory therapies for children with learning disabilities and behaviour problems are controversial and the hammock therapy is no longer recommended, but we were pleased we used it.

Like most of the therapies we had tried, it helped Rebecca but was not a magic cure. At the end of six months in the hammock, plus motor-sensory classes, her vestibular function was found to have improved greatly and had reached the low end of the normal range.

DEVELOPMENTAL COORDINATION DISORDER

Signs include · difficulty with sports participation · some gross motor problems such as clumsy walking or running · difficulty climbing or jumping · some fine motor difficulties such as tying shoelaces · poor handwriting · some balance difficulties such as unable to stand for 15 seconds feet together, arms out · unable to tandem stand 15 seconds with eyes closed · unable to hop in place alternating feet.

Management includes · a supportive environment · appropriate sports participation · activity with a chance of success such as swimming · academic activities tailored to motor abilities · occupational therapy.

www.fpnotebook.com/PED98.htm

Grandparents' visit

Several months after our arrival in Darwin, my parents drove up for a visit during the month-long school holidays. Rebecca attended an intensive motor sensory class every morning and the rest of the time we visited the sights of Darwin.

On the first day back at school we got up early to farewell my parents on their long trip home. At seven o'clock that night there were two policemen at the door. 'There's been an accident. Your father is dead.' My mother was in Tennant Creek hospital where she was too injured to be moved.

We all lay on the double bed with our arms around each other, crying ourselves to sleep. I caught the next plane to Tennant Creek and stayed in a motel, spending my days at the hospital with Mum. My parents had been an exceptionally close and loving couple for more than fifty years. I could not imagine how my mother would face this tragedy. She made a determined effort to recover and as we left the doctor told her, 'You've been an inspiration to us all.'

We returned to Darwin with Mum in a wheelchair. The house was overflowing with flowers sent by relatives and friends down south. She stayed with us another five weeks, letting the broken bones heal and, as she said, 'watching the mangoes grow'.

A new preservative in bread

One day, while my mother was still with us, we ran out of bread. Howard walked to the corner store. 'I could only get this bread,' he said, showing me a local brand. 'Why don't we ever buy it?'

Since we had started avoiding additives two years before, I automatically read the ingredients list on every product before buying.

'It contains a preservative,' I answered. Darwin was one of the first regions in Australia to use high doses of the bread preservative which is now widespread. Howard started his career as a food technologist, so he understands food additives – at least from the technical side. He looked at the ingredients on the label. 'Code number 282, what's that? Calcium propionate, that shouldn't be any problem. It's a mould inhibitor found naturally in some cheeses.'

'It's on our list of food additives as "possible adverse effects",' I said, 'but we can try it with Rebecca and see what happens.'

Her IQ had plummeted

Rebecca ate some sandwiches with no problems, so we continued eating this new brand of bread. After about five days Mum and I visited the school to watch the athletics carnival. We were alarmed to see that Rebecca had no idea of what was going on, thought she was attending a birthday party and could not manage to walk in a line with the rest of the class. It was as if her IQ had plummeted. She appeared to be intellectually handicapped.

I puzzled over this until the next day, when I remembered seeing Rebecca helping herself to dry bread for breakfast instead of cereal. Again she was like an addict, wanting more and more of her fix. Over the last few days she had been requesting nothing but sandwiches, then bread only, and then helping herself to it. I rushed off to the school with a different lunch. 'Has Rebecca's behaviour been all right this week?' I asked her teacher.

'Not exactly,' she replied. 'She's been lying on the floor at odd times during class and her handwriting has been getting bigger and messier every day.'

Rebecca started improving within a few hours of having the bread withdrawn from her diet. The teacher exclaimed, 'I wouldn't have believed it could affect her so much.' I felt the same way. The effect that calcium propionate had on Rebecca was a slow build up of learning disabilities, coordination problems and lack of energy.

> Ten years later, researchers in Brazil were to find that giving daily propionic acid to young rats for three weeks, in doses not much greater than can be eaten in Australian bread, 'alters normal development and induces long-term behavioral deficits'.
>
> Brusque AM and others, 'Effect of chemically induced propionic acidemia on neurobehavioral development of rats', *Pharmacology Biochemistry and Behaviour* 1999;64(3):529–534.

I was lucky that my mother witnessed for herself the dramatic changes in Rebecca. Anyone who ever sees these changes is convinced and my mother was very supportive of my efforts. Many mothers have to struggle with unsympathetic relatives who sabotage their attempts to avoid food chemicals.

'Your daughter will never do ballet'

A few months later, it was time for the physiotherapist to re-test Rebecca. By this time he knew her and her capabilities well. On the way to the appointment we had stopped for a strawberry pure fruit ice-cream. Rebecca was progressing through the assessment as expected, showing improvement in some areas, when right in the middle of a set of questions, she stopped concentrating. The physiotherapist tried hard to complete the test, then sent her out of the room.

He was obviously curious and could hardly wait to talk. 'What's going on? I can't finish it. She's unassessable.'

All I could think of was the ice-cream. Perhaps there was an artificial colour in the cone. Or could it be salicylates? Strawberries, especially in concentrated pulp, are high in salicylates. Rebecca had eaten those ice-creams before, but we'd never seen an effect. Perhaps it was because we hadn't been doing careful motor sensory assessments at the time the effect kicked in.

'You've had more success with diet than any other mother I've seen,' the physiotherapist commented.

Rebecca continued attending the motor sensory group twice a week for six months. The physiotherapist warned me that her problems were serious. 'Your daughter will never be able to do ballet,' he said. We were to remember that many years later.

Since Rebecca was already attending a beginners' class, I went to talk to the ballet teacher. 'My daughter has coordination problems,' I began.

'Oh, I know that!' the teacher exclaimed, 'but send her along. We have had worse and sometimes we see big improvements.' I decided to encourage Rebecca at ballet for as long as she enjoyed it and felt comfortable.

Learning piano

One of the physiotherapist's suggestions to develop fine motor coordination was to learn a musical instrument, so Rebecca started learning the piano. Out of interest I had checked Howard on one of Rebecca's tests. The blindfolded subject holds one hand out, palm up. The experimenter then joins, for example, the subject's index finger and thumb together. The subject has to say which finger is touching the thumb. Both Rebecca and Howard had difficulty doing this. Howard was sceptical about piano lessons.

'She won't be able to play with both hands, or read music. I'd love to be able to play the piano, but I can't.' Rebecca kept up lessons for eighteen months. We noticed a big improvement and she played quite well with both hands, but what she and Howard simply could not do at all was understand how to read music.

To help Rebecca learn a new piece I would put my hands over hers and press her fingers on the correct notes. This helped her to memorise the music. I only realised what she had done one day when I saw her playing a piece of music which was not on the page in front of her. She was actually working much harder than she appeared, because she had memorised the whole book while appearing to sight read.

There are some very famous musicians who are unable to

learn to read music. Former Beatle Sir Paul McCartney is one. Presumably it is a form of dyslexia but Rebecca's piano teacher had no understanding of this problem.

The medical view

Rebecca was now seven. Our problems had escalated so much that I decided to take her to a pediatrician. We were referred to one who, unusually at that time, had been interested in hyper-activity/ADHD for many years. In the early 1990s in Australia, children's behaviour problems were increasing but few people had any understanding of this. Most people thought if they hadn't heard of it, it couldn't be real. They blamed the mothers for poor parenting and most doctors said, 'There's nothing wrong with this child.'

SOME SYMPTOMS OF ADHD

Inattention: makes careless mistakes, has difficulty paying attention, seems not to listen, fails to finish tasks, disorganised, dislikes or avoids certain tasks, forgetful, easily distracted, low motivation, forgets instructions.

Hyperactivity–Impulsivity: excessive activity, leaves seat, feels fidgety and restless, difficulty playing quietly or relaxing, constantly 'on the move', talks excessively, difficulty awaiting turn, interrupts others, impulsive and impatient, mood swings and short temper, accident prone.

ADHD (technically AD/HD) was formerly called hyperactivity or attention deficit disorder (ADD). The American Psychiatric Association's *Diagnostic and Statistical Manual of Mental Disorders* (DSM-IV-TR) identifies four types: inattentive, hyperactive, combined and other. DSM definitions are written by committees and are purely descriptive. They do not explain causes or give an overall 'big picture'.

Diagnostic details: http://student.admin.utas.edu.au/services/options/adhd.htm.

The pediatrician listened to everything I had to say and observed Rebecca, who was quietly eating her way through a box of sultanas and was outrageously awful after we left. When I had finished, he said, 'Congratulations. You have worked it all out for yourself. These are the treatments we use,' as he ticked

them off on his fingers: 'Medication, diet, behaviour management, counselling, physiotherapy.

'In your case, the diet is obviously working well. I'll send
you to a dietitian to make sure it's all right nutritionally and
you can go to counselling if you like. You're already doing the
physiotherapy.'

Then, leaning back in his chair, he continued gently, 'What's
her father like? Always on the go, is he?' 'Well, yes,' I agreed.
I had seen a connection. Rebecca had inherited her problems
from Howard, although she was much worse.

At that time it was thought that because children could inherit
ADHD, the condition had always been around, but there is
another possibility. Animal studies show that behavioural
effects of low level toxic exposures – for example, though contaminated food – can be passed down through the generations.
DDT, the first of the powerful new synthetic pesticides, was
introduced in 1938 and thousands of other pesticides and industrial chemicals followed. Howard and I were in the first gener-
ation of children to be exposed to these new pesticides and
industrial chemicals. Experts now think that effects of chemicals contribute more than previously realised (see p. 148).

'Fish living in the Great Lakes are contaminated with a large
number of persistent toxic chemicals . . . rats fed Lake Ontario
salmon are hyper-reactive to unpleasant events but react normal
when "life is pleasant". We have also shown the same behavioral
changes in the offspring of rats fed Lake Ontario salmon. These
results occurred when the offspring were tested as juveniles or as
adults, even though these rats had never been fed the fish.'

Daly HB, 'Laboratory rat experiments show consumption of Lake Ontario
salmon causes behavioral changes', *J Great Lakes Res* 1993;19(4):
784–788.

Going to a doctor about a child with behaviour problems can
be an ordeal. I always worried about whether the doctor would
believe me, and whether he or she would know enough to help
or would be patronising and dismissive. I usually came out
feeling depressed, angry or wrung out. Most mothers I've talked

to feel the same way. This time it was good to have my worries confirmed but there were no miracles being offered to help us. I didn't want medication but I had been hoping there would be some magic answer.

Worst case scenario: a 'healthy' diet

Rebecca had so many problems that I decided it was time for us to take diet seriously. The dietitian was not helpful. 'I don't believe the Feingold diet works,' she said, 'and it's not my job to help hyperactive children.' She persuaded me not to try the elimination diet which I had requested. 'It's very difficult, and you've done most of it already.' If only I could have talked to a sympathetic dietitian at this stage. I was finally ready to hear what they had to say, and it would have saved us years of anguish. I listed a typical day's food for Rebecca and we debated calcium intake, a problem for us.

'Which vegetables does she eat?' the dietitian repeated. 'Vegetables are very important, you know.' I was embarrassed to realise that she ate as little as possible.

How to eat vegetables

The result of this interview was that I decided to feed my children much healthier meals. I started on a program to get them to eat blended vegetable soup with home-made chicken stock. On the first night, the children only had to put a tiny spoonful in their mouths to get a small reward. The next night they had to lick the spoon as well. After that, every day the amount was doubled until by the end of two weeks they were eating a cup of soup and the rewards ceased.

I found I could get any vegetable into the children if it was in the soup. It became a rule of the house that soup must be eaten. Meals were served earlier, and on time. Everyone had to sit at the table and make interesting conversation. This worked so well I wondered why I hadn't tried it before. Afternoon tea was limited so that appetites were good.

The main course, usually meat, chicken, fish or eggs with potatoes or rice and salad could be negotiated but a reasonable portion had to be eaten before dessert could be served. Dessert was often carob, a sugar-free chocolate substitute, with a selection of fresh fruits such as grapes, strawberries and melons.

I thought I was feeding my children good food but the dietitian could hardly have given me less helpful advice. I had decided we didn't have to worry about salicylates. I couldn't have been more wrong. We embarked on a two-year period of even worse sleeping problems than we had already encountered.

Researchers comment that mothers rarely see a correspondence between food and behaviour. It was true. I did not relate Rebecca's increasing inability to go to sleep at night and worsening problems in other areas to the 'healthier' diet we were eating.

Meanwhile, in New Zealand . . .

The other result of my visit to the pediatrician was the realisation that, because of the genetic connection, Howard's donated children in New Zealand might have problems too. We decided to warn them and managed to find news of the family from a mutual friend. We were distressed to learn that the couple had split up. Marriages involving children with behaviour problems fail more often than average and I wondered if this could have been a contributing factor.

I wrote to their mother, Beth, 'We have finally had a diagnosis for Rebecca's problems which have worried us from her birth. She has inherited ADHD from Howard.'

I included a list of symptoms that I had noticed in Rebecca, then aged seven.

- Difficulty getting to and staying asleep
- Ordinary discipline doesn't work, it just escalates the problem
- Can get violent and abusive
- Difficulty concentrating (not always)
- Good days and bad days (very unpredictable)
- Panics easily
- Never satisfied – always wants more
- Craving for sugar and sweet food
- Picky eater; doesn't recognise when she's hungry
- Very difficult if she doesn't eat regularly

OTHER CONDITIONS

Today, it is common for ADHD children to be diagnosed with 'comorbid' (associated) conditions. A child presenting with Rebecca's problems might be given the following list including a possible dash of the shyness from Asperger's disorder. All of these conditions have a large overlap with food intolerance symptoms.

ADHD, see p. 47.
Opposition defiant disorder, see p. 61.
Developmental coordination disorder, see p. 43.
Food intolerance, see p. 155.

Specific learning disabilities involve difficulty acquiring and demonstrating knowledge and understanding in areas such as reading, writing, listening, speaking, reasoning or mathematical ability. This results in a discrepancy between achievement and intellectual abilities.

http://www.washington.edu/doit/Faculty/Strategies/Disability/LD

Restless legs syndrome consists of an irresistible urge to move the legs often accompanied by crawling sensations in the legs. The sensations are only relieved by movement, and become worse at night. It is usually related to food intolerance, side effects of medication or overtiredness, although experts don't know that yet.

www.rls.org

Asperger's disorder involves social shyness, impairment of social interaction, impairment of imagination such as imaginative play and ability to write fiction, and restricted, repetitive patterns of behaviour, interests and activities.

http://www.udel.edu/bkirby/asperger/aswhatisit.html

- Mixed laterality – dominant eye, hand and foot not on same side
- Not very sure about dominant hand
- Minor coordination problems becoming more obvious as she gets older
- Difficulty reading and writing; persistent reversals, for example, 'b' for 'd', 'p' for 'b', 'was' for 'saw'
- Vagueness and lack of commonsense

- Hypoactive episodes – shuts down when under stress
- Teachers sometimes complain 'too quiet'
- Hyperactive episodes – can't keep still or quiet.

I wrote about the treatments I had tried. My letter finished, 'Since this problem has been so difficult to diagnose we thought we should let you know in case Emma or Matthew has it.'

Beth answered, 'It seems that Matthew has the same condition, which has remained undiagnosed . . . certainly his school performance was below what I expected of his innate abilities. Many of the symptoms you described are ones that Matthew has . . . I have been watching his diet very carefully especially the last few years, with elimination of sugars and dairy . . .'

I found this letter exciting. Two children with the same father being raised in different countries, with no communication between the families, and their mothers had independently discovered that foods exacerbated their symptoms.

It obviously wasn't all in my mind, as so many well-meaning professionals, relatives and friends had implied. There was another woman in the world who knew exactly what I was talking about. Beth's other news to Howard was a shock. 'I had intended to write to you about this time. I have decided to tell Emma and Matthew that you are their biological father.'

We sent a photo and waited anxiously for news of Emma and Matthew's response. Beth's letter described the children's shock then curiosity and Emma's questions. 'Is he tall? Is he skinny? Has he got freckles . . . As she sat glued to your photos she exclaimed, "Oh my God. I look just like him."'

'I'm a stranger'

Emma and Matthew asked for Howard to write to them. 'What will I say?' asked Howard. 'I'm a stranger. I don't even know what twelve- and fourteen-year-olds are interested in.' He carefully wrote a letter to each about his job and interests, and that he would like to hear from them soon.

Beth told us of the response to this. 'I think Matthew committed the information in your letter to him to memory. It was immensely important to him . . . I am not so informed about

Emma's response because she lives with her father, but she told me delightedly on the phone about the letter and the photos which she took to school.'

Emma replied, 'Mum and Dad have just told Matthew and me that you are our real father. It came as a bit of a shock, and I felt angry that they hadn't told me sooner . . . but now I've had a chance to settle down . . . Mum thinks that we look the same.' Matthew's card was short. He talked about his interests. 'I think I've inherited your love of travel,' he wrote.

Photos of Emma and Matthew arrived. To our astonishment they were taken in a hotel in Bali where we had stayed during the Christmas holidays. We had missed them there by only two months. It was five years since we had left New Zealand. We had been thinking of visiting, so now we wrote to say we would come in the summer holidays and we would like to meet the children. In the meantime I exchanged letters with both Beth and Emma. Howard and I were alarmed by some of Emma's letters about accounts of late-night parties and drinking. We hoped it was teenage exaggeration and wrote back about other things.

An antidote for food reactions

Around this time I stumbled across a home remedy for food reactions. It was a combination of bicarbonate of soda, calcium carbonate and potassium bicarbonate. In the past, these ingredients were often recommended by family GPs for stomach upsets and other symptoms of food intolerance. We found this antidote worked like magic when Rebecca ate the wrong thing.

One night after we had eaten at Darwin's famous sunset beach markets, Rebecca was unusually jumpy and restless. We realised she had inadvertently eaten monosodium glutamate (MSG). I gave her the antidote and she quickly calmed down. 'What does it feel like?' I asked, curious.

'It tastes yucky,' she said, 'but then it feels like coming home after a long, hassley holiday.'

After this episode she started taking the antidote, often at night, and it helped her get to sleep. Eventually we discovered that bicarbonate of soda or calcium carbonate – in plain calcium supplements available at any pharmacy – worked just as well and were easy to obtain.

'This is Rebecca'

In 1990, the first Australian book about ADHD appeared. It created an explosion of awareness about these children, at least among desperate mothers. I kept reading it over and over. Rebecca's symptoms were there, described in detail, and I kept saying, 'This is my daughter,' while Howard read it saying, 'This is what I was like as a child.' It was such a relief to see it in print.

The downside of this book was that it dismissed diet and enthusiastically recommended medication as the first and most important treatment for children with ADHD. There was a lot of public resistance regarding giving mind-altering medication to young children. As a diagnosis of ADHD automatically came to mean a medicated child, controversy about 'does ADHD really exist?' and 'is ADHD medication safe?' obscured more important issues such as the desperation of families who needed help, what has caused the upsurge in children's behaviour problems and how can we prevent it.

Word was spreading among mothers that I had successfully improved my child's behaviour with diet. I started to get telephone calls. The mothers would often burst into tears with relief at finding someone who understood what they were going through.

Telling the teacher

At the start of the new school year in which Rebecca turned eight, once again my explanation to her teacher was greeted politely, but with a lack of comprehension.

It was to be six months before we made a mistake and her teacher would run down the corridor after me to say, 'What happened yesterday? Rebecca couldn't sit still for two seconds. Every time I turned around she was in a different place. If I hadn't seen it with my own eyes I wouldn't have believed it was the same child. Now I know what you are talking about.'

This year was to be a good one for Rebecca at school. Her teacher reported, 'She can read anything,' and I heaved a premature sigh of relief at having escaped the learning difficulties which so often accompany behaviour problems, not realising that a learning delay in maths becomes apparent at age eight or later, which is when attention problems are identified.

Rebecca was enjoying ballet, and for the first time appeared to be retaining friends. Sleeping still remained a problem though. She often took up to three hours to get to sleep at night or woke in a panic during the night calling out, 'I'm scared.'

Arran started preschool and hated it. I had hoped at least he would be easy at school.

Life in the Territory

One night we were woken by a storm. There was a continuous roar of thunder, flickering lightning and the house was shaking in the violent winds. Just outside there was a massive explosion. A tree had been hit by lightning and came down over the power lines. Darwin is a very exciting place to live and Howard was more settled than I'd ever seen him. Perhaps the unpredictable environment satisfied his need for constant adventures.

With the finish of the wet season in May, we resumed our exploration of the Territory. Everywhere we visited was better than the tourist brochures. Canoeing the Katherine Gorge was my favourite, with a surprise around every corner, whether a sandy beach, waterfall or a freshwater crocodile.

'I'm tired'

Kakadu Stage Three became another favourite area, with its waterfalls, every one perfect and different. We spent several happy weekends at a particularly idyllic rockhole. One morning after breakfast we climbed up to the top of the falls and spent hours exploring the pools and canyons. It was such fun we spent longer than we intended, eating all the snacks we had brought but still reluctant to leave.

Suddenly Rebecca said 'I'm tired' and lay down. She was panicky and uncoordinated and we had to almost carry her down the steep, slippery path. When we reached the tent she lay unmoving, refusing to eat. I forced her to drink some juice and soon she got up and started playing as if nothing had happened.

Episodes like this always seemed to happen when we were away from home. On the worst occasion we were staying in a cabin and I remember over the week Rebecca had been eating a lot of bread and marmalade. When she suddenly said 'I'm tired' I decided to see if she would sleep it off. I left her lying on her bed in the twilight.

About an hour later, expecting her to be asleep, I found her crouched under a bench in the now dark room. She did not seem to recognise me, was incapable of speech and appeared terrified. I led her gently to the kitchen and stuck a spoonful of sugar in her mouth. In a few minutes she was back to normal.

I tried to find out how to prevent these alarming episodes. The doctor I talked to said, 'She's probably got hypoglycemia, but she's too young to have a glucose tolerance test.' He also suggested that her night waking with panic may be due to hypo-glycemia and that we might have to wake Rebecca and feed her in the middle of the night.

We took his advice on feeding her before sleeping. If she spent several hours trying to fall asleep, as usual, then she ate some more supper. This did reduce the night panic and if she woke eating helped her to get back to sleep.

I thought I could see a pattern. The episodes usually occurred when we were out of our regular routine and they seemed to be associated with exercise. If Rebecca ever mentioned she was hungry I learned to feed her immediately, as the feeling quickly passed. This lack of self-awareness characterised both Howard and Rebecca.

Arran frequently complained 'I'm hungry', but food could be delayed without any ill effects. Rebecca rarely complained of hunger. I was more likely to observe, 'You are getting grumpy. I think you need to eat.' She would often deny this and have to be cajoled into eating, but improved quickly after eating. If Rebecca actually said she was hungry I regarded this as a red alert situation and fed her immediately. Five minutes delay was too long. The feeling would have passed, soon becoming 'I'm tired', refusal to eat, and lying down. Sometimes there was another stage, 'I want some sugar,' before the tiredness.

Many years later I would find the explanation. Salicylates can impair production of glucose in the body while increasing glucose utilisation. This causes an imbalance, resulting in salicylate-induced hypoglycemia. Rebecca's problems while on holidays or bushwalking were related to our higher consumption of salicylate-containing foods such as dried fruit. The effect was worsened by exercise, which increases the body's need for glucose.

Problems in many areas

Rebecca had problems in many areas and with each professional I saw I risked being treated as neurotic. If they did help it was only within their area of speciality. I was getting the most helpful information from books. Parenting felt like a difficult and lonely job to me. No matter how much effort Rebecca put into something, other children were winning prizes for various sports, doing well at ballet or having other successes.

At swimming classes Rebecca would listen to the long list of instructions and forget what she was supposed to do. She dropped out of Brownies because she didn't seem to understand what was going on or make friends with the others. She dropped out of gym, which she never enjoyed.

When she came home in tears after a special ballet class with an authoritarian teacher who relied heavily on sarcasm I took her out of that class. Other mothers talked earnestly to me about teaching children not to be quitters but I felt my child already had enough difficulties in life. Why should she persevere when it led to continual failure and criticism? But I found it disheartening to have a child who often failed, despite extra effort on her part and my feeling that she was capable of better.

Some alternatives

I looked at some alternative therapies. The first naturopath turned out to be interested in megavitamin therapy. I don't feel comfortable with this, as I can't see any difference between drugs and large doses of synthetic vitamins but I decided to give his recommendation a go. Rebecca was to take chromium tablets every day for two weeks. I couldn't see any change during this time. Then she was to start on a low dose of phenyl-alanine, an amino acid. The result here was startling. The ballet teacher greeted me with, 'When Rebecca has a day like today, we all hold our breath and say, "Wow, here comes Rebecca!"'

I noticed improvement in coordination and Rebecca's atten-tion seemed more focused. These improvements didn't last. Then I discovered a whole string of tablets stuck under the table. Rebecca had stopped taking them. Despite the improvement the phenylalanine made, I felt sufficiently uneasy about using what I saw as a drug to stop using it if Rebecca didn't want to take it. That was the end of that experiment.

Later we also tried evening primrose oil. Rebecca's teacher told us, 'Before I had to remind Rebecca to do things about ten times a day. Now it's only about three.' This was a help but not the whole answer and after a while we realised it made her depressed. No more evening primrose.

Increasingly, Howard was required to go away on business trips, which included meetings all over Australia, trips to Alice Springs and Katherine, flights over Kakadu wetlands to inspect weed control programs, 4WD trips in central Australian agri-cultural trials and the occasional trip to Indonesia. 'I suppose I do have a more exciting job than the average Canberra bureau-crat,' Howard said, although he disliked interstate meetings because they required so much travelling. I hated the amount of time he had to spend away from home but thought the job suited him because it contained enough variety and adventure to keep him interested. 'Look at this,' Howard would often say as he arrived home from work, and we would all sit down for a ceremonial tasting of an exotic fruit.

Because of his interest in this area we bought unusual fruit such as tropical jackfruit, starfruit and pomelos at the Asian-style markets every week. Some of these fruits obviously affected Rebecca and the pomelos, large green citrus fruit with a delicate pink flesh and exquisite flavour, affected us all badly in different ways.

'Walking on eggshells'

Rebecca's inability to sleep was still a major problem. Our three bedroom house was set up with a study and a guest bedroom. The large master bedroom contained the only air conditioner, our double bed, Rebecca's hammock and Arran's bed. This unconventional sleeping arrangement proved the easiest because Rebecca needed company and constant reassurance to get to sleep. She went to sleep most easily if we were all in the room and woke at the slightest noise.

If Howard and I wanted to watch a video we would have to get her to sleep first, which sometimes took two or three hours, or let her sleep on a sheepskin in the hall where she could see us but not the screen. If the music was too scary she would complain, so we gave up trying after a while. Howard recalled, 'I remember my parents saying they used to find me asleep behind the sofa when I was meant to be in bed. They always said I got easier at the age of eight when I started reading.'

My days passed in a blur of exhaustion. I frequently felt numb from fatigue and unable to cope, and napped in the after-noon while the children were watching television. I usually fell asleep the instant I lay down regardless of the time of day, although when my sleep was disturbed too frequently I became unable to go to sleep for hours. This was accompanied by emotional outbursts, loss of confidence and inability to make decisions.

When Howard was away on business trips I felt as if I was on duty all day every day. Rebecca would not leave me alone. She had many fears, of the dark, of dogs, of being alone, of pain. She was often irritable, demanding and uncooperative. I had to treat her very gently especially in the mornings or she was likely to respond with a temper outburst.

'Like walking on eggshells,' said one mother. Sometimes I would have to spend hours sitting with Rebecca to get her to sleep. I felt I had no time or space to myself. At these times I often thought to myself, 'I want to resign. This job is too hard and the hours are too long. I never agreed to these work conditions when I took it on.'

Darkest hour

Many mothers have shared with me that they have fantasies of packing their bags and walking out on the children just before their husband arrives home and some of them have carried it out. I often felt like this too, particularly during business trips. Howard hated coming home after these trips and was angry with my inability to cope. I was usually exhausted but too wound up to sleep and we often fought.

One night while he was away it was all too much for me. I lost control and screamed at Rebecca hysterically, 'Go to sleep or I'll bash you to a bloody pulp.' Darwin houses are not soundproof. With open louvres and still tropical nights sound carries. I heard a muffled exclamation from the neighbours.

'What am I doing?' I thought. 'How can I say this to my own daughter? I can't manage by myself. I need help.'

I had always tried to keep to our rule of 'No smacking'. I felt if I ever started I would not be able to stop and Rebecca would be a battered child. Now I started having thoughts of killing her and how quiet it would be afterwards. I was frightened by how I felt.

With my sanity, Rebecca's life and my marriage under threat, I made an appointment at the Department of Health and Community Services centre and spent an hour crying about my problems to a counsellor. She listened kindly, and summed up, 'I don't think I'm the one to help you. You are depressed, but it sounds as if there's a good reason for it. I suggest you go to the child and family section and see if they can help you as a family.'

It would be years before I would see a list of the symptoms for oppositional defiance (see the box on p. 61) and realise that all of them, except the last one, were what I found so difficult about Rebecca.

I wish the counsellor could have said then, 'Look, these are the symptoms which are driving you mad. You can get rid of all of them by getting your daughter's diet right. Go to a dietitian and do the RPAH (failsafe) diet strictly.' At least she didn't try to fob me off with antidepressants. She was right about one thing – the pressure I was under was intolerable. We had to make some changes.

OPPOSITIONAL DEFIANT DISORDER

Children with ODD like to say 'no'. *Irritability* is the main feature of this disorder. Symptoms include:

- losing temper
- arguing with adults
- defying requests or defying rules
- deliberately annoying others
- blaming others for their own mistakes
- touchy and easily annoyed
- angry and resentful
- spiteful and vindictive.

ODD develops between one to three years; consists of a pattern of negative, hostile and defiant behaviour lasting at least six months; includes at least four of the above features; can exist with or without ADHD; and runs in families.

The child's behaviour depends on others:

- normal when 'life is good'
- overreacts to negative interactions.

If untreated, ODD can progress to conduct disorder which often involves law-breaking.

Treatment

Diet can be 100 per cent successful. All the above symptoms can melt away, as shown in the remarkable video the *Shipley Project* (see p. 243). Children do not have to be diagnosed with ODD to improve on diet.

Behavioural approach

- stay calm, avoid confrontations, be positive, offer options
- *never* back the child into a corner
- a critical, authoritarian, punitive or violent approach can aggravate the condition.

Medication has limited success. ADHD medications can make oppositional defiance worse because children can focus better on being defiant.

It was hard for Howard to find time to make appointments but we managed and were assigned to a team of psychologists. The process of talking about our problems was very useful for us. We had trouble saying exactly what our problems were.

The counsellors helped us to focus on the issue of getting Rebecca to sleep and suggested a simple little trick to help us. We set up a clock at Rebecca's bedside and said, 'Go to sleep. I'll come in and see you in five minutes.' The next night it was ten minutes and so on. This didn't help Rebecca to get to sleep but it gave us a breathing space. After she had tossed around for a few hours we would often get her up and give her some more supper, otherwise she would wake later with nightmares.

The counsellors now recommended that we come for marriage counselling. As a family, our situation had deteriorated. Howard was often away at work. When he was at home he felt I was too easy on the kids and responded by being what I saw as too strict and authoritarian.

Overwhelmed by fatigue and Rebecca's incredible resistance to requests, I found it easier to give in. Howard and I were not presenting a united front. All children need limits and want their parents to be in control, difficult children especially so.

The best environment for any child, but especially a child with behaviour problems, is a close, loving family where there are clear rules. This was not happening for us. I spent most of the sessions with tears rolling down my face. 'Why are you crying?' the counsellor would say. It was hard to explain. I felt relieved that the load I had shouldered alone for so long was being shared, angry with Howard for sometimes leaving me in what I felt was an impossible situation and humiliated that I couldn't cope with my own child.

The counselling on our marriage, painful though it was, worked and we became a loving couple again, learning to listen, hear each other's needs and work together on our problems.

Throughout the sessions, the counsellors encouraged me to stop trying to help Rebecca and to come to terms with the way she was. They were wrong. There was a solution for her, I just hadn't found it yet.

School problems for Arran

Towards the end of the school year we moved into a house with wide verandahs and sea breezes, which met all of Howard's criteria of outlook, privacy and potential garden and unlike the others was convenient to live in as well. The catch, in this case, was the size of the mortgage. In the evenings we ate on the verandah, watching formations of magpie geese against the sunset sky. I can feel overwhelmed by Rebecca in a confined space but this house was set up for outdoor living. As well, the children moved into their own bedroom.

On the last day of school, the preschool teacher called me in. 'You can send Arran to school next year if you want to,' she told me, 'but I recommend he spends another term in preschool.' I was aghast. He hated preschool. I had been hoping he would enjoy school more.

'Why don't you think he's ready for school?' I asked. We thought of him as bright and competent. The teacher was perplexed.

'It's hard to say. I know he's articulate. He's been assessed as three years ahead of his peers in the language area, but there are some areas I worry about. Social immaturity. Poor pencil skills. Perhaps another term will give him a chance to catch up.' I had always regarded Rebecca as the one with problems.

At home, I found Arran a charming companion who could entertain himself for hours. When he was good, which was most of the time, he was excellent. But when he was bad he was terrible. He would whine unceasingly if I stopped to chat to a friend. Arran could be very inflexible, and was capable of extraordinary temper outbursts. It was impossible to reason with him at these times. Even when locked in his room he would continue ranting for hours.

Very active

Despite a high level of activity I didn't think of him as hyperactive but often when he was in a group such as a swimming class the instructor would say to me 'He's a bit hyper, isn't he?' We had noticed him completely out of control after eating junk food one day, but as he was on Rebecca's diet too, this was not usually a problem. While he rode a bike well, his fine motor coordination was poor. As well, he still had the stomach aches and chronic diarrhoea which dated from the age of ten months.

I told the preschool teacher that Arran's sister had ADHD. 'I don't like labelling children,' she said. Some experts recommend that the greater their understanding, the more likely teachers are to be able to help the child.

With misgivings I agreed to send Arran back to preschool the next year. I now know that in general repeating a grade because of social immaturity or poor fine motor skills has been found to be unhelpful because it may lead to boredom, which is exactly what happened to Arran. It is more constructive for an understanding teacher to provide help with particular problems.

At the end of our second school year in Darwin, we had come a long way in our understanding of Rebecca's condition. We had an official diagnosis and more treatments. I was, however, starting to recognise a pattern. Whenever I started to think I had things under control, another problem area became apparent.

The symptoms of both food intolerance and ADHD change with age, and can persist throughout life. It used to be thought that children grew out of hyperactivity. In fact, a reduction in activity level at about ages five to seven may lead parents to report an improvement, but at the same time coordination problems may become apparent through difficulties with school sport, or social problems with peers may become more obvious. If reading is to be a problem the teacher may start to notice that now, and the secondary behaviour problems which arise from the child's feelings of inadequacy may begin. With our eternal optimism we were prematurely congratulating ourselves on Rebecca's having escaped learning difficulties.

A New Zealand holiday

A few days after school finished we departed for a holiday in New Zealand, exchanging the humid heat and dramatic lightning displays of the wet season build-up for a cool and grey Christchurch. We stayed with my friend Robin and her family who were now living on a small farm. It was good to see Rebecca and her babyhood friend Rosemary playing together again. Robin was intrigued to see how Rebecca had grown up and how sensibly she ate.

'The tables are turned,' she said. 'I don't know how you keep her off sugar. It's hard when all the other children eat so many sweets. When they come here Rosemary insists they eat sweets too.' In the old days it had been Rebecca who was the fussy eater, not Rosemary. Now Rebecca was eating regular, balanced meals. Rosemary had become more fussy: 'No, I won't eat a sandwich. Only with chocolate sprinkles.'

We meet the children

After leaving Christchurch we spent a week camping in our beloved mountains, and then headed towards our meeting with Howard's other children, Emma and Matthew. We were very anxious about this. What would we say? What would they be like? Feeling apprehensive, we arranged with their mother, Beth, to meet at our motel. While we waited Howard and I walked to the corner store.

We were on our way back when a small white car pulled up beside us. It was full of eyes and suddenly there we were. All just looking and looking. Emma and Matthew staring at Howard. Howard staring at Emma and Matthew. Beth and I hugging, everybody hugging, wiping their eyes.

Dinner at a restaurant that night was a great success. We looked at the menu and there was a chorus of 'I can't eat cheese,' 'I can't eat wheat,' 'I can't eat sugar,' and we all laughed. It was good to be with people who understood. Matthew turned out to have the same gift as Rebecca and Howard of enjoying young children and took Rebecca and Arran out for a walk. There was so much to talk about.

Beth had planned a magical mystery tour for us, starting with a stately old home. Rebecca and Arran were fascinated. On a beach the children went for a swim and explored the sand hills, then we had a cliff-top walk. All the time we were getting to know each other.

Beth and Matthew share our love of nature and wild places, while Emma shares Rebecca's obsession with books. It was interesting to see the family resemblances, both in looks and personality. Beth and I were surprised to find that Emma and Rebecca had similar sleeping patterns as babies.

'Emma only ever slept for half an hour during the day,' Beth told me, 'and she often had to sleep in with us.'

'I don't have to worry about food'

There was a sense of negativity about Emma. She obviously wanted to get to know Howard yet didn't want to join in with some of our excursions. 'I think she's got ADHD too,' Beth explained, 'but she doesn't want to know about it. She's never done as well at school as I expected.' Emma was failing in some subjects and just passing in others, despite everyone's feeling that she could do better. When we ate out she ordered colas while the rest of us drank soda water. 'I don't have to worry about food,' she said. We agreed with Beth that the only possible approach was uncritical acceptance. We liked her as a person and hoped she would grow out of this stage of defiance.

Looking at all four children and their father together we were fascinated to see the similarities and differences. It was as if they had been offered a set of behaviours at birth and all had chosen a different number and combination. Rebecca had the most problems, then Matthew, Emma, and Arran.

It was hard to know where Howard would have fitted in if he was a comparable age. At school I suspect that Howard played the role of the class clown, continually making jokes which were not always appreciated by teachers, whereas Emma said she could be loud and stroppy in class. Rebecca and Matthew were the dreamers who got nothing done. Howard, Emma, Rebecca and Arran were all excellent readers. Matthew had a learning disability in reading, Emma and Rebecca had difficulties with maths. Three of them had coordination problems, but not in the same way. Four out of five had sugar cravings. Matthew had a sensitivity about food textures and lumpy food which he shared with Howard's father. Rebecca disliked dry food and hated chewing. Arran was sensitive to loud noises and scratchy clothes, especially garment labels. Howard, Emma and Rebecca shared the sleep problems, difficulty getting to sleep and staying asleep. Matthew slept long hours and was hard to wake and Arran slept well – when he wasn't eating food colouring – and woke early.

This is what makes labelling children's problems so difficult: no two children are the same, and behaviours change with age. At this time Emma was nearly fifteen, Matthew nearly thirteen, Rebecca eight and Arran just five.

After a few days we left, arranging to meet up again on a tiny island off the south coast in a week's time. As we said our goodbyes, Matthew slipped into our car, pretending to stow away. He sat silently in the back seat. 'What was that about?' Howard asked me as we drove off. 'Does he really want to be with us, or was it only a joke?'

'I don't know,' I answered. 'It felt like a cry for help, but perhaps I'm wrong.'

We were off to rugged Fiordland. Emma and Matthew's legal father, Colin, and his new partner were also in Fiordland for a tramping holiday and came to visit us. We sat comfortably indoors and chatted about old climbing trips while the rain drummed on the roof. Like many fathers, Colin was wary of the diet-behaviour link.

An impulsive decision

With Donna, our wonderful babysitter, who was now a doctor in a nearby hospital, we joined Beth, Emma and Matthew on Stewart Island. Donna and I talked non-stop, trying to catch up on three years in three days. She was worried by Arran's skinny appearance combined with his history of chronic diarrhoea and suggested consulting a pediatrician. We all explored the island together and went fishing. During this time we were forming an impression of Emma and Matthew.

Their upbringing was similar in many ways to our family lifestyle. Camping, adventurous outdoor trips, nature and a healthy lifestyle were a big part of their lives. We envied their family canoeing and hiking trips. For Matthew, there was also sailing with his father. I admired the way Beth had pursued the naturopathic approach to health far more than I, raising Matthew to the age of twelve without antibiotics and only a tiny quantity of paracetamol. Food additives had been avoided. She was using a therapy called spirionics, similar to, but more involved than, the educational kinesiology which had proved so useful for us.

Before the family split up, they had lived in an idyllic place in the country which possessed in abundance all the features we value – outlook, privacy, a vegetable garden and easy access to beautiful nature reserves.

It was obvious that the marriage breakdown had been traumatic for everyone. Emma was in a teenage stage of negativity and rebellion. Matthew was lacking in confidence and doing badly at school. 'Do you think there's anything we can do to help?' Howard and I asked each other. Emma was happy with her group of friends at school but Matthew was about to attend a new school for just one year before starting high school.

We made a quick decision. With less than a week of school holidays remaining we suggested that Matthew would be welcome to come and spend this school year with us. Beth must have found this a terribly hard decision to make but came to the conclusion that it was an excellent opportunity for Matthew's personal growth. Colin and Emma were both opposed to the idea but gave in to Matthew's great determination.

Thus we found ourselves heading back to our new house in Darwin, with Matthew arriving on the plane the next day, to stay for ten months. There were many times during the next month when I thought, 'What have I let myself in for? We've invited a virtual stranger to share our home for nearly a year.'

4 Matthew's year

I admired Matthew's courage. It couldn't have been easy to come and live with strangers in another country, and he was homesick at first. It was interesting to observe him closely. Rebecca and Matthew were at opposite ends of the spectrum. She had difficulty sleeping. He slept like a log and took a long time to wake in the morning. At school she found maths difficult. He had trouble with reading. You wouldn't have thought they suffered from the same problem.

Hyperactive children can change from 'flippers' to 'floppers'. Matthew was a flopper. It was hard to get him going. Perhaps he had once been a flipper. He was accident prone, we noticed almost straight away, quite apart from the scars he was covered with. If he deviated from his additive-free diet at all, there was usually some small accident. Hearing crashing noises from the kitchen one night, we found Matthew ankle deep in broken crockery, having broken nine plates in one go.

'Everything he touches seems to wear out,' I wrote to Donna. 'He's an academic failure, clumsy, used to acting dumb and playing the fool to cover up the hurt from failure and criticism. My heart goes out to these kids, because it is a cycle they cannot break out of by themselves.'

It was hard for us to know how to explain Matthew to other people. I usually said, 'This is my stepson Matthew from New Zealand,' and left people to construct their own story, but this didn't explain the obvious lack of relationship between Howard and Matthew. We told our families and close friends the whole story. Most were open-minded and supportive.

It was clear that Emma and Matthew wanted to know about their biological father, in the same way that adopted children often make huge efforts to seek out their birth mothers. These days adopted children and children from artificial insemination by donor schemes are encouraged to meet their biological parents. It is not because they want to replace the loving relationship with their nurturing parents. The children just want to know their background as a part of understanding themselves.

Term one

Matthew was one of the oldest and tallest in the class. With his size he stood out. Right from the start he disliked school. 'How was school?' I'd ask.

'Boring,' Matthew would answer.

I already knew and liked Matthew's teacher. When I described Matthew's problems to her she commented, 'Great, I think I've got a bit of that myself.' She was sympathetic and took care to bolster the children's self-confidence. Matthew liked her. After a few days, she recommended a special reading and spelling program for me to do at home with him.

'He needs to improve his reading and writing before he goes to high school,' she warned. 'He doesn't do much in class, and never finishes anything. I'll refer him for assessment.'

Karate

I also talked to Rebecca's physiotherapist about Matthew's coordination. 'Motivation is a problem with older kids,' he said. 'Martial arts are good. You need an activity where they have to think about their actions and do them properly. You'll probably need three sessions a week to make a difference.' We were able to get Matthew into a karate class which he liked straight away.

From the time he arrived, Matthew started eating our diet. His presence made cooking more complicated, as he did not eat meat, except chicken. I wrote to Donna, 'Arran's chronic diarrhoea has been diagnosed as possible gluten intolerance, so every night I have to plan a dairy-free, sugar-free, meat-free, gluten-free, additive-free, moderate-salicylate meal.' It was easy to write about it flippantly, but a couple of times in the first week I sat down and cried in despair.

Textures

I discovered that Matthew could not eat certain textures like lumpy soup if a million dollars depended on it. His range of food was limited to mainly chicken, mashed potato, eggs and blended vegetable soup. We started eating a lot of chicken. After a while we introduced him to some favourite Territory specials, such as barramundi fish and mango ice-cream made from pure fruit. Gradually he widened his range of foods.

Matthew was going through a growth spurt and ate more than any of us. I had to think of new and filling foods in a hurry. I baked fresh damper over campfires and at home. I baked scones, muffins, cookies, loaves and cakes, all sugar-free. For every batch I had to cook a corresponding gluten-free lot for Arran and me.

When Matthew ate the wrong foods, he became clumsy and generally had some kind of accident. He would become talkative, but the quality would deteriorate. Rebecca sometimes does this. After a while I would realise, 'This is rubbish. I don't want to listen to this.' His concentration would evaporate, but detecting this was more subtle and I didn't notice unless we were doing homework together.

Matthew's level of activity was higher than Rebecca's. While watching television he constantly fidgeted. We tried to teach him to sit still by using gentle reminders. I wish I'd known more about the failsafe diet then. What I thought of as a moderate salicylate diet was still way too high in salicylates.

At first I was bothered that, unlike Rebecca, Matthew would never have a quiet time with a book. 'He can't entertain himself,' I complained to Howard. 'He wants to be with other people all the time, or watch television and play computer games.' However, in an extended family, there's always someone doing something interesting. Matthew, Rebecca and Arran enjoyed each other's company and got on amazingly well together considering the age differences. Matthew was nearly thirteen, Rebecca was eight and Arran had just turned five.

On the weekends we showed Matthew the Territory. With his enjoyment of camping, water sports and wildlife, Matthew fitted into our family perfectly.

Reading program

Within a few weeks of Matthew's arrival we started on a reading program which consisted of working our way through a book of graded word lists, doing twenty minutes every night, with a mixture of spelling, reading and writing. We visited the library to apply for a library card. Matthew was obviously uncomfortable. He sat in the middle of the library trying to avoid looking at the books.

Matthew's parents had both explained their concern about his reading ability. Although he could read words slowly and laboriously he was not really a functional reader in that he did not read for either information or pleasure. I couldn't understand how he had got to the age of twelve without a teacher pressing the panic button until I realised that, like Rebecca with her sheet music, he gave the appearance of having more skills than he really possessed.

It wasn't until I started a systematic program with him that I understood how many problems he had. There are some bizarre stories of illiterate adults who have achieved extraordinary success while keeping their illiteracy secret, including an American who graduated from university, worked as a teacher and became the millionaire owner of a real-estate business while unable to read or write.

Matthew's main trick, which worked well, was to smile disarmingly at whoever was handy and ask politely for help. He had some clever questions which drew the helper into explanations, such as, 'What do you think they mean here?' or 'I don't quite understand this one.' When he appeared to be reading he was mostly looking at pictures.

Apparent laziness

I had noticed at the museum that, although he wanted to know about the exhibits, Matthew avoided looking at any written information. Now I understood why. His teacher explained that he used delaying tactics like looking for a pencil in class and proceeded slowly with no intention of finishing the work. His lack of skill was hidden by apparent laziness.

When I first got him to write a sentence, virtually the only words he spelt correctly were 'a' and 'the'. Even common words like 'chair' and 'table' were wild guesses. We went right back to the beginning and started with the alphabet and in particular short vowel sounds. We then worked our way through carefully graded lists of words using these sounds, progressing through the various elements of spelling, such as consonant blends and long vowel sounds, at Matthew's own pace. He had to go right back to the beginning and learn everything again.

Literature immersion

I started borrowing up to forty library books a week between the five of us. There were books in every room of the house. For Matthew and Arran I chose picture books with a wide range of topics, or anything about nature. These were the books we used in our first reading sessions. I deliberately left cereal packets and magazines on the table.

This is a remedial reading technique called literature immersion. The idea is that children must be surrounded by books and see people reading in order to understand the need for reading.

Matthew's mother, Beth, had obviously spent huge amounts of time reading aloud to Matthew, as he knew and loved a wide range of the books which good readers of his age would normally read. This was an excellent way of helping Matthew, as it fostered a love of literature and helped Matthew to want to read.

A television ban

'I don't know what to do about television,' I said to Howard. 'With such a big age range, the kids want to watch different shows and the TV will be on a lot. Now I understand why Beth doesn't have one.' Matthew would have been happy to sit and watch television non-stop.

We ended up with a ban on television, except for family shows that we could all watch together. I was pleased with the television ban. The house was quieter, the children were more interesting, they read more, and the times we did sit down to a favourite show were family times that everyone looked forward to.

Computer games were different. One of our favourites then was a science fiction adventure game in which instructions had to be keyed in. It didn't work unless they were spelled correctly. Some of the first words that my children learned to spell were 'thermal detonator' and 'nuclear reactor'. I was pleased that their brains were being engaged but I still had to remind them, 'Go and look at the sky. It's time for some fresh air and exercise.' The kitchen timer was invaluable. If I didn't limit the time they spent on the computer, Matthew would have stayed on it all day.

Karate for Matthew, ballet and piano for Rebecca and gym for Arran were keeping me busy after school. As well, we visited the toy library often, partly for stimulating toys like Lego Technics, and partly for educational aids and games.

Darwin was having an exceptionally good wet season, almost as good as the one in which Cyclone Tracy dumped a lot of rain. Nevertheless we went ahead with our plan to install a swimming pool. 'Swimming pools are a necessity in Darwin,' the bank manager said, and extended our mortgage.

Exercise

From the time we had arrived in Darwin I had come to think that a swimming pool is the very best way for children to wear off energy. It takes up a relatively small space, occupies hours of time, and they don't have to be well coordinated to enjoy splashing around. The advantage of having your own pool is that you can have pool toys and by now we had an inflatable rubber boat, masks and snorkels plus whatever we thought of. Upturned plastic buckets provided good flotation. There was always something. The water in Darwin is so warm the children would stay in for hours.

Now that Matthew was with us, Howard could join me on my morning beach walks. Because of the huge tide range in the Top End, sometimes we ended up wading around cliffs with the incoming tide above our knees. The rising sun on the yachts, the birds in the lagoon and, in the wet season, the excitement of storm clouds or a quick tropical downpour made these walks very special. We caught glimpses of the occasional dolphins, manta rays, turtles, crocodiles and dugongs. 'Where else in the world could we get a walk like this?' we would say. I had never seen Howard so settled. The Territory was providing the adventurous lifestyle he and Rebecca thrive on.

Homework

We expected homework to be done conscientiously. Matthew employed his usual technique of looking interested, getting all the books out and then saying, 'What do they mean by this question?' If I wasn't careful I found myself doing it all for him.

I realised it was taking him hours of painstaking effort to complete what should have been manageable in half an hour. The effort was not worth the result. He was too far behind to be able to learn from work at this level. No wonder he found school boring. 'Can he leave out the harder sections?' I asked his teacher.

'Good idea,' she replied. 'He's doing all that extra work at home anyway. Keep it up. I can see the results already.'

For the major term project Matthew had to complete a book review. This took hours of work nearly every day for two weeks and, as I was determined not to do it all for him, meant a large number of spelling errors per page. It was awarded a 'C'. Throughout the year Matthew was extraordinarily willing to work long hours at what were for him very difficult tasks. I admired his persistence and was only too pleased to help him.

Nine weeks after Matthew joined us, the guidance officer phoned me. She was supportive of the reading program I was doing with Matthew and assessed him straight away. We had already seen an improvement but the assessment showed a nearly four year learning delay in spelling and an over two year delay in reading. 'I'll try to get him into the Language Development Centre,' she said. 'It's a small class of intensive language study every morning for a month.'

'Will he catch up to grade level by the end of the year?' I asked, thinking of his return to New Zealand.

'No,' she replied. 'There's no way he can catch up a delay like this in a year.'

End of term one

During the short school holiday at the end of Term One I enrolled Matthew in a sailing course, partly to give us a break from each other and partly to increase his confidence. Matthew had done some sailing with his father in New Zealand in his own dinghy. 'I'm the only one in the class who hasn't capsized,' he grinned.

My mother joined us for the holiday. Over Easter we went canoeing on Katherine Gorge with two canoes for the six of us and visited Mataranka Hot Springs and Edith Falls.

My mother disliked Matthew. She thought I was spending too much time with him and not enough time with my own children. 'You are running around in circles looking after all of them and he's so lazy, he doesn't lift a finger to help. You're wasting your time with him,' she said. 'He's dumb.'

Victim mode

So this was her assessment of him. She had been a school-teacher for more than twenty years. Her approach was to lick him into shape with endless criticism. Matthew responded by going into what Beth calls 'victim mode'. He stopped trying and deluged us with endless questions, some reasonable, many unnecessary: 'Where's the butter? What's this for?'

Although he was aggravating to live with, I could understand what he was doing. He was under an unreasonable load of crit-icism and had no other avenue of fighting back. I watched the fragile self-confidence I had fostered crumbling. 'He has improved so much since he came to us. Please try to praise his good points and avoid criticism,' I begged. 'He's had that from his teachers all his life.'

It was hard for Mum. She felt that Matthew was an intruder in the family. But after that she kept her mouth shut, even if she was gritting her teeth. My aim was to not overload Matthew. It was true that he did nothing in the house unless asked but we had made a start. He was working willingly on reading and homework.

We sometimes felt overwhelmed by Matthew's endless questions. One of the counsellors who'd helped with Rebecca had a session with us about Matthew. At her suggestion we started answering every question with, 'What do you think?' or 'I think you might know the answer to that.' We were fortunate that the education department provided an assertiveness training course for Matthew's class. He looked forward to these sessions and gained in confidence from them.

Term two

At the start of second term, Howard began an intensive evening course in Indonesian, to be completed with a week in Timor at the end of the term. His job involved Indonesian liaison which he enjoyed, but he needed more language skills. He was very busy and we saw little of him except on weekends, although he made a point of collecting Matthew from karate during the week.

Arran finally started school, aged five and a quarter. For a few weeks he was happy but disenchantment quickly set in. He refused to read the readers which were sent home, which perplexed me because I knew he could read. He would sit on my lap while I read *Time* magazine, reading the headlines and sometimes whole sentences aloud. I had always thought that Arran was bright and wondered why his teachers did not think so. I felt the same about Rebecca.

Part two of the bread preservative story

Rebecca and her new teacher were not getting on at all. There was an emphasis on mental arithmetic and maths tests which she failed badly, and she began to cry about going to school. My explanatory talk to the teacher had backfired in a way. When I talked to her about the maths problems it became obvious that she had decided Rebecca was a difficult child and had a low expectation of achievement. In light of subsequent discoveries I don't see how she could have thought otherwise.

I enrolled Rebecca in a remedial maths class. The initial assessment was worrying. She appeared to have little concept of maths and was assigned to the lowest level, counting dots, then progressing to adding one to the numbers under ten. She did not improve as well as the instructor expected. At this time she was eight and a half. It was hard to reconcile her lack of performance with the child who had read the entire C. S. Lewis *Chronicles of Narnia* series by herself around her seventh birthday. In ballet Rebecca was also failing to live up to expectations.

Reaching for our familiar brand of bread one day in the supermarket I noticed with a sinking heart that the packaging had changed. Quickly scanning the ingredients list, I found what I feared: 'mould inhibitor (282)'. I rushed home and phoned the manager of the bakery.

'When was the recipe changed?' I asked.

The manager was friendly but evasive. Although he would not give me a date, it was clear that the recipe had changed some time ago while the old packaging was being used up. Unknowingly I had been feeding Rebecca her old enemy. No wonder she had been having trouble at school and ballet. I was surprised that I hadn't picked the problem myself. Effects of bread preservative are cumulative, and the onset of symptoms is slow and subtle. Rebecca's new teacher could not be expected to see the problem as she had no basis for comparison.

I found a new brand of bread clearly marked 'No Preservatives', although I had a half-hour round trip to buy it. Rebecca's maths and ballet showed immediate improvement.

Matthew starts to succeed

In the fourth week of second term I wrote to Beth. 'In the three spelling tests so far this term Matthew has come top, done very well, and got 100 per cent, and last week he came home proudly with a merit certificate for his science project. For this they had to choose an animal. Matthew chose a platypus "because he didn't know anything about it", typed the information into the computer, used a spelling checker then added line drawings on each page. He put hours of work into it. His mark was 87 per cent, compared to a "C" in the last project.' Matthew was starting to savour success, the best motivator.

He also became interested in finishing a Roald Dahl book we were using in the spelling program. It was the first novel Matthew finished of his own accord. 'I'm going to read all of Roald Dahl's books,' he announced, reaching this goal within a few months.

Matthew's attitude to spelling had changed. 'I'm going to learn each word properly,' he explained. 'I know I can learn all the words in a spelling list.' The lists he was learning were structured so that he was learning spelling rules at the same time. He still made a lot of mistakes but the wild guesses had gone.

At karate, Matthew was proud of his new uniform and passed his first grading. I wrote to Donna, 'Now he looks like a winner instead of a loser.'

A letter came from Emma. 'I felt angry when I first heard Matthew was going to Australia. I thought you were stealing my brother. Now I realise it is the best thing for Matthew. He sounds much happier in his letters.'

It was time for the half-yearly report card. Matthew's teacher gave me the report with a big smile and said, 'Read it first. I've got some good news for you.'

Despite this, I felt disheartened by the report card. All the important subjects, spelling, reading, and maths, as well as handwriting, were rated below average. The good news was that recent diagnostic tests showed Matthew's learning delay in spelling and reading had improved by ten months in one term. 'He is the most improved in the class,' his teacher said. 'If he keeps it up, he'll be doing well by the end of the year.'

Social problems

Socially, Matthew was having a terrible time at school. He was finding it hard to make friends and was constantly teased by one boy. At home the three children and I discussed methods for coping with teasing and practised them with role plays, which was fun, although I don't know if it helped.

'We've always taught our children no hitting,' I said to

Howard, 'but this time I think the whole problem would vanish if Matthew would just hit the boy. But how can I say that?'

Beth agreed with me. 'We've always felt he needs to be able to express his anger,' she replied.

This was one of the situations where I felt I'd been thrown in at the deep-end, trying to parent a thirteen-year-old. It made me realise how much parents grow with their children.

The situation improved suddenly as Matthew made friends with a new boy who also had a learning disability. Both agreed, 'This school is more violent than the ones we've come from.' Matthew and his new friend played endless games, both on and off the computer. I was relieved that Matthew had found a friend, although the teasing continued.

Behaviour management program

Fed up with lack of help in the house, I started a new system of credit points like the old star charts which I hadn't used for a while. First I made a list of what bothered me most. I would have said we had problems in all areas, but it was mainly doing household chores, getting ready for school, going to bed and listening to my instructions. I started giving clearer instructions, establishing eye contact first and keeping it simple and positive.

The children had to pay 10 points for rewards such as half an hour of computer

EXAMPLE OF SCORESHEET

	Plus	Minus	
unload dishwasher	20		
made sandwich	20		
computer time		-20	
ready for school on time	30		
movie		-50	
good bedtime/ sleeping	100		
clean school shoes	20		
maths homework	30		
video time		-20	
grizzle		-10	
cash		-50	
Total	220	-150	70

time, friend to play or family board game. A special dessert, video hire or the waterslide cost 20 points. They could earn points by being ready for school on time, chores and homework. There were bonuses for willingness and occasional small fines for complaining but overall we kept it positive. To stop the rewards from escalating, the program was used during alternate months.

The results amazed me. I reported to Beth, 'Rebecca and Matthew have been literally fighting each other to do chores, fighting over possession of the broom and elbowing each other away from the sink. It would have been funny if they hadn't been so serious. I had to modify the system to prevent an outbreak of hostilities. The more I observe the three of them the more I realise how different Rebecca and Matthew are.'

I had discovered that Arran would do what he was asked and would respond to praise. He didn't have to be bribed or reminded to do things. On the other hand, Rebecca and Matthew didn't understand the concept of doing something just for the praise or job satisfaction, but were extremely bribable. Arran didn't care so much about the bribe.

The reward for a certain age-related number of credit points was a whole block of the chocolate substitute, carob. Matthew always ate his immediately. Rebecca hoarded hers carefully, eating a little at a time and always knew how much she had left. Arran generally ate some and forgot about the rest.

Eisteddfod

The next event on the school calendar was the Darwin Eisteddfod. Matthew's class entered in the verse-speaking section, reciting an amusing poem about a biker gang of nuns. Matthew felt a special sense of kinship with this poem as he had recommended the book to the class. We all enjoyed learning it and recited bits at the dinner table. His teacher did a wonderful job preparing the students. The class had to appear on the main stage in the Darwin Entertainment Centre and the recital was a great success.

Mid-year break

At the end of term my mother arrived. She was astonished at the change in Matthew. 'He's like a different person,' she exclaimed. 'I thought you were wasting your time, but I have to admit I was wrong. I admire your determination, Sue.'

In the Northern Territory there is a long school holiday during the dry season, in the middle of the year, which is more like a summer holiday for us. The day after school finished the six of us caught a flight to West Timor in Indonesia.

From Kupang we travelled in an Indonesian fishing boat to a sparsely-populated island, staying in a palm weave bungalow on the beach. There were no roads or cars. Every morning we went out snorkelling in a boat and in the afternoons we walked up a path through rice paddies for a swim in a freshwater spring. Matthew and Rebecca joined up with some other tourist children while Arran, now aged five and a half, played with the village children and their animals. One morning I noticed a line of red flea bites on his tummy but was not alarmed because at the time I had no idea that diseases like typhus could be carried by fleas.

After a week on the little island, we took the inter-island ferry for another week on the volcano-studded island of Flores. Between our major destinations was the hard work of low budget travelling, rock bottom hotels, crowded public transport, long waits and strange food. But the children managed the holiday well. Processed food is unknown in the eastern islands of Indonesia, so additive-free eating was easy.

Term three

Third term was to be turbulent for us. After three days at school Arran came home with a sore throat and headache which eventually became high fevers, a peculiar bruise-like rash and migraine-type headaches with visual disturbances. It took numerous blood tests and the whole term to discover that he had contracted typhus from the flea bites in West Timor.

Rebecca started the term auspiciously with a pass in her ballet exam. I was delighted as it showed how far her coordination had improved since her initial assessment. The next day she too came down with a mystery illness, which turned out to be the intestinal infection, giardia. She missed three weeks of school but she didn't ever seem to recover from the tiredness which accompanied this infection, and spent the rest of the year underachieving and dispirited. We were eventually to discover the reason for this was yet another battle with calcium propionate, the preservative in bread.

Thank goodness for Matthew, though. With two down, it was good to have one child I didn't have to worry about. He was glad to be back at school with his friend again. He competed in the school athletics and had a good time at the school bush dance. His homework was being completed in half the original time and with a lot less questions, he won his yellow belt at karate and completed a seven-page story for homework when only five pages were required. This project would have been impossible for him six months before.

In August I wrote to Beth, 'Matthew seems to have gathered momentum of his own and continues to improve. We have done about three-quarters of the spelling program. The spelling homework from school is now relevant instead of being an impossible chore. Matthew read the *Wizard of Earthsea* by Ursula La Guin and found it very exciting. He wrote a profile of a wizard based on the character in the book and won a merit certificate for it.'

When I collected the children from school, I no longer asked, 'How was school?' knowing that the answer would be either 'OK' or 'boring'. Instead I invited everyone to tell me one good thing and one bad thing that happened at school during the day. One day Matthew could hardly wait to tell me, 'I was put in the advanced maths class today. I asked my teacher, "Why me? I don't think I'm good enough."'

I was pleased for Matthew. His achievement in maths had been hindered by his inability to read the problems, and he still couldn't multiply. I knew we would have to address that problem sooner or later but didn't want to overload him.

Each term, Matthew's class was expected to submit a book

review. For the first one he had received a 'C', in second term a 'B plus', and now he received an 'A'. 'I want to get an "A plus" next term,' he grinned.

Rebecca had been continuing with remedial maths classes. I now decided that Matthew was coping so well with all the other work that he could start the class too, if he wanted. 'I'd like to work at multiplication,' he said. He had to complete some preliminary levels, which he raced through. The instructor could not have been more supportive. Seeing how motivated Matthew was, she encouraged him to do double assignments every day. 'I'd like to work on 7 and 8 times tables,' he'd say, and she would give extra assignments on those. He had taken responsibility for his own learning. When we went camping Matthew and Rebecca sat in the bush waving the flies away and doing their maths.

Term four
The pediatrician who had been seeing Arran for his typhus suggested that Arran may improve at a different school: 'I think you might be sitting on a bright child there.' We had Arran assessed and moved him to a small alternative school where he was more likely to be treated as an individual.

But Arran was a real puzzle. He hated school, achieved virtually nothing and made few friends. His fine motor coordination problems made handwriting almost impossible. He frequently complained of headaches and stomach aches. We wondered if he was ill, from typhus or some other problem, or if he was faking the headaches to get out of school. Perhaps his underachievement was due to boredom, or maybe he had ADHD. I had accepted long ago that his diarrhoea and stomach aches were symptoms of food intolerance. So why didn't I consider this as a cause of his headaches and lack of progress?

Part three of the bread preservative story
Rebecca took one look at Arran's new school and said, 'I want to go there. Tomorrow.' It was a school which guaranteed class sizes of no more than twenty and individual programs tailored

to the children's needs. The emphasis was on positivity and mutual respect. I wish all schools could be like this. Soon we reduced our mortgage repayments and arranged for Rebecca to move too.

I discussed the move with her old teacher. 'I have a feeling she's not well,' she said. I considered taking Rebecca to a doctor but there wasn't much to complain about except fatigue and lack of achievement. She loved the new school but made no progress in maths.

'She'll never be any good at maths'

Howard told me, 'You are going to have to accept she's handicapped. She'll never be any good at maths.'

Then the ballet teacher called me in. 'She's worse than ever. It's as if she's in a dream. She's not with us.'

It had to be a food. I kept a food diary for a week. She was eating a lot of bread, but it was labelled 'All natural. No preservatives'. It was from one of our large supermarket chains. I rang the bakery, then the flour mills.

Whey powder

After weeks of discussion we discovered that an extra unlisted ingredient was added to the bread only during the summer months. This ingredient, a cultured whey powder, is a natural method of adding a propionate preservative to bread without having to list it on the label.

WHEN IS A PRESERVATIVE NOT A PRESERVATIVE?

'Propionic acid or propionate salt must be labelled as a preservative when added to a food, thus precluding the use of the desirable term "all natural" . . . Alternatively, the propionibacteria may be grown in a natural medium such as milk or cheese whey, and the entire medium . . . may be dried and used as a natural preservative.'

Glatz B, 'The classical propionibacteria: their past, present and future as industrial organisms', *American Society for Microbiology News* 1992;58(4):197–201.

Although the dose was less than the maximum allowed in bread, for a sensitive child it was enough to cause problems. By the time we found this out we didn't need to be told, because we had stopped eating the bread and Rebecca had made, in her teacher's words, 'A huge improvement in maths.'

There was now no reliable source of preservative-free bread in Darwin. I bought a breadmaker. Our run-in with calcium propionate (282) had cost Rebecca more than a year's worth of learning, and a big loss of confidence, and would ultimately cost us thousands of dollars in private school fees.

The most difficult aspect of detecting this additive for us was that the effects were subtle and cumulative, the additive was unlisted and she was eating it all the time.

Propionate preservatives (280–283), whey powder, which contains propionate preservatives, or other preservatives are now used in most supermarket breads in Australia, and are rapidly spreading in New Zealand. You can't tell the dose by reading the label. An Adelaide survey in 1999 found that half the breads tested contained near maximum amounts of calcium propionate (282) while the other half contained tiny amounts or none, despite the listing. Fortunately, there is now an alternative for some consumers. Brumby's and Bakers Delight hot bread chains, as well as some small bakeries, pride themselves on their preservative-free bread.

Food labelling

Food Standards Australia New Zealand (FSANZ) acknowledge that 'a small number' of consumers will suffer from 'adverse reactions' to food additives.

That is why food additives are labelled, they say, so that people who are affected can choose to avoid the additives. But how can you choose to avoid an additive:

- if you don't know you react to it?
- if it isn't listed on the label because of new packaging?
- if it isn't listed on the label because food technologists have found a way to avoid that?
- if there is no alternative?

We had just experienced all of those problems.

I frequently hear from families who have avoided the bread preservative and noticed a big improvement in their children. Sometimes it is the only additive they have to avoid, although more often it is an indication they need to avoid other food chemicals as well.

Some wins for Matthew

One day, my mother sent me a logic puzzle. 'Can I try that?' asked Matthew. We started working on it at the same time and I got my answer first, but when Matthew finished he explained to me why mine was wrong. I was astonished. I had just glimpsed an organised, logical mind I hadn't known existed.

Matthew's next big win at school was a surprise for everyone. In the national Westpac Maths Competition he won a Distinction Certificate. These are awarded to the top 16 per cent of each state and Matthew was one of only two in his class to win this. The competition had taken place while Matthew was still classified as below average in maths. By the time the results came out, he was in an advanced class and his teacher was enthusiastic about his progress. Matthew's ability had been hidden earlier on because he had trouble reading the questions, and he lacked basic skills such as long division and methods of calculating fractions. When these were explained to him, he quickly caught on. I loved doing maths with him, as he had a quick and logical mind.

Language centre

The pre-monsoon storms which announce the approach of the wet season and the school holidays began. Matthew started a four week course at the Language Development Centre. We were lucky to get him in. Due to funding cuts he was in the last course before the centre closed. 'What will happen to all the other children who need a course like this?' I fumed.

The emphasis at the centre was on motivation and self-learning. All the students had to fill out a form and could be refused entry if they didn't make an effort. Matthew answered the question, 'Why do you want to attend this course?' with 'I want to improve.' He was in an excellent position to benefit from the course as he had improved so much already. He realised how handicapped he was in every area by his poor reading. 'You're lucky, Rebecca,' he said once. 'You're only bad at maths. Because I'm bad at reading it affects every subject.'

At the Language Centre, Matthew reported with surprise about the boy sitting next to him, 'He's worse at spelling than I am.'

All the children loved the course. They were a group of ten highly motivated children who worked hard. 'It's so much easier to work in a room where the other kids aren't mucking up. I wish our regular class could be like this,' they enthused.

Matthew worked hard on the course, read a lot and received a glowing report from the teacher.

Up to grade level

The next time I saw Matthew's class teacher, she told me, 'Congratulations. You should be very proud. Matthew has done so well. He has caught up to grade level.' I understood what she meant. Matthew was now enjoying school, reading novels appropriate for his grade, and coping with homework.

I told her about Arran. 'I'm starting to wonder whether Matthew could be bright, too,' I said.

'He must be,' she agreed, 'to have caught up so much in a year.'

Matthew attended a photography workshop, open to all children, run by the Northern Territory Association for the Education of the Gifted and Talented. He made friends with a boy his own age. Later I told Matthew about his new friend, 'He's clever at maths and attends a special unit, but he has dyslexia too and for years they thought he wasn't very bright because he couldn't read.' Matthew seemed pleased to know he wasn't the only one.

At karate Matthew passed his orange belt grading. Coordination and confidence weren't the only skills he had learned here this year. 'I can see how coming here three times a week has made a difference,' he said. 'The others who started with me and missed classes have dropped behind.' He was hoping to continue with karate on his return to New Zealand.

A fight

A flight to New Zealand was booked for the last day of school and Matthew was busy buying presents, sorting out clothes and getting school reports together. I fitted in a last letter to Beth before Matthew's departure.

'Even more news to report. I am amazed. I thought Matthew would be just filling in time for the last few weeks after the Language Centre course, but it seems as if he's determined to squeeze every last ounce of experience out of this year. Yesterday he came home with a bruised face and torn T-shirt. He and the boy who teased him had finally had a real fight. I think Matthew was pleased with himself, although shaken. I was astonished at what he said. "If I'd had that fight with him earlier on this year he would have beaten me because I didn't know what to do. Karate has helped me because I know what to do now. When the others tease me in the playground I just tease them back and if they want to hit me, I'm not afraid. I used to be chicken but I'm not now. I feel confident."'

The last week went quickly. I attended the school presentation assembly. There are only two prizes awarded for each class. I watched with tears in my eyes as Matthew walked up to the stage to receive one of them. He was so pleased. I thought of how far he had come in the last ten months.

The Year Seven Social was a success and on his last day I collected Matthew from the gate. He was covered in shaving foam and grinning broadly. 'I'm going to miss them all,' he said. 'I never thought I'd feel like that. I've learned a lot this year.'

'It's been a hard year for you,' I agreed, 'but it's worked out well in the end.'

'Thank you for asking me over,' he said. 'I'm always going to take opportunities that are offered to me, after what I've learned this year.'

The next day he caught the flight to New Zealand and we

waited anxiously for letters from the family. His father's letter arrived first. 'My first surprise (shock!) was seeing how much taller Matthew was! And then when he spoke it sounded like a new person. All Emma could say was "My God!" . . . At the swimming pool he impressed his cousins with his suntan, muscular build and diving ability . . . he is looking forward to school getting started . . . in many ways you have rescued him from failure.'

Beth told us, 'Matthew feels much more confident about himself . . . his time in the Territory has been very important to him . . . What you offered was exactly right for him.'

Matthew wrote, 'I really enjoyed it, especially the holiday to Indonesia, the waterfalls and the family . . . Thanks for the experience. I learned a lot.'

Emma

Emma's letter was a big surprise. 'Matthew is still on the diet, and I began mine about a month ago, noticing the difference in living with Matthew and how he had improved so much at school . . .'

Later, she explained: 'I didn't actually believe it until I saw the changes in Matthew when he came back from Darwin. He went away being so unintelligent and came back being rather above average, so I thought, "May as well give it a try".'

Five months after starting her diet, and into her final year at school, Emma's marks had improved in all subjects by an average of 25 per cent. 'Everybody around me says they can see it, so it must be doing something for me . . . It probably took six weeks after going on the diet for me to understand that I had a concentration span . . . I didn't even know I had the potential to do well. The grades don't come easily just because I'm on the diet. They come because now I've got the concentration to be able to work.'

For the first time in her life she was able to go to sleep easily: 'All my life I was always tired because I couldn't sleep properly. Even if I did go to bed I couldn't sleep for hours. Everyone else would be asleep and the house would be quiet.'

Emma's parents arranged for her to have a tutor 'just for motivation – in getting all my work done'. She found it a great help, especially writing lists of what needed to be done and 'the joy of crossing the task off when completed'.

A COACH

'Your coach can help you to get organised, stay on task, give you encouragement or remind you to get back to work.'

'50 Tips for ADD Adults' from *Driven to Distraction* by Edward M Hallowell MD and John Ratey MD.

Only three years before, Emma had been averaging in the fifties and saying 'school's boring'. She did well in her final exams and spent the long holidays before the start of university with us. It was lovely getting to know her properly after years of letters. Of the four children she is the most like Howard in looks and mannerisms and I loved seeing them together. Like him she tries to be super organised. 'I have to work at it,' she says. 'If I don't make a list I'll forget things.'

An update

Matthew and Emma are now happily settled with university degrees, partners and jobs. Like most food intolerant boys, Matthew developed a tolerance for food chemicals as he grew up and, like most food intolerant girls, Emma didn't, and must watch what she eats. We have spent many wonderful holidays with them and their partners, and will be forever grateful for the day that they came back into our lives.

5 Howard the adult

When Rebecca was diagnosed with ADHD, I asked, 'Will she grow out of it?'

'If you want to know what your daughter will be like when she grows up, look at her father,' the pediatrician answered. While some children with ADHD may end up as alcoholics or criminals, he reassured me that this was unlikely to happen to Rebecca 'because she's diagnosed, she's bright and she's loved'.

It was a shock for Howard at the age of forty to discover that he had a life-long disorder of which he had been unaware. But it helped to explain certain aspects of his life which had always bothered him. 'I spent all my free time at primary school down at the cricket nets,' he said. 'Other kids would stand there, a ball would come, and they'd catch it. In all the years I did that, I never caught a ball. I couldn't understand it. Did they know something I didn't? It was frustrating and I was very envious of the others.'

I asked other people who had known Howard then about his early life.

'Oh no,' said his mother. 'Howard wasn't hyperactive. Active, perhaps, but not *hyperactive*.' It is an interesting fact that most mothers who telephone me say at some stage, 'My child isn't hyperactive, but . . .' An outsider's perception of hyperactivity, and the mother's perception of living with a hyperactive child, are obviously different.

'Howard?' said one of his brothers. '*Of course* he was hyper-active!'

Recollections of an ADHD childhood

It is hard to know exactly what Howard was like as a child because long-term memory is notoriously unreliable and everyone has a different version of events. His mother recalls he did well at school. One of his brothers describes frequent family camping holidays, enjoyed by everyone. I asked Howard to tell me how he thought having ADHD had affected his childhood. This is how he remembers it.

I was regarded as a discipline problem by virtually all the teachers I had. In primary school I was caned quite frequently compared with other children in the class, on an almost daily basis in one class, because I was often seen as being rude, disobedient and cheeky. I think I was a smart alec, although I wasn't trying to be difficult. I teased the other kids very badly and never knew when to stop. Throughout primary school I didn't have any close friends.

A difficult child
While I was growing up I remember having an uncontrollable temper. My brother still has scars on him where I hit him with a brick. You can't get much more aggressive than that and that was only one incident of many.

I remember my mother saying I was a difficult child at least until I was eight when I was able to read all the time and entertain myself. She described me as very stubborn and inclined to contradict and answer back. She used to say, 'He's typical of this family. They're all obstinate, they won't listen to other people and if they're reading you won't get through to them.'

My grandfather was like that. I can remember him at the holiday cabin sitting up at night with the pressure lamp on and he'd be reading. If I was in bed in the same room and asked for a glass of water he'd never hear me. He wasn't deaf, just reading.

My father was often away on building sites leaving my mother alone with four young children. She was a loving mother and worked hard but I felt I didn't get much attention at home. Or, more likely, I was never satisfied with what I got, like Rebecca. We had a very large and close extended family, who were generally accepting of me and supportive. My grandparents regarded me as an extremely difficult child. When I was seven one of my uncles taught me to play chess. He related to me as a person instead of as a discipline problem which was the position I felt I was in most of the time.

I was the only one in the family my father ever hit. He only beat me a few times but he threatened me frequently. He didn't like team sports and took me fishing or shooting. That's where my love of the bush comes from.

When I was eight I joined Cubs which gave me a place to let off a lot of energy. It was in a big hall. They didn't go camping in those days. I enjoyed being in a group. Even then I was bossy. Very early on I was in charge of a group and later went on to be Scout patrol leader, troop leader and Queen's Scout. In many of these activities I was a leader. Maybe that's the way I relate to my peers and I'm still doing it. Once I accidentally overheard two of my friends talking about me and one said, 'He's very bossy, isn't he?' The other one agreed. I was actually quite hurt at the time, but it was probably true.

At primary school

My handwriting was terrible and I used to do a lot of reversals, like 'gril' for 'girl' and 'was' for 'saw'. Some of my most humiliating primary school memories was the choosing of the various sports teams, where the teachers sat at the back of the room and the classes were led in one at a time. The teachers chose alternately until I was left as the last person because everyone knew I was terrible at sport.

Right through school I disliked team sports and this was the only thing offered. I've talked about standing at the cricket nets and never catching the ball. The interesting thing is that I didn't regard myself as poorly coordinated. I ended up with a poor self image but nobody ever said to me, 'The reason you find this difficult is that you have coordination problems. It doesn't mean you're not intelligent.' I could never work out what was wrong with me. Perhaps the other kids didn't like me for some social reason. The hierarchy amongst the boys was all sport. I wasn't part of that. I felt lonely and different.

A family crisis

In my first year at high school, when I was nearly twelve, I had to take a lot of responsibility suddenly because my mother couldn't cope. My memory is that nobody told us what had happened or where our parents were. My eldest brother and I were put into a hostel, which was a horrible experience. We were there for six weeks and the other boys beat us up unmercifully. We felt we were battling for our lives, my brother and I, in this dreadful hostel with a whole lot of hostile kids all around. Perhaps fifty of us slept in a large room with rows of double bunks, all in together, but each age group had a separate locker room where clothes were kept. These locker rooms were dark, dingy holes. You'd walk in and you'd be grabbed and thrown on the floor while they rubbed toothpaste or boot polish in your hair or genitals. It felt like a continual battle. In the end we refused to stay there any longer. Our empty house was next door to my aunt and uncle, I was quite capable of cooking and we could walk to school. My memory is that we did this for a short time until my mother came back.

Because I'd had arguments with her where she'd said 'I can't cope' if I argued or was noisy, I always assumed that I was responsible for her problems. I carried that burden of guilt until I was thirty or so. I wonder how many ADHD children are left with a burden of guilt for how difficult their parents find them?

Sport

At high school my problems with sport continued. At hockey and soccer I thought I did pretty well but I was the leader of the D team. On the other hand, drama was enjoyable and I often played the lead. Schoolwork was all right except for French. I could never come to grips with that. I tended to go in cycles, working extra hard at a subject I was behind in while getting behind in my good subjects.

Through Scouts and family outings I came to love bushwalking, rockclimbing, abseiling and caving. By the time I was fourteen I had started leading overnight bushwalks and developed good fitness. School cadets provided me with another opportunity to lead groups and learn interesting skills. Again I clawed my way up through sergeant to cadet under-officer.

Getting organised

All through Scouts I used to organise camps right down to the food and equipment but often something was left behind. It came to the crunch when I went for my Master Cook's Award about age fifteen. It was an evening meal for forty people, consisting of saveloys, mashed potatoes, undercooked onion and burnt custard over tinned fruit. The examiner said, 'That's not good enough.' I was dreadfully hurt about it and decided to become more organised.

Applying my organisational skills to schoolwork, I realised that my best way of learning was to write my own summaries of everything I'd written in the last couple of months before the exams, then go through all the key points and learn them. This was successful and I realised I could get a reputation for reliability by being more systematic instead of relying on my memory. This was a coping skill which hid my weaknesses.

My grandfather was important to me and about the time that he died we had an English teacher who explained about the decision of the poet Keats to live life very intensely. That's how I felt but no one had ever acknowledged that you could make that choice before. I decided to live life intensely too, because life is so short and I wanted to do everything. I still do!

At university Howard chose to study food technology, then a relatively new course leading to a Bachelor of Science degree, because he was interested in food. He lived in a residential college which is where we met, both in our second year of study, both aged nineteen. Howard was leading the full life he had always wanted, being president of the caving club and vice-president of the Students' Union. He went away most weekends, caving, bushwalking or fishing and on big expeditions to the outback during the long holidays.

We had a brief relationship based on our common interest in outdoor sports. I enjoyed the bush and found Howard an interesting companion, but I had difficulty making contact with him emotionally. His relationships with women were for many years short and superficial.

'When they talk about it as a brain immaturity, that's what it feels like,' Howard says. 'I've always thought I'm about ten years behind everyone else in developing personal relationships. I don't think I went through adolescence as a teenager. I think it happened in my twenties.'

Moving to New Zealand

After university in Australia, Howard moved to New Zealand and I didn't see him again for ten years. During this time he continued to live life at the same pace, climbing mountains, backpacking around the world and working at a variety of jobs. Changing employment and addresses is typical of ADHD adults. Howard's seventeen jobs to date include chemist, crayfisherman, truck driver, ski-lift operator, fire-lookout, geologist's assistant in Antarctica, station leader in Antarctica, and seasonal millhand at a wheat research institute. It was the director here who discovered that Howard had a degree in food technology. 'Would you like to try working upstairs in the laboratory as a research scientist?' he offered.

Howard enjoyed the work. The director gave Howard the perfect encouragement. He was permitted to follow his ideas and given plenty of leeway. 'He believed in me,' Howard remembers. 'I still don't know why he did it. He took me on when I was a hippie in plaits with nothing but a broken work history and went in to bat for me. With his belief in me I was able to start moving forward. God knows what would have happened to me if he hadn't. I decided to do a doctorate. I couldn't have done it at university, but I thought I could do it now.' Howard was awarded his Ph.D. at the relatively late age of thirty-four, establishing an international reputation in the field of starch chemistry.

It was during this period in New Zealand that Beth and Colin approached Howard about becoming a sperm donor. It is a comment on the subtlety of ADHD symptoms that they chose someone with this disorder. By his mid-twenties, Howard must have presented an image of an intelligent, energetic person with strong outdoor interests. Emma and Matthew were born two years apart and, as arranged, were not told of Howard's part in their birth. We know two other couples who have children born in similar circumstances, so I suspect this is more common than is generally recognised.

Transcendental meditation (TM) was spreading widely through Australia and New Zealand during those years. Howard became interested and undertook two advanced full-time residential courses of three months each. 'Meditation gave me a feeling of wholeness and confidence I had never experienced before,' he reports. Brain scans show that meditation activates brain structures involved in attention and positive emotions, so it seems reasonable to expect that it can help adults with attention disorders.

EFFECTS OF MEDITATION

'The left prefrontal lobes of experienced Buddhist practitioners light up consistently (rather than just during meditation). This is significant, because persistent activity in the left prefrontal lobes indicates positive emotions and good mood . . .'

Flanagan O, 'Colour of happiness', *New Scientist*, 24/5/2003. 44.

The one aspect of food intolerance that Howard found meditation could not override was sleep disturbance. During the courses, meditators were fed an additive free vegetarian diet extremely high in salicylates. 'We just about lived on tomatoes and eggplant,' Howard recalled. He suffered increasingly from twitchy, restless legs and difficulty falling asleep. Unable to explain this, the course instructors phoned the TM headquarters in Switzerland. The TM founder Maharishi himself taught Howard some effective techniques for overcoming the problem but no one realised their healthy diet was the cause.

Meanwhile, in Australia I was enrolling in my first meditation course. In the intervening years I had spent three years backpacking, working as a cook on a yacht in the South Pacific, living on a beach in Morocco, spending a winter in Vermont, and trekking in the Himalayas – unknowingly staying in many of the same places as Howard had a few years before.

In the mountains

Howard and I met again in Australia after ten years. My first thought was that he related to me now as a person rather than a bushwalking companion. We went on a long trip together in the rugged mountains of Tasmania. I was impressed by his bushcraft and intuitive skill as a navigator.

I fell in love with this man of the mountains and we conducted a year long trans-Tasman courtship through letters and phone calls, with a few flying visits. The second of these was a long weekend in winter at a hot springs resort in the mountains. On the drive up from Christchurch we stopped at a tea-room where Howard bought a plate of sugary coloured cakes. 'Why did you buy those?' I asked, puzzled. They were so unlike the wholefoods we usually ate.

'I thought you might like some,' Howard replied, and tucked in with great enjoyment. I never ate food like that and found them sickly sweet. During our journey Howard became progressively more withdrawn and remote and when we arrived he informed me that he had really only brought me there to tell me our relationship was over. I was absolutely furious and screamed at him that I didn't need to pay hundreds of dollars to come to New Zealand to hear this when a letter would have achieved the same purpose.

His replies seemed depressed and illogical. The next day he told me he'd changed his mind and apologised. I was so confused I didn't know what to think and by the time I left we had made up, uneasily. I felt as if he had been like two different people, the sensitive, happy person who met me at the plane, and the depressed, uncertain person in the mountains.

In the spring Howard flew over for a quick bushwalking trip and persuaded me to move to New Zealand by asking me to marry him. When I packed up and moved at the beginning of summer, we really didn't know each other very well. Despite both being in our early thirties, with a number of broken relationships behind us, we were committed to the idea of children and determined to make our marriage work.

Puzzles

I quickly learned that Howard thrived on impulsive, unplanned adventures. One Sunday morning he said to me, 'I'm going for a walk before breakfast. Do you want to come?' The 'walk before breakfast' turned into an all-day hike along the top of the hills behind Christchurch. It was three in the afternoon before we limped back into civilisation for a late lunch.

On another 'hour's walk for a bit of fresh air' we found ourselves several hours later in knee deep snow and fading light with nothing to eat but a chocolate bar. After a while whenever he suggested a short walk, I learned to organise a daypack, saying, 'Hang on a minute while I get a few things: food, water, raincoat, torch . . .'

There were other puzzles. Howard seemed to be like many different people. There was the calm, interesting person I was in love with. Sometimes he was cold and remote for no obvious reason. Then there was the loud, brash person he became at parties and in hiking huts.

'People must wonder what on earth I see in him,' I would think. 'This is not what he's like at home.'

Parties

I soon learned to spend my time at parties as far away as possible from Howard and when we were hiking we often had terrible rows, sitting down for snacks a couple of hundred metres apart. He mostly walked well ahead of me so I rarely saw him. When I look back and think of party food, and the hiking food we carried, loaded with colours and preservatives, I'm not surprised at what happened.

Sometimes on weekends and holidays we would explore New Zealand in our campervan and here Howard often stopped at tea-rooms for tea and cakes. On many of these trips I would feel the closeness between us evaporate and Howard would retreat into the superficial, remote person that I hated. It was difficult living with a husband who seemed to veer unpredictably between loving and rejecting me. His moods seemed to change for no reason I could recognise. I had also brought my own

Additives to Avoid card

Pop out and keep handy in wallet

ADDITIVES TO AVOID

Artificial colours

102	tartrazine
104	quinoline yellow
107	yellow 2G
110	sunset yellow
122	carmoisine
123	amaranth
124	ponceau
127	erythrosine
129	allura red
132	indigotine
133	brilliant blue
142	food green
143	fast green
151	brilliant black
155	chocolate brown

Natural colour

160b	annatto

Preservatives

200–203	sorbic acid and sorbates
210–213	benzoic acid and benzoates
220–228	sulphur dioxide and sulphites
249–252	nitrates, nitrites
280–283	propionic acid and propionates

Antioxidants

310–312	gallates
319	TBHQ
320	BHA
321	BHT

Flavour enhancers

620–625	Glutamates, MSG, HVP, HPP
627	Disodium guanylate
631	Disodium inosinate
635	Ribonucleotides

problems to the marriage and I was unassertive and unclear about asking for what I wanted. Six months after our wedding we had a big fight and agreed on a trial separation.

This was good for me. I moved into a shared house and started making my own friends, enjoying parties and going climbing, rapidly regaining my confidence. In the meantime, I attended assertiveness training courses.

Separately and together Howard and I attended personal and joint counselling sessions, psychodrama groups, support groups and an intense encounter group weekend. These sessions were painful but we were doing everything possible to make our marriage work. Howard recalls that the counselling sessions were of least use to him because he doesn't learn very well from listening. Group work, especially psychodrama with its emphasis on role playing, was the most helpful.

The strategies we learned for dealing with stress during these personal growth sessions helped us through our siege years with Rebecca. We had also learned to seek professional help when things got too much for us. We meditated regularly together. I could see the difference when we did this. We were calmer and life seemed to flow more smoothly.

Effects of food

It was not until years later when we removed food additives from our diet because of Rebecca that I started enjoying Howard's company at social occasions. By the time we had tightened our diet to lower overall salicylate intake, Howard as well as Rebecca was sleeping better than ever before, and performing well at a high level job. 'Meetings used to be a problem,' Howard recalled. 'I would feel unsure of myself. Now I feel in control.' Then he surprised me by adding, 'I don't think I could have got this job without managing my diet and I wouldn't have been able to achieve what I have.'

Doctors originally thought the symptoms of ADHD were outgrown in mid- to late-adolescence. Now they realise that although there is usually a significant improvement in symptoms about this time, in many people the condition continues throughout adult life and symptoms can range from mild to disabling, threatening careers and marriages. As with children, everyone is different and the problems change with age. The kind of problems most likely to be encountered by adults are impulsiveness, restlessness, discontent, irritability and mood swings causing problems with interpersonal relationships, and disorganisation and being easily distracted leading to work problems.

There have been times when I have felt as if life with Howard and Rebecca was a rollercoaster ride, fast, exciting, sometimes frightening and a bit out of control, but never dull. It took a while for me to realise it was up to me to say, 'Stop. Enough,' because no one else in the family would do it. In our family it is not a matter of the ADHD person feeling out of place, it is I who seem lazy because I have comparatively so little energy.

As Howard says, 'I've got lots of energy. Everybody else in the world seems to have not enough.'

6 The big answer

It was the beginning of the great surge in medication for ADHD in Australia. We mothers had previously been told our children's behaviour was our fault. Now we were told our children had been born with a chemical imbalance in their brains. ADHD clinics sprang up. Doctors travelled Australia telling parents that 'medication is magic' and desperate parents agreed. Medication often *is* magic at first. Hundreds of scientific studies confirmed the short term effects of medication and it was assumed that there would be long-term benefits.

I wondered if I was denying my daughter a treatment which would improve her quality of life. Like many mothers I had resisted the idea of medication for my daughter because, 'My child isn't bad enough for that.' I could live with her now without having a nervous breakdown. Rebecca's teacher had pointed out to me that she saw 'spasms of brilliance' but that Rebecca was underachieving. We were using diet but not the right one, and it wasn't enough.

A trial of medication

Not long after Rebecca turned ten we went on a holiday to a big city. We took the opportunity to visit a clinic which deals entirely with ADHD children. One possible complication for us was that Rebecca had a relative who has had a facial tic since he was a child. From my reading, I knew that children with a family history of motor tic are often advised to avoid the stimulant medications as they can provoke the onset of an irreversible tic in some children.

Breakfast on the day we visited the clinic consisted of croissants, raspberries and yoghurt. We know Rebecca reacts to both the salicylates in the raspberries and to dairy foods. Over the years I have learned to provoke a food reaction in my child before taking her to a doctor. There is no point in taking along a perfect child.

We were the first patients to arrive at the clinic early in the morning and were ushered in for a consultation. Because we had made a last minute appointment we had been assigned to a temporary and relatively inexperienced doctor.

Since Rebecca had been diagnosed several years before by an experienced pediatrician I had hoped we would be able to discuss our problems but found instead we had stepped onto a diagnostic conveyor belt. The doctor was obviously uneasy about our claims of the effectiveness of diet and became quite exasperated and hostile about our inability to provide her with current examples of how Rebecca had ADHD. 'But it's con-trolled by diet,' we kept saying.

Rebecca of course was sitting quietly and the doctor became openly sceptical about the possibility that our child had ADHD. She explained the six tests Rebecca would undergo and made it clear that there were no absolute answers, only trends, which children sometimes displayed on these tests. Her implication was that we would not see these with Rebecca.

The neurotic mother

I felt I had been cast once more in the role of the neurotic mother being patronisingly interrogated by a doctor whom I felt knew less than I did about the subtleties of girls with ADHD, the effects of diet on behaviour and the side-effects of stimulant medication with regard to motor tic. There was no recognition of the possibility that parents might actually know something about this child they had lived with for ten years.

As usual I felt powerless in the face of such determined authoritarianism. We were finally sent away while Rebecca had some tests. I was shaking with anger and ready to cancel the whole procedure.

When we collected Rebecca, she felt the same as I did and Howard had to convince us to stay. Rebecca agreed to return only on the condition that I accompany her to the tests, so I watched, fascinated, while a paired-associate learning test was administered, then Rebecca was given a tablet of dexamphetamine. My anxiety about the medication was so strong that I felt almost physically ill when Rebecca took the tablet.

After an hour, with Rebecca noticeably settled and focused, the paired-associate learning test was administered again, the time with slightly different elements. Rebecca had to remember random place names assigned to a set of pictures of fruit and vegetables. The number of tries she took to memorise them was recorded.

Uncooperative

After this test, we returned to the doctor to hear the results of the tests. The change in her attitude was astonishing. She was all smiles. Rebecca had 'passed' the tests with glowing colours. Her results on every test strongly suggested ADHD. The trial of dexamphetamine had produced a 40 per cent improvement in learning ability in the before-and-after tests.

Rebecca had been observed to be restless and impulsive. She had shown a big discrepancy in her achievement tests and a large delay in maths, another trend. Her brain scan had shown typical ADHD patterns. As parents we were exonerated from the suspicion that we were neurotic. Our child really had ADHD.

The doctor told me how Rebecca had been hostile and unco-operative in the tests and was surprised when I laughed. 'Now you know what we have to live with,' I thought.

Side effects

Leaving the surgery, we boarded an interstate train for the first leg of our journey home. Rebecca was exceptionally quiet and creative. She and I had attended a holiday drawing class at the museum and she spent the next eight hours practising the tech-niques she had learnt there. The drawings were excellent. Howard and I were impressed by the effects of the drug, although for the next two days, Rebecca's behaviour was horrible.

Shortly after we arrived home, I received a telephone call from the doctor. She was sorry, but she had done some more reading and discovered that a family history of a motor tic meant that Rebecca should not take stimulant medication, as I had said all along. Instead she recommended another drug.

Since we lived interstate, I had to visit my own pediatrician to have this prescribed. Our pediatrician was not prepared to prescribe the drug she recommended for us because it had recently been associated with three sudden deaths due to heart attack in prepubescent children given the drug for ADHD in the United States. I agreed. I wasn't prepared to take that risk either.

Having seen the dramatic effect on my daughter's learning ability I was at first disappointed that this avenue of treatment was not available to us.

State-dependent learning

Eventually, Howard decided he would like to trial medication too. At his age, the tic warnings didn't apply. It was difficult for him to control his diet during his frequent business trips. What if medication really worked?

While medication did help him to sit through long, boring meetings, he quickly discovered there were drawbacks. Although at its peak effectiveness it was useful, he felt uncomfortable each time the effect of the medication kicked in and out.

The trial came to an abrupt end during a business trip to Indonesia. Howard speaks Indonesian fluently but when he opened his mouth to direct the cab driver, he was horrified to find he couldn't remember a single word. As soon as he stopped the medication, his previous proficiency returned. This is an example of state-dependent learning, where what is learned in one state – such as under, or not under, the influence of medication or alcohol – can only be recalled in the same state.

The medication merry-go-round

When we look back, we are glad our family avoided the use of medication. I know many families who found that after six months the dose had to be raised, or different medications used. If they stopped using the medication, their children were no better than they had been previously. So the answer was, keep taking the medication. They were on the medication merry-go-round. Side effects included rebound, appetite suppression and growth suppression.

> 'I have taken my ADHD son off medication since being on the diet. My family and friends cannot believe the difference. After three years on medication, eight weeks on this diet seems nothing.'
>
> —*Mother of a seven-year-old.*

Because medication works in the short term, the families had no need to learn behaviour management strategies and the children had no opportunity to learn self-control. By the time the children refused to take their medication in high school, it was too late.

There is no evidence for the long-term effectiveness of ADHD medication. The human body has a tremendous capacity to fix itself, given the right circumstances. These include good food, exercise and sleep. What *we* needed was a diet that worked just as well as medication, and we were about to find it.

The water-only diet

We were still worried about Rebecca's lack of energy during exercise. When I explained the symptoms in detail to our pediatrician, he agreed to have her tested for hypoglycemia and booked her into hospital.

Rebecca spent twenty-four hours in hospital on a water-only diet, having regular blood tests to see if her blood sugar level changed. It didn't. The hospital doctor was contemptuous. She thought that ADHD was overdiagnosed, that Rebecca's problems were due to poor parenting and that food intolerance was 'clutching at straws' but we noticed a remarkable change.

From a rude and angry start, Rebecca progressively became more polite and cooperative, sweet-natured and clear-thinking. That evening she was fun to be with and played the best game of checkers ever. We thought she was lovely. 'That is how I want my daughter,' I joked to our pediatrician on our follow-up visit. 'We've discovered the right diet for her. Water only!'

I was surprised to find he took me seriously. Hadn't he ever believed me before?

'Perhaps the hypoglycemic symptoms are being triggered by a food sensitivity,' he suggested. The upshot was that he arranged a case conference with a new dietitian.

The big answer

In 1993, four years after I had first asked a Darwin dietitian to supervise an elimination diet for us, we finally embarked on the diet recommended by the Royal Prince Alfred Hospital Allergy Unit in Sydney. There are as many elimination diets as there are allergy clinics, but none of them are as effective or have been as thoroughly researched as this one. It was tested over a period of twenty years with 20,000 patients. Since 1978, research using the RPAH diet has been published in medical journals all over the world studying food intolerance symptoms as diverse as urticaria (hives), asthma, behaviour problems and depression (see pp. 244–245).

The diet involves removing all possible offending food chemicals, as well as strong smells such as perfumes and cleaners. I call it failsafe because that's what it is: Free of Additives and Low in Salicylates, Amines and Flavour Enhancers. After a few weeks, food chemicals are carefully reintroduced one at a time, as challenges.

Preparing for D-day

Some families start their diet immediately. Others have a food binge first. And others think about the diet for months or even years before acting. We avoided some social occasions and chose a Monday six weeks on. I talked to the children separately.

'I know this is going to be very hard. I don't know if you can do it. What's it worth to you?' I asked.

'$5 a day,' Rebecca answered immediately.

I bargained her down to $2.50 a day plus a bonus at the end to make it up to $100 if she stuck to it all the way through. Arran agreed to less. Compared to the costs of doctors, psychologists and tutoring we have paid for, this was a real bargain.

Next I asked the children, 'Here is a list of the foods you're allowed to have. What do you think you might like for breakfast?' and so on. We tried out recipes and they agreed on what they might like. If it was a failure, I asked, 'How do you think I could improve it?' I tried to involve them in the decision-making.

We used up all our non-failsafe food and on the weekend before we started, binged on fruit and takeaways. It probably made our subsequent withdrawal symptoms much worse. Starting the diet was like entering a monastery, but we had a sense of sharing an adventure.

Our first step was to eliminate all foods containing additives, salicylates, amines, wheat and dairy products. Most families don't have to avoid milk and wheat unless they suspect problem symptoms are severe. It does make the diet much more difficult, but we already thought Rebecca reacted to dairy products and Arran to wheat.

For the first two days hunger was a problem. If we got too hungry we were tempted to break the diet, so we ate a lot of puffed rice breakfast food while I organised alternatives. As time went on it became much easier as our tastes changed and the cravings stopped.

Withdrawal symptoms

The effects of food chemicals are like drugs and include addiction and withdrawal. The children and I all suffered from withdrawal symptoms on days four and five. This is an encouraging sign that the diet is working, but at the time it can be difficult. You can take an antidote (see p. 183) but we didn't know that then. When Howard – who had declined to do the diet although offering moral support – ate an off-diet mango in front of me, we were both surprised at my uncharacteristically aggressive response. After that he stayed failsafe at home.

Improvements

By the end of the first week on the diet we were all feeling better and the improvements continued. It was obvious that I had *never* taken food chemicals seriously enough. *Despite my previous efforts, we were all dramatically better on the elimination diet than we had ever been before.*

Sometimes the children found it hard, especially when we were out. I often said, 'I really admire you for sticking to your diet. I think you deserve a trip to the toy shop.'

We had lots of hugs. I frequently told them how brave I thought they were and how much I liked their new behaviour or Arran's better health. I provided substitutes for treats at school and parties and rewards for refusing unexpected offers of non-failsafe foods.

Challenges

Challenges help to pinpoint exactly which food chemicals have been causing problems. I was glad our dietitian pushed us to reintroduce foods because I was reluctant to disturb our new family harmony.

'Do we have to do challenges?' Rebecca asked. 'I feel so energetic and organised. I like feeling like this. I don't want to spoil it.'

Compared to the capsule challenges used in teaching hospitals, food challenges can be slow, but my children enjoyed them. 'Challenges are fun,' they would tell new failsafers. Parents expect they will see an immediate reaction to a challenge, but most reactions are delayed.

TYPES OF FOOD REACTIONS
- Type 1: starts within a few hours (or minutes) and lasts for a few hours or longer depending on dose.
- Type 2: starts within five to eight hours and lasts for a day.
- Type 3: builds up slowly over several days and lasts for several days or longer; in rare cases, up to a month.

Except for food colours and MSG, our reactions occurred the next day or built up slowly. Sleeping problems would usually happen either twenty-four hours after consumption of food chemicals or develop in cycles. I found irritability the hardest to understand. Sometimes the children would play happily, but if something went wrong – such as a dispute over a toy – then Rebecca would overreact. If you're expecting instant hyperactivity, then a child who is uncooperative or easily annoyed the next day may not seem to be affected by food. As one mother said:

> 'At last we have two children who get up each morning, dress themselves and start the day without having to be cajoled, asked, reminded, told, spoken to sternly and yelled at. (Why did it take 20 minutes plus to put socks on before the diet?)'

Additive challenges

We decided to skip additive challenges because we didn't want to eat additives anyway. We had already seen that Rebecca's behaviour was related to additives and our asthma was related to sulphites.

In retrospect, additive challenges would have been useful. It is easy to think, 'we'll probably get away with that'. It took me years to realise that one dose of annatto natural colour (160b) in a vanilla ice-cream was enough to cause a grumpy Rebecca for the whole of the next day and that even unlisted BHA (320) in butter blend could affect her if she ate small doses every day.

Keeping a diary

During challenges, I wrote down all foods and behaviours in an exercise book which I kept on the table. Rebecca's most troublesome behaviours soon became apparent. Uncooperative, irritable, defiant, aggressive, difficulty falling asleep, night-waking, panic attacks, nightmares and 'can't think straight' occurred most often. As well, such behaviours as cooperative, thoughtful, 'remembered to take her sports uniform', and 'helped without being asked' started appearing.

Learning ability

It is hard to notice effects on learning ability unless you are really looking so I tested Rebecca by asking her multiplication questions in the car. Sometimes she would give me the answer straight away, sometimes there would be a long pause followed by the wrong answer and at her worst she'd say, 'I can't be bothered doing that.'

At first I had intended to zoom through the challenges in minimum time but as our tastes adjusted we found we could live with the diet. It suited our lifestyle to do the challenges on weekends so we could observe changes.

Wheat was first, because I wasn't sure whether it affected Rebecca, and it didn't, although the effects of food chemicals can be subtle. It would take us years to realise that Rebecca could be affected by too much whole grain wheat, as in Weet Bix, but not refined wheat as in white bread. Arran and I reacted with irritable bowel symptoms, although we were to develop a tolerance eventually. It is easier to regain a tolerance to wheat than any other food.

Amine challenge

Foods to be consumed on challenges are strictly limited, because a challenge will be ruined if foods contains other food chemicals as well. Amines are food chemicals which occur naturally in a wide range of foods, especially chocolate, cheese, tomatoes and wine. Having to eat 100 grams of dark chocolate and two ripe bananas a day was good fun, except that Arran and I reacted within two days. Since I hadn't thought I was much affected by foods and was only doing the elimination diet to support Rebecca, the improvement in my quality of life, and my reactions to challenges, were a surprise.

Amines made me tired and unable to concentrate. In small doses they gave me mild, daily headaches I had attributed to dehydration or eyestrain. In large doses, amines caused fatigue and migraines which usually started a day and a half after an amine-rich meal, slowly building up then wearing off over another day and half.

We suspected that Arran's frequent headaches and tummy aches were an attempt to get out of going to school. His teachers always complained, 'He doesn't do anything.' He had always been a loner. Now it became obvious that there was a reason. Kids can't explain how they feel and even if they do, they are generally not believed. Arran's reactions were the same as mine. Freed from continual headaches, tiredness and inability to concentrate he became happy about school, working well and fitting into a group. Since Rebecca didn't react to amines she was able to add amine-containing foods back into her diet.

Salicylate challenge

People say the salicylate challenge is the hardest. Ours was a mess. Salicylates are natural chemicals in plant foods, especially citrus fruits, pineapple, tomatoes and peppermint. In the morning of the first day, we started eating permitted fruit. Rebecca was going to a birthday party that afternoon, so we sent her with a plate of party food to share, plus ten Minties, which at that time were permitted challenge foods.

She ate only the food we provided for her, which we appreciated, but by the time she got home from the party, she was so restless I couldn't bear to be in the same room with her. We stopped the challenge immediately. That night Rebecca took hours to go to sleep and woke during the night. The next day she was vague and couldn't think clearly.

Minties were subsequently withdrawn from the salicylate challenge because they contained blue food colouring and a preservative. When she came back from the party, Rebecca was almost certainly reacting to the food colouring which is a Type 1 reaction for her. The next day she was probably reacting to salicylates and preservative. Later mistakes showed us that she has a Type 2 reaction to both salicylates and preservatives.

We had abandoned the salicylate challenge on the first day. Arran and I seemed to be OK but eventually, we would realise we had a Type 3 reaction to salicylates. I had forgotten to look for delayed reactions.

Dairy challenge

Less than half an hour after her first glass of milk, Rebecca's physical appearance changed while I watched in fascination.

Her face became puffy and her eyes looked glassy. She became irritable and defiant. Howard, with less chance to observe Rebecca, agreed about appearance but was unsure of behaviour so we repeated the challenge.

This time he saw the extraordinary physical change happening. After three days Howard still wasn't sure about behaviour so we kept going. By the end of the fourth day Rebecca was irritable and uncooperative. Rebecca commented, 'I want to stop drinking milk. When I drink it I don't feel hungry for any other food.'

In the past we have noticed that when Rebecca drinks milk she consumes huge quantities and loses her appetite for other food. She tolerates other dairy foods such as ice-cream, cream cheese and cheese better than milk, so they have become 'use occasionally' items. She has to be careful. Even a small serve of yoghurt every day for ten days can cause symptoms to build up slowly.

For Arran, the main effect of dairy products is impairment of memory and concentration, difficult to see until his school marks drop. At first, he restricted dairy foods to holidays and less than once a week during term time, although he developed better tolerance over time. For me, dairy foods cause a susceptibility for rhinitis, otherwise known as hayfever – stuffy or runny nose, and sneezing when I am exposed to pollen. I can manage small amounts, except in the hayfever season. Both of us limit dairy products because of nosebleeds.

Sugar challenge

For nearly six years we had been convinced that Rebecca reacted to sugar and had avoided it in our diet. Refined white sugar is permitted on the elimination diet – as part of a balanced diet – and the children were now eating sugar to compensate for the restrictions on fruit sugar.

I had to admit Rebecca did not seem to be affected, but when she had a big reaction five hours after eating a lemonade icy-pole, I blamed sugar. To confirm this, we did a challenge with ten sugar cubes. No reaction. Still unconvinced, we tried again with twenty sugar cubes. Still no reaction. I had to accept that Rebecca did not react to sugar and that I had been wrong for all those years. Lemonade icy-poles contain small amounts of salicylates. I had finally seen for myself that Rebecca's hypo-glycemic symptoms had been related to salicylates not sugar.

In the years that followed, I came to understand salicylate-induced hypoglycemia. When Rebecca avoids salicylates, she can eat sugar with no problems. If Rebecca eats too many salicylates, especially while exercising, under stress or skipping some meals, she suffers a hypoglycemic episode and improves instantly with a spoonful of sugar. I would prefer my daughter to be able to eat fruit rather than sugar. But that's not the way it is.

Results

For years we had thought that we had Rebecca's behaviour under control with her diet but she was now more settled and communicative than we had ever seen her. It took us six weeks to realise that the effects of the elimination diet on Rebecca's behaviour and learning ability were dramatic and widespread. Her face lost its usual pallor, she looked healthy, was more cooperative and communicated far better with us. Her sleeping problems improved.

Although her teacher did not notice the change straight away, the friendship between Rebecca and a schoolfriend seemed to blossom. When I listened to their conversations in the car, I realised that Rebecca's conversation was more meaningful than previously. I asked this friend if she had seen any difference in Rebecca and she looked at me as if I was mad.

'Yes, of course,' she exclaimed. 'She's concentrating so much better. When we are told what we have to do in maths at school, Rebecca listens and she understands what she has to do.'

Diet is not a cure for ADHD. There were still ADHD quirks. We still needed to provide routine, and the classic ADHD management which minimises weaknesses and emphasises strengths. But without constant oppositional defiance, life was a joy.

After several months Rebecca's teachers at school and ballet reported 'amazing' changes. Her school teacher reported, 'There's a fantastic difference. I cannot believe the changes I'm seeing. Everything is completed. It's all being done on time and she's keeping up with maths. She's being more social, willing to have a go at sport, interacting with me more. She is a pleasure to teach.'

A jump in IQ

It was in the area of learning ability that the biggest change occurred and was hardest to detect. I could only see this if I was regularly doing the same kind of homework with Rebecca. In the ADD clinic tests fourteen months earlier Rebecca's IQ had been assessed as slightly below average. Now a reassessment found her IQ had jumped an astonishing *twenty-four* points to put her in the bright category. Her school performance at both times had mirrored her score.

Rebecca summed it up, 'People like me more, I'm doing well at school and I'm a lot more organised these days. I like this diet.'

By the end of primary school, Rebecca had been on the failsafe diet for over a year. In that time, she had made a remarkable recovery in many areas. She had won some prizes for her short story writing and art, and had become passionate about ballet, although was still not very good at it.

She was also starting to enjoy maths. Somehow she had learned all her multiplication tables.

'How did you do that?' I asked.

'I saw them written on the back of an exercise book and realised I needed them,' she laughed. 'So I memorised them'.

I hated to think how much time and money we had spent on trying to get her to learn her tables before diet.

> 'Lost – one learning disorder: Guess what, Anna has learned her tables! I am very excited. She has worked hard for about six years nearly every morning and until now she hasn't been able to retain them.'
>
> —*Mother of a twelve-year-old, after three months failsafe*

When I saw the dramatic changes in our daughter due to diet, I felt angry that it had taken so long for us to find this answer. Nearly all of the health professionals, psychologists and teachers we saw, people who were meant to be helping us and were happy to take our money, had denied, downplayed or ignored the effects of foods.

'Everyone should know about this diet!' I thought. So I wrote a book about our experiences, called *Different Kids*, and was very surprised when it became a bestseller.

7 High school

After a promising start at high school, Rebecca, aged twelve, had some bad luck. While recovering from mycoplasma, a mild lung infection sometimes called walking pneumonia, she was rushed to hospital with a ruptured appendix.

The hospital episode was a nightmare. There was a ten-hour wait for her 'emergency' operation. The antibiotics she had to take made her desperately ill. Rebecca grew worse, not better. 'She'll be back at school in two weeks,' said the surgeon. It was to take two and a half *years*.

The sleeping beauty

Rebecca became deathly pale, was tired all the time and slept sixteen hours a day. In an ironic twist of fate, the little girl who could never sleep became a teenager who slept all the time. Eventually she was diagnosed with chronic fatigue syndrome (CFS). After a while, Rebecca dropped school, but refused to give up ballet until a ballet concert left her bedridden. With her waist length dark hair spread out on the bed around her, she really did look like the sleeping beauty.

At her very worst she would lie in bed, too tired to roll over. There were months when even getting up and going outside were too much for her. The hardest part was not knowing how long she would be like this.

The start of homeschooling

At first I enrolled her in distance education. The staff were wonderfully sympathetic about chronic fatigue but Rebecca was not capable of doing schoolwork. She dropped everything except her favourite subjects – English and Art – but still couldn't cope and dropped those too. As the weeks dragged into months and then dragged into years, I encouraged her to follow her interests. I kept her supplied with heaps of library books and videos.

During the first year she was too tired and forgetful to read. She spent a lot of time watching ballet videos.

Rebecca did teach herself to play the piano, however. It was one thing she could enjoy when she felt out of sorts. Remember Howard's advice – 'She'll never read music'? Too ill to go out for piano lessons, after a few lessons from me Rebecca taught herself to read music from a library book and kept going from there.

It's very lonely having chronic fatigue. Rebecca was too tired to socialise. She rarely watched television but every evening I would watch a video with her. These were times we both enjoyed.

Diet again

As soon as we realised Rebecca had chronic fatigue we did the full elimination diet again. She still didn't react to wheat or amines, but salicylates now had a different effect – they made her tired and depressed, so she had to follow her diet more carefully than ever. It took us a long time to realise she had developed an extreme sensitivity to chemicals and smells. Eventually we banned household cleaners except vinegar, soda bicarbonate and detergent; perfumed toiletries including shampoo; pesticides including mosquito sprays and cockroach baits; and cancelled some house renovations.

CFS has only recently been officially recognised as a medical condition, although the cause is unknown. Researchers are excited by findings that nearly 70 per cent of chronic fatigue patients test positive for mycoplasma, compared to about 10 per cent of people without CFS. So far, there is no cure.

'I spent two miserable years of bouncing from one medical practitioner to another trying western medicine and other alternatives such as acupuncture . . . It took nearly three months on a very strict elimination diet before I felt my old self again and the glands in my neck no longer felt like golf balls. It wasn't long after the three months that I was back working in the outdoors . . . I seem to be very sensitive to strong smells such as deodorant and perfume . . . Without a doubt, going failsafe saved me from years of depression and frustration.'

—*Former CFS sufferer, Victoria*

In the second year of her chronic fatigue, Rebecca started to have some good days amongst the bad, and halfway through the next year she caught a cold. People with chronic fatigue don't get colds because their immune systems are in overdrive so Rebecca knew it was the end of CFS, although it would take years to regain her strength and fitness.

Recovery

When she could manage, Rebecca and I went to the gym several times a week to rebuild the muscles she had lost through enforced bed rest.

Realising she would be able to go back to school, she started working her way through the maths textbook and a weekly tutor gave her a three-month crash course covering the last two years.

At last well enough to attend piano lessons, Rebecca had to explain to her disbelieving new teacher that she had progressed from beginner to Grade 6 – with some gaps – by herself. 'She absorbs everything I say. She is a gifted musician,' said her teacher. In this, as in many other ways, Rebecca was the opposite of what she had been before the diet.

Rebecca regrets that she lost several years of her life sleeping, but she enjoyed other aspects of her time at home. It gave her the chance to discover her interests. She had always liked English and Art but through reading she came to realise that she enjoyed science. Studies show that homeschoolers have better self-esteem and do better at university than school students. They learn organisational and self-directed learning skills which help them throughout life.

'I started homeschooling my son aged seven when they painted his classroom and he was too sensitive to the fumes. It was much easier than I expected. Homeschooling has taken all the pressure off us. Now my daughter is at home too. Both kids are doing much better than they did before. As a family, we are all happier. And it is easier for them to stick to their diet.'

—*Homeschooling failsafe parent*

Senior college

After missing most of the first three years of high school, Rebecca enrolled in a senior college for the last two years of schooling. The college had just been rated eleventh in a national newspaper feature on the top schools in Australia. It is a large, no-frills public senior college with a reputation for accommodating school drop-outs in a small remote city. How could it earn a place on a list dominated by elite private schools?

The secret to the college's success lies in its flexibility and tolerance. Rules have been reduced to the essentials and students are encouraged to be independent.

There are no detentions, parent–teacher interviews, dress requirements, bullying or discipline problems. Students and teachers treat each other with respect. Students are also encouraged to choose subjects they like and to change teachers or subjects if unhappy. Students with good attendance get first choice for the teachers they want in the next semester. There is strong competition because teachers are friendly and dedicated. Students are free to skip classes, although rolls are called and parents are notified of excessive absences.

The need for self-control

Some parents say 'that would never have worked for my kid'. The biggest childhood predictor of adult success is not academic achievement but self-control. A school with this amount of flexibility suits ADHD students if they have self-control and in my experience, those who have used diet from a young age are much more likely to have developed self-control than those who rely only on medication.

Provisional entry

Since Rebecca hadn't even done Year 10, let alone passed any exams, she was given provisional entry in the top maths course. 'There's no way she can do that with her background,' said the assistant principal, 'but she can give it a try for five weeks.' Rebecca knew how to work hard and valued achievement. After five weeks, she was awarded entry to the class, although she had to work extra hard for the rest of the year to catch up, attending school maths tutorials, after school maths coaching and seeking help from her teacher for assignments.

We finally realised that English essays were a problem because Rebecca had never written one before, so her teacher provided some pointers, but overall it was surprising how she managed despite missing years of school.

Needed encouragement

Senior college was perfect for Rebecca and she did well. After being ill for so long, she was very shy. When she told her friends she had ADHD they laughed at her because she seemed the opposite – quiet, attentive, conscientious and high-achieving. However, I could see glimpses of ADHD in the way she found it almost impossible to do something she found uninteresting. It was crucial for her to choose the right subjects. She was enjoying science but twentieth century Art History was a killer. In this situation, a choice of topics would have been helpful. As it was, she needed lots of encouragement.

Back to ballet

Rebecca was glad to be back at ballet, although I didn't think she'd last two weeks. She had always been one of the worst in the class, she had missed two years, she was now in a particularly strong senior class and she was weakened by chronic fatigue.

She begged us for a ballet mirror at home. I remembered the physiotherapist's advice: 'she relies on visual cues'. Perhaps if she could see herself, she could improve. We bought a mirror and she practised every day.

I don't know how Rebecca managed the first year. It was hard work and she was often tired. She was pleased to get a mixture of Bs and a few As at school. She spent all her spare time at ballet and the highlight of her year was the ballet concert. The senior class had been heavily involved in the production and performed eight items, ranging from classical to jazz and contemporary. Rebecca loved every minute of it.

During the holidays the ballet school was sold and under the new teacher, senior students now had open classes which focused on preparing dancers for performances rather than syllabus work which focused on exams. Performance-oriented learning suited Rebecca.

Gifted teacher

In the next term, Rebecca attended ballet classes with a visiting expert teacher who had trained internationally. This woman was one of those rare gifted teachers who inspire their students to achieve far beyond their expectations. When Rebecca showed an interest, she was invited to audition for a position as a full-time student with the teacher's small ballet school and company. After the physiotherapist's warning that she would never do well at ballet, I thought Rebecca was wasting her time, but she was offered the position. I hesitantly mentioned past coordination problems. 'There's no sign of that now,' replied the teacher, 'and I give your daughter ten out of ten for attitude'.

Rebecca's former primary school teacher was amazed. 'You know, we had to change the way PE [physical education] was done at our school, because there were some exercises that Rebecca just couldn't do,' she confided.

End of school

Rebecca was so devoted to ballet that she fitted her trial exams around rehearsals for a ballet performance.

In her final exams, she achieved a brilliant tertiary entrance rank. Her score in the mid-90s, including an A in top maths, would get her into the science degree of her choice at any university. Despite a previous learning disability in maths and missing half her high schooling, Rebecca had outperformed most of her old friends.

Her science teachers assumed she would do science, her art teachers assumed she would do art and her ballet teachers wanted her to do ballet. She was awarded the Senior Dancer of the Year trophy at the ballet studio. I wasn't too keen on a ballet career. A ballerina's life consists of long hours, hard work, sore feet and low pay. But Rebecca didn't have to make her choice straight away.

Around the world

A week after the exams, we set off on our trip of a lifetime, a six month backpacking trip around the world using Howard's long service leave. We had already postponed it for two years because of Rebecca's chronic fatigue. Now everyone said, 'you're not taking the kids?'

Teenagers are supposed to be unpleasant to live with, but the teens were a non-event in our family. We were already established on the failsafe diet long before our children got to their teens. When you look at the symptoms of oppositional defiance, they are exactly how teenagers are supposed to behave. We joke that Rebecca went through her teenage years at primary school, before the diet.

Parents are always saying to me, 'My teenagers aren't affected by food. They just can't get themselves motivated.' Inattention and lack of motivation are two sides of the same coin. With big appetites, some teenagers eat such large doses of food additives – such as the bread preservative – it would be surprising if they weren't affected. In my experience, maybe 10 per cent of teenage behaviour is due to hormones, and the other 90 per cent is due to processed food. Take out the food chemicals and you can handle the rest with communication, compromise and respect.

Rebecca had just turned eighteen and Arran was nearly fifteen. Arran was not happy about leaving his friends or his computer, so we made a deal. We agreed to visit internet cafés every day when available and planned our itinerary together.

Arran wanted to ski and visit an internet friend working on state-of-the-art virtual reality. We spent two magical weeks skiing in Austria and made a huge detour to see his friend's virtual reality site at an American university. Rebecca wanted to go to Egypt and to catch some ballet in Europe. We spent two weeks in Egypt and attended ballets in Paris and London. Howard and I wanted to hike, especially in Nepal. Our month's trek in the Annapurna region was a highlight for everyone.

Towers and tunnels

Friends who had travelled with children in Europe said, 'Forget cathedrals and art galleries. Go for towers and tunnels.' So we climbed volcanoes, mountains, minarets, bell towers, the Eiffel tower in Paris and Trump Towers in New York. We explored underground tombs near the pyramids, the Paris sewers, World War One trenches, Roman ruins and an Austrian salt mine. We rode bikes through a smattering of fresh snow in a Dutch national park and camels through the Sinai desert. We explored ancient temples and futuristic science displays. We caught ferries down canals in Amsterdam and Venice and a fishing boat behind the Taj Mahal. We hiked on cobblestones through old seafront fortress villages in Italy and mule trails in the Grand Canyon. We stayed with old friends in Italy and the US and met new ones on our travels.

There were a lot of fantastic times and some very hard times. Our descent from Annapurna base camp became a survival situation when we were caught in a ferocious Himalayan blizzard. On our first day in Italy we were nearly arrested. We stayed in some appalling fleapit hotels. The worst times were with travellers' diarrhoea. Whoever wasn't sick had to take over and we all had to rely on each other.

Friends could not understand how we could spend ten weeks living in a campervan in Europe with two teenagers and wrote 'are you still talking to each other?' Pre-diet, Rebecca could drive me mad in a caravan in ten minutes. During our holiday, the few arguments were between Howard and me, and usually involved my navigation!

Overall, our trip was a remarkable family bonding experience. It confirmed my opinion that the greatest gift parents can give their children is time spent together.

The failsafe traveller

When we left Australia, we had been strictly failsafe for seven years and I had been gluten intolerant for three years. My biggest worry was how we would manage to stay failsafe.

On the first half of the trip we visited cheaper countries where it was still possible to eat traditional peasant foods and to avoid Westernised foods. In those countries we stayed in backpacker hotels and ate in cafés. The rest of the trip covered the expensive, Westernised countries. We used a mixture of campervan, tent, youth hostels and low budget motels with self-catering.

The trip was a perfect chance for me to compare food additive use in different countries. While Howard shopped, I would read labels in supermarkets. There is a more detailed account of each country on my website. I discovered that eating without adverse effects was much easier in some countries than others.

In Nepal, India, Bali and Egypt we ate in cafés, avoiding Westernised foods and following the travellers' dictum 'if you can't cook, boil or peel it, don't eat it'. We avoided meats other than chicken or fish and often ate vegetarian. We were on a low budget holiday and cheap local foods were all natural and virtually failsafe. Within days we had realised we could eat many more fruits and vegetables than at home. It is common for people with food intolerance to have greater tolerance when less stressed during holidays, but that was not the whole explanation.

Peasant foods

Traditional peasant diets were noticeably lower in salicylates and amines than the affluent or processed Western diet with its emphasis on strong flavours, especially through fruit. Local fruits and tomatoes were small, soft, ripe, sweet, juicy and obviously lower in salicylates than their Western supermarket counterparts which have been developed to be large, firm and unripe. Salicylate levels decrease with ripening. These local fruits were picked so ripe they had to be eaten the same day, otherwise most would be rotten by the next morning.

In the countries which had the safest foods, we were also exposed to the least numbers of toxic chemicals. In the West we have become used to surrounding ourselves with pesticides and solvents, cleaning products and perfumed toiletries.

Nepal was the easiest country for us to eat in. Of course we had to avoid Western products in Kathmandu and the main trekking routes. Other than that, we all enjoyed being able to walk into a cheap restaurant or tea house and order any local food we wanted.

'This isn't like visiting another country,' Rebecca said, 'it's like visiting another time – hundreds of years in the past.' Rebecca was able to eat all the local food without a sign of ADHD or oppositional defiance.

It made the ADHD industry in our country seem absurd. 'This is what we should do with the kids with behaviour and learning problems,' I thought. 'Load them onto planes and bring them to Himalayan villages.'

Nepal is one of the poorest countries in the world, yet their children don't have the behaviour and learning problems which bedevil so many Western families. 'My children think my wife and I are like gods,' said our guide.

'Learning is the one we desire'

Nepalese children have excellent coordination and a willingness to learn. In 1961, Everest climber Sir Edmund Hillary opened a school for poor Sherpa children after one of his Sherpa climbers told him 'Of all the things you have, learning is the one we most desire for our children.' One of those first students became a Boeing 767 pilot, others became important executives in travel, business and nonprofit organisations.

Ironically, it is now many Westerners who most desire learning for their children, not for lack of schools but because of learning disabilities or inattention.

It appears that poor villagers are better able to raise attentive children than the residents in rich, powerful, high-tech countries. Are the material possessions and convenience foods of the Western lifestyle really so important that it is worth sacrificing the wellbeing of an increasing number of our children?

Sadly, the additive-free era in Nepal is coming to a close. Monosodium glutamate (MSG) is aggressively marketed everywhere, sold loose as 'tasty powder' in farmers' markets, and popular in flavour sachets with instant noodles. I met a Nepalese woman who complained of headaches that lasted four days. She also ate lots of MSG. I stayed in houses where children eating this new Westernised food were fretful and sleepless. I never saw that twenty years ago on my early travels.

I also met trekkers convinced that their irritability, restlessness and inability to sleep was due to altitude sickness. This was at only 3,000 metres (10,000 feet). It was more likely due to tartrazine in the several packets of orange flavoured drink they were drinking per day.

Back to the Western world

After three months of traditional village foods, arriving in Europe was a shock. Nathan Pritikin used to say if you want to stay healthy, eat like a peasant, not like a king, meaning rich people eat more fats and sugars. Villagers generally eat simple, fresh low fat foods they can grow themselves, mainly vegetables, pulses such as lentils and grains and home made yoghurt or cottage cheese. If there is meat it is generally in small quantities.

Now I could see that affluence also involves an increase in amines and salicylates because it allows people to eat more expensive protein foods and stronger flavours. Protein foods such as meats and cultured cheeses will be high in amines through aging and fermentation. Highly flavoured fruits and vegetables are the ones highest in salicylates. Food processing – such as fruit juicing – which concentrates these flavours increases the salicylate content even more. As well, the development of supermarket varieties of fruit and vegetables designed to be firm and unripe has led to higher salicylates.

Within days of arriving in Europe we realised that we would have to stop eating fruit the way we had in Nepal and Egypt. 'These aren't *real* bananas,' said Arran in disgust.

Additive-free foods

For our ten week stay in Europe we hired a campervan because it was the cheapest form of accommodation and we could cater for ourselves. It would have been difficult to avoid overdoing salicylates and amines if we'd had to eat out all the time – but not as difficult as eating out in Australia. We were surprised at the wide range of fresh, additive free foods.

Europeans – on the Continent, that is – don't like food additives and use them as little as possible. It was such a delight to walk into a bakery and know that everything was preservative free. Europeans in general eat healthier, less processed foods than Australians. Even in processed foods, they use fewer additives. In Italy, packaged foods are usually labelled *senza coloranti, senza additivi*: colour-free, additive-free.

It took me half an hour to read all the labels on confectionery displayed in a large Italian supermarket in Naples. Only 5 per cent of the sweets in the display contained harmful colours or preservatives, compared to about ninety-nine per cent of a similar display in an Australian or North American supermarket.

Multinational products were the biggest surprise of all. I would have thought that a particular brand of orange flavoured fizzy drink sold all over the world would contain the same ingredients, but no. In Australia, it contains an artificial yellow colour known for its adverse effects. In Europe, including Britain, it is coloured with betacarotene (160a), a safe yellow colouring which is rarely used in Australia because Australian food technologists consider it too difficult and expensive to use. Likewise, a well-known brand of chocolate-covered vanilla ice-cream on a stick in Australia contains annatto (160b), already mentioned above for its adverse effects. In Europe it contains 160a which is OK. In the US, it is colour-free.

FSANZ

In Australia Food Standards Australia New Zealand (FSANZ) regulates additives in our food. During our trip, it became clear to me that FSANZ could be doing a much better job of protecting the health and wellbeing of children in Australia and New Zealand compared to their European counterparts.

There are many more food additives in the UK than the rest of Europe but there is also a greater awareness of their effects than in Australia and more additive-free options. The same potentially harmful food additives are used but, for example, when sweets are sold from bulk bins – even in cinemas – their ingredients are clearly labelled, unlike bulk bins in Australian supermarkets where the ingredients are unknown. My favourite English souvenir is a grocery bag from a supermarket chain which proclaims 'WE HAVE BANNED ARTIFICIAL COLOURS AND FLAVOURS'.

In the USA

After England, we flew to New York. Arran wrote: 'a bunch of dark skyscrapers huddled together on the horizon, very dramatic looking'. It was just five months before the events of September 11 would change the world.

Everything seemed bigger in the US: cars, parking lots, skyscrapers, kids' hyperactivity, fat content in foods, food portions, hospitality, stunning scenery – think giant redwoods, the Grand Canyon and Niagara falls – and food additives.

The food was *loaded* with additives, much worse than Australia, although our food manufacturers are quickly catching up. We spent the first three weeks staying in motels. The only failsafe foods in the free breakfasts were Rice Krispies and Philadelphia cream cheese. Two of us developed rashes from the washing powders used on the sheets. Although we self-catered, it was difficult to buy even the most basic foods – rice, rolled oats and bread – without harmful additives. Additive-free staples have become alternative foods and you can't get them in mainstream supermarkets.

We flew into Denver, Colorado, and travelled south. On

reaching the end of the snow, we bought a dome tent and four sleeping mats from Wal-Mart. Camping in beautiful national parks and forests for our last two weeks was low-chemical, cheap and much more scenic. So that is how we ended our trip to the most powerful and high-tech country in the world: quietly sleeping in a small tent under huge trees, and cooking for ourselves over a wood fire.

Back home

Soon after we arrived back in Australia, Rebecca left home to start her ballet course in Alice Springs. I stayed with her for a few weeks to help her get settled. At first she shared a house with another failsafer, which made things easier.

Since she was required to work long hours at the ballet studio, she would have to be organised. I bought her a small freezer so she could shop for food and bread once a week, and prepare her meals in advance. She drew up a weekly menu and I gave her a copy of the *Failsafe Cookbook*, one of my books. 'I am so lucky to have a direct line to the author,' she joked. I stocked the freezer for her before I left, but her new home was a sixteen-hour drive away. Now she was on her own.

It was hard for Rebecca at first. Not only did she have to go through the usual trials of homesickness and getting established, but she could never relax and buy takeaways. She always had to be organised and have suitable food on hand. When she made mistakes, her performance suffered.

Reactions

It is easy for people to understand that additives might cause hyperactivity, and Rebecca's ballet class saw an example of this when she suffered a tartrazine-like reaction to fluorescein sodium yellow diagnostic dye used by her optometrist.

What was much harder to identify – and the others at the ballet school didn't understand – was a build up of oppositional defiance caused by a food chemical overdose. To them Rebecca would appear withdrawn and uncooperative. She wouldn't realise she was affected. I would start to suspect foods if she reported she was having problems and then responded to every one of my suggestions with an immediate 'no'. Each time, it took us a while to work out what was wrong as the effects built up slowly.

The culprits were mostly foods she could tolerate in small amounts but occasionally she went over her limits with salicylates, dairy foods, wholegrain wheat in breakfast cereals and antioxidants in hot chips, a treat during a study tour.

A birthday surprise

As the months passed, Rebecca became more confident. The ballet company became a home away from home. Everyone was supportive of her diet and even bought Sara Lee Chocolate Bavarians, which as a non-amine responder Rebecca can manage, as birthday cakes to share so she could join in. On one of her birthdays, she attended the evening class at the studio to discover it was really a surprise party for her.

I soon changed my mind about her choice. From classes in classical technique, pointe and partnering, to Pilates and anatomy, assisting with productions, costumes, performances, teaching and study tours, Rebecca enjoyed it all. She used her computer graphics skills to design posters and programs for each performance. Her days were busy and interesting.

Arran

In the year we left to go overseas, Arran had found himself in an unusual situation. The class around him had disappeared when the last few students from the top year in his small school left. Faced with starting at a new high school for a few months, dropping down to the year below, or homeschooling, he chose the latter. So for the second time I had a student at home.

Homeschooling was just as useful for Arran as it had been for Rebecca. He had rarely done well at school. When he started correspondence lessons, he generally got Cs, until he started using a keyboard. Immediately, he started achieving As. Like Rebecca, he gradually dropped the subjects he didn't like and concentrated on the subjects he loved – which hadn't even been obvious until he started homeschooling. English and Social Education became his favourites and he chose a computer-based topic for a large independent research report.

He learned to do well, and to enjoy doing well. He also learned to be highly organised. When he eventually went to senior college, he agreed with Rebecca: 'Homeschooling gave me a taste of senior college. Some people wag all the time. I know that if I miss class, the work still has to be done.'

Handwriting

Arran had been born with poor muscle tone in his hands. This led to fine motor control problems with scissors, cutlery and especially to poor handwriting, despite otherwise excellent motor control. There was a near universal lack of understanding regarding this problem amongst school teachers.

'He'll grow out of it', or – looking him firmly in the eye – 'Arran, you just need to go home and practise', were common responses to his condition.

We followed all the recommendations from an occupational therapist – piano lessons, ball games, pencil grips, sloped desk, exercises, use of the keyboard instead of joystick at the computer. But as she predicted, it didn't make much difference. At the end of each year, Arran's school books would have only a few pages of widely spread writing in them. His teachers never understood that he could write more or less legibly for a short time, but it was so exhausting and physically painful he could not keep it up for long.

'That's not too bad' they would say. 'There are others as bad as that.' But I was furious. Our whole education system is based on writing. Marks are awarded based on neatness and legibility. Here was a student who had a whole world in his head which he couldn't express, yet as he progressed through school, some of his teachers didn't even realise this. They would look at his bookwork and think 'this kid isn't trying'. Some probably thought he was disruptive because he wouldn't work continuously.

He avoided writing

Whenever possible, Arran avoided writing, used the shortest words and wrote the shortest answers he could, and generally got poor marks. He couldn't do maths unless he could do it in his head. If he could use a computer, he would produce long assignments lavishly illustrated using computer graphics packages. Some teachers marked him down for these because they couldn't believe the same student could produce such different standards of work.

We thought a laptop class at school would be the answer, but disappointingly, the students used their laptops for only small amounts of class work.

Special exam provisions

By comparison, correspondence lessons were fantastic. Suddenly, Arran could use the computer for everything. He learned to use maths symbols although it was time consuming, wrote a small program to draw graphs and enjoyed projects which required graphics illustrations. His teachers raved over the quality of his work, and he enjoyed doing it.

When he enrolled in senior college (like Rebecca he had never passed his School Certificate and needed special entry) we applied for exam provisions. We needed a report from a pediatrician and one of his correspondence teachers wrote a letter of support about using a keyboard: 'This decision had dramatic and instantly positive results for Arran's performance [allowing him to show] his true academic potential, understanding and intelligence . . . I recommend that consideration be given to his unique learning style . . .'

At first Arran took his laptop to class. It was essential in English but heavy to carry and most classrooms lacked power points. Eventually, he realised he could leave the classroom to do essays in the school computer laboratories. He dropped subjects such as Maths and Geography which required intensive handwriting, graphs, maps or diagrams. But the problem remained, how could he take notes in class?

Arran's alphabet

Because he had difficulty with curved lines, Arran developed his own system of writing, like *Lord of the Rings* style runic writing. It is based on straight lines. For example, he uses a dash for the letter O (see below). He became so proficient in this that he learned to write as quickly as his classmates and now writes exclusively in rune – class notes, phone messages, lists, essay drafts. It's not tidy, but it works. He can use it anywhere, unlike a keyboard; he can write pages of it; and he can read it back, unlike his previous style.

After a while, Arran's rune became very cool at the college. His classmates and teachers were intrigued by his workbooks which were filled with writing they couldn't read. They said it looked like Japanese and wanted the code. After thirteen years of schooling in which his handwriting had been misunderstood or perceived at best as a handicap and at worst as lack of intelligence, it became a social asset.

Outside school, one of Arran's main interests was the local youth newspaper where he was in great demand as a sub-editor for his fast typing and good spelling. He also won an award for his 'endless supply of good quality fiction'. Just as the girl who couldn't dance became a dancer, the boy who couldn't write became a writer.

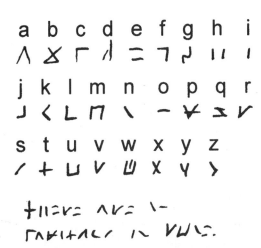

Effects of food

Like many boys, Arran developed better tolerance for food chemicals as he grew bigger. In his final years at school, he stayed failsafe at home and took his own lunch to school but he could manage more salicylates and amines than previously. He ate the occasional hot chips, pizza and ice-cream with friends, although he often requested a 'Dengate takeaway' – dinner in a takeaway container – for sleepovers.

When he first started at senior college, he liked to take muffins and home-made cookies to share. He also enjoyed buying failsafe pretzels from the college vending machine. Soon his diet became accepted by his friends, one of whom was gluten free.

During term time Arran stayed mostly dairy free but ate more dairy products during school holidays. His marks were usually As and high Bs. We learned by experience that if he started getting Cs or below, it was because either he had submitted something in his own handwriting, or he was eating something wrong.

In his second last year of school, Arran started a month-long trial of lactobacillus GG in yoghurt. Although it worked for his gluten intolerance (see pp. 245–246), daily dairy foods affected his ability to concentrate. After a set of Cs in end-of-term assignments, he called a stop to the trial on day twenty-five.

Arran understands clearly what most medical and education experts do not: that some foods can affect his learning ability very badly indeed.

8 The end of the story

As families around Australia discovered the failsafe diet, my life became a busy round of answering questions, giving talks, writing books, starting support groups and running a website. Through email, I talked to thousands of failsafers. The more stories of suffering I heard, the more I was convinced that our children were not getting the protection they deserved.

> 'We see many parents who are really at crisis point with their young children. While spending time in their homes, I have noticed that what the family eats is probably a major contributor to their children's behavioural issues.'
>
> —*Family support worker*

Mothers often told me, and I had seen for myself, that the preservative in bread was the worst, because it is in a healthy staple food which is eaten every day. In most shops and some entire towns in Australia you cannot buy a loaf of failsafe bread.

Bakers in Darwin were probably the first in the world to use high doses of this additive. At first I had thought my daughter was the only one affected, but as the years went by I realised there were many families suffering as much as we had. 'Consumers should be warned about the possible effects of this additive,' I thought.

I complained frequently in writing and by phone to our national food regulators.

'There's no evidence,' they said. Eventually, I told them I would start a petition.

'Even if you give us a petition with 50,000 names on it,' the acting head of food labelling told me one day, 'it will end up in the bottom drawer of a filing cabinet. We don't want to hear from consumers, we're only interested in the findings of scientists.' So I decided to become a scientist. A community pediatrician kindly agreed to help me.

'Don't do it,' said Howard. 'It will be a huge amount of work and take you years to get published.'

The bread preservative study

Howard was right. In Rebecca's second year of chronic fatigue, I raised funding, applied for ethics committee approval and carried out the field work for a double blind, placebo controlled study with families of twenty-seven children. I spent years writing it up, and submitted the manuscript to a medical journal just before we left for our overseas trip.

But in 2002, the year after we came back from overseas, the study was finally published in a medical journal, accompanied by nationwide publicity. The day after publication, shops selling preservative-free bread noticed a strong increase in sales.

People from all over Australia contacted me to tell me how they had realised the bread preservative was affecting them. You can see their stories on my website.

The stories include many families of children whose behaviour improved; some families whose children who had been able to stop using ADHD medication when they switched to preservative-free bread; adults whose mood and work had been affected; breastfed babies who screamed constantly when their mothers ate preserved bread; several people with heart irregularities related to the bread preservative; and a high powered executive whose diagnosed chronic fatigue turned out to be '70 per cent due to the bread preservative'.

> 'Within days of switching to preservative free bread, my ADHD son started improving and we halved his dose of dexamphetamine medication. After four weeks on preservative free bread, he was able to go without medication altogether. You've no idea how much this child has changed. It's huge.'
>
> —Mother of ten-year-old

It wasn't only behaviour, sleeping disturbance and heart

problems that were associated with the bread preservative. People reported eczema, irritable bowel symptoms, migraines and asthma. The bread preservative is not the only food additive which can cause these problems, but it is probably the additive eaten most often by people who think they are eating a healthy diet.

Despite all this, soon after my study was published the new Food Standards Code came into effect, allowing a big increase in the maximum level for propionates in bread and their use in many more foods.

In the medical journals

At this time, while I was researching my asthma book, I noticed increasing articles in the medical database about a new metabolic disorder called propionic acidemia which is characterised by developmental delay and mental retardation. Propionic acid (280) is one of the propionate preservatives and food authorities have always assumed that propionate preservatives are safe because propionic acid occurs naturally in the human body. However, some people have a defect in the enzyme which is supposed to metabolise propionic acid. In these people, propionic acid accumulates in their tissues. This condition was only identified as a distinct disorder in 1971. At first I didn't think there could be any connection between propionic acidemia and propionate preservatives.

A medical murder mystery

In July 1989, at the same time we were discovering the effects of the new preservative in our bread, a young mother in Missouri rushed her five-month-old son to hospital with worsening lethargy, vomiting and harsh breathing. Laboratory blood tests reported antifreeze in the baby's blood. Baby Ryan Stallings was placed in care, where he died within a month.

Then unknowingly pregnant, Patricia Stallings was arrested and gave birth to her second son while awaiting trial. When the new baby was diagnosed with a rare metabolic disorder, doctors confirmed that his older brother Ryan had also been affected.

Although this disorder could account for Ryan's symptoms and death, the trial verdict was based on laboratory tests.

Stallings was accused of putting antifreeze in her baby's bottle, convicted of first degree murder and sentenced to life in prison. A university professor who had seen the case on television realised that antifreeze and propionic acid can be easily confused in laboratory analyses. At his urging, new tests showed that the so-called antifreeze in Ryan's blood was really propionic acid and Patricia Stallings was freed. This was the first time that propionic acid had come to the attention of the general public.

Propionic acid and brain damage

In people with propionic acidemia, propionic acid building up in the body results in lethargy and neurological deficits which can be subtle at first. If untreated, propionic acidemia can be rapidly fatal. Even when treated, it can lead to mental retardation and brain damage. Other effects include frequent infections related to reduced immune function, and less commonly, heart problems and dermatitis.

At first, researchers thought the symptoms of propionic acidemia were due to metabolic crises. Only recently, when patients without obvious crises were found to have the same effects, they started to realise that propionic acid itself might be the cause of the symptoms.

In Brazil a group of researchers wondered if they could induce symptoms of propionic acidemia in young rats by giving them daily doses of propionic acid.

'Surely the dosage involved would be very different from the use of propionic acid as a preservative?' I thought, but there wasn't such a big difference. The principles of toxicology require a substance to be demonstrated as safe at ten times the usual dose. These doses were only four times higher than the amounts of propionate which could be eaten in a normal diet by a young child.

Lasting deficits in learning ability

At doses which could be consumed by an Australian child eating large quantities of preserved bread, the rats showed deficits in their learning ability in a water maze and changes in their brains which lasted into adulthood. Could the same thing happen in children? We don't know. The researchers also found that giving the rats ascorbic acid (Vitamin C) at the same time could prevent the adverse effects. Does this work in humans? We don't know.

Not thoroughly researched

What we do know is that propionic acid was not very thoroughly researched before the World Health Organization gave approval for propionates to be used as preservatives. There were consumption tests on frogs, rats, rabbits, cats, dogs and *one* man.

As with all other additives, there were *no* tests of effects on learning ability or behaviour in either juvenile animals or children. It was assumed that because propionic acid occurs in the human body it is safe at all doses, although other naturally occurring substances essential for life such as Vitamin D and iron are not safe in high doses.

In a period of less than twenty years, most Australian consumers went from eating almost none of the bread preservative to eating several times every day. It is unlikely that any food additive in the history of the world had ever been introduced so quickly and completely into a population – and we really don't know what the consequences might be.

In Australia, there is no avenue for consumers to register complaints about adverse effects and there is no way of warning consumers that certain effects may occur. Despite government reassurances, I don't think consumers are adequately protected.

'Ribo-rash' – the scandal of ribonucleotides (635)

Propionates are not the only additive to slip into our food supply without adequate testing. In the mid-1990s, a new flavour enhancer was approved. I quickly realised that this additive and its components were very different from all other additives. They can cause an unbearably itchy rash and/or potentially life-threatening swelling of the lips, throat and tongue. What makes these additives different is that symptoms are most likely to be

WHAT THE RESEARCHERS SAY

'Scientific studies emphasise the need to include behavioural testing in food additive safety evaluation.'

Weiss B, 'The behavioral toxicity of food additives' in Weininger J and Briggs GM (Eds) *Nutrition Update* Vol 1, New York: John Wiley & Sons, 1983, pp. 21–37.

'The recognition that food and food components can alter brain function and influence behavioural patterns indicates the need for appropriate neurobehavioural test procedures to be included in the test protocol for food additives.'

Rowe KS and Briggs DR, 'Food additives and behaviour: an overview', *Aust J Nutr Diet* 1995;52:4–10.

'The FDA should require certain new and existing additives to be tested for behavioural effects.'

Jacobson FJ and Schardt D, 1999, 'Diet, ADHD and behaviour: a quarter-century review', Center for Science in the Public Interest, Washington DC; www.cspinet.org.

'The present study supports the recommendation that testing for behavioural toxicity be included in food additive safety evaluation.'

Dengate S and Ruben A, 'Controlled trial of cumulative behavioural effects of a common bread preservative', *J Paediatr Child Health* 2002;38(4):373–376.

delayed for up to thirty hours after consumption, can last for up to two weeks and can occur in people who don't normally get skin rashes. The delay in reaction means that victims rarely realise what caused the symptoms.

I was alerted to the effects of this additive when a pediatrician enquired which ingredient in chicken-flavoured instant noodles could cause a dramatic skin rash in a young boy. I described the incident in my newsletter and asked if anyone else had a similar reaction. People phoned me from all over Australia; they had only realised the cause when they saw my report.

Soon afterwards, one Saturday night when Howard was away, Arran woke me. An angry raised red rash started from a line across his chest and was slowly creeping down his body like an alien invasion. The itch was unbearable. We spent the night trying ice packs, soothing baths and lotions but nothing seemed to help.

When the pharmacy opened next morning, I was on the doorstep. The assistant was aware of similar recent cases, both associated with pies, although the exact ingredient was unknown. Because Arran was failsafe, we knew the culprit had to be in some party pies he'd eaten at a class party thirty hours before. I checked at the supermarket. Flavour enhancer 635 was an ingredient he'd never eaten before.

'Where is the evidence this additive is safe?'

On my next encounter with ribonucleotides, I was at the gym with Howard. We were in a class lifting weights to music when I saw the now familiar rash moving slowly up his arm. He normally never gets rashes but by the end of the class it had travelled up his neck and reached the side of his face.

'You've been eating 635,' I said.

'No I haven't'! he protested.

Howard went back to work. At a staff party the afternoon before, he had eaten 'a handful' of corn chips. The packet was in a rubbish bin; Howard pulled it out and scrutinised the ingredients list: another product with flavour enhancer 635. It couldn't have been any of the other ingredients because he'd eaten those before. Like Arran, he had to take antihistamines for more than a week. Howard was angry.

'These reactions are so extreme, and so many people are affected, they should have picked it up during assessments before approval,' he said. 'They don't look for behaviour and learning problems, so you can't expect them to find anything, but this is different. They should have found this. Where is the evidence that this additive is safe?'

This experience marked the turning point in Howard's attitude to food additives. As a student, he had idealistically chosen food technology because he wanted to help feed the world's starving millions. He thought that food technology was about making more and better food.

A job as chief chemist with a large multinational food company quickly disillusioned him: testing sulphites in glucose syrup, which always seemed to be over the limit, and making chicken soup without chicken – 'it was all about keeping costs down'.

Disgusted, he left the food industry, eventually settling into a career in agricultural research and administration. When I started finding out about the effects of food additives, he was at first sceptical, then accepting, then supportive. But it wasn't until his experience with 635 that he became proactive.

'Minutes from death'

We submitted a formal complaint about ribonucleotides to the food regulators, telling them about a number of reactions, including one boy who was 'minutes from death' according to the doctor, by the time he reached a doctor's surgery. The regulators replied they didn't want to hear about anecdotes. We described reactions – with graphic photographs – on our website, talked to doctors, contacted the media.

As stories kept coming in, we submitted a formal request to the regulators for an official investigation. This time the regulators suggested it was up to *us* to organise a clinical trial!

I wrote about ribonucleotides in my book, *Fed Up with Asthma*. It led to a big newspaper feature followed by a segment on a current affairs program on national television and I was inundated with stories about 635 from around Australia.

People told me similar stories (many are on my website) which included twin ten month boys who suffered two months of severe lower body and nappy rash caused by flavour enhancing ribonucleotides in butter; a two-year-old who suffered life-threatening swelling of her face minutes after eating a packet of flavoured chips while waiting to see a doctor in hospital – which probably saved her life; and a woman in her seventies whose lower body rash was so bad for nine months she could hardly walk, sit or lie down to sleep.

> 'I don't want to end my trip to Australia looking like a leper and feeling like I fell in a bag of fleas.'
>
> —Clare, a young Canadian tourist, after eating 635 in instant noodles

Parents also reported grouchy or aggressive behaviour. Doctors had no idea about this additive. They variously mis-diagnosed the rashes of ribonucleotides as a virus including chickenpox and pityriasis (a scaly skin rash which lasts about eight months), psoriasis, shingles, chronic eczema, dermatitis, dandruff, allergy to soaps and detergents, food allergy – 'but it could be any one of a thousand foods, you'll never work it out', a 'non-specific reaction which will eventually disappear', allergy to sunlight (rash on face and neck), pregnancy related rash, foot-and-mouth disease (rash inside mouth), ideopathic anaphylaxis, and 'it couldn't be a food additive because the reaction wouldn't last that long'.

Consumers are outraged

When people with skin rashes find an additive is the cause, they are outraged and choose to avoid the additive. Effects on behaviour and learning are different. Victims are usually too irritable, oppositional or inattentive to realise they are affected and so cannot take steps to protect themselves.

After the segment on the television program, FSANZ finally decided to act. The Royal Prince Alfred Hospital Allergy Clinic is now conducting a study. But in my opinion, this should have been done *before* approval was granted.

How can authorities continue to ignore the effects of food additives on our children? The evidence confirming the adverse affects of additives has gone from a trickle to a steady flow. Soon it will be a torrent. Eventually, one successful court case will open the floodgates.

Independent scientists look at ADHD and diet

In 1999, independent scientists at the Center for Science in the Public Interest (CSPI) in the US reviewed a quarter century of research including twenty-three major studies concerning behaviour, ADHD and diet.

They found that some foods can affect some children's behaviour very badly and criticised the US Food and Drug Administration (FDA) for publication of a 'misleading pamphlet' cosponsored by the food industry which denies that food colours affect children's behaviour.

One study using electroencephalograms (EEG) to monitor brain activity during food challenges found changes in brain electrical activity associated with provoking foods. Another found increase in beneficial REM sleep and number of arousals during sleep when ADHD children avoided provoking foods.

The review authors recommended that:

- **Health practitioners should advise diet first:** '. . . health practitioners concerned about children with ADHD and other behavioural problems . . . should advise parents to consider modifying their child's diet as a first means of treatment'.
- **Parents should consider diet first:** 'Parents should consider dietary changes (along with behavioural therapy) as the first course of treatment for children with behavioural problems before turning to stimulant drugs'.
- **Test food additives for behaviour:** 'The FDA should require certain new and existing additives to be tested for behavioural effects . . .'.
- **Consider banning food dyes:** 'The FDA should "consider banning from foods consumed widely by children any dyes and other additives that affect behaviour"'.
- **Food manufacturers should minimise the use of additives:** 'Fast food chains and manufacturers of foods, drugs, and vitamin supplements popular with children should minimise the use of dyes and other unnecessary additives'.
- **Schools should minimise the use of additives:** 'Pediatric hospitals and psychiatric clinics, as well as schools and camps, should minimise the use of food additives that may contribute to behavioural disorders'.

The CSPI's forty page report can be downloaded from www.cspinet.org. The first seven pages include the executive summary, useful for giving to schools and doctors. Anyone who denies that diet affects children's behaviour is out of date.

'I know several mums with ADD kids who want to hear about a different approach than the meds they are currently on.

When she heard about your talk, one clutched my arm and said, "Do you mean she might give us some hope other than tablets?" When I said yes, she said "Get me two tickets, we're going!" '

—*Failsafe talk organiser*

A number of schools in England have eliminated additives from their tuckshops since an Isle of Wight study showed that significant changes in preschool children's behaviour could be produced by the removal of artificial colourings and sodium benzoate preservative from the diet. The result of removing only these additives was less than the effect obtained by methylphenidate medication but similar to the effect found for clonidine medication in the treatment of children with ADHD. Researchers from the University of Southampton Psychology Department estimated that removing these additives from the diet would reduce the prevalence of hyperactivity from 15 per cent to 6 per cent.

At the Dingle School in Cheshire, nearly 60 per cent of parents reported improvements in their children's behaviour and sleeping patterns when an entire class of six-year-olds avoided thirty-nine additives for two weeks. The British ITV television network provided additive-free food and filmed the trial. Professor Jim Stevenson from Southampton University was able to identify which brother in a set of identical twins was in the additive-free class by observing the twins' behaviour and testing their concentration before and during the trial.

FOUR ADDITIVE-FREE SCHOOLS
- Barnabas School in Drakes Broughton, Worcestershire: pupils better behaved, sleeping better.
- Tywardreath School in Cornwall: fewer detentions, children calmer.
- Seaford College, West Sussex: calmer classrooms.
- New End Primary School in Hampstead: pupils noticeably better behaved, calmer in the afternoons.

You can read about improvements in four additive-free schools on the BBC website (see p. 247). This trend is likely to increase as schools begin to appreciate the delicacy of their long-term legal position. How can anyone defend the right of schools to sell to students, every day for profit, substances which were shown to impair learning ability as long ago as 1980?

Johnny can't sit still

Until the mid-1990s, experts were unable to explain the majority of cases of ADHD. They knew that some cases were genetic, and that a few per cent were due to abuse of alcohol and illicit drugs during pregnancy. They suspected that many more cases might be related to environmental neurotoxins.

A range of studies has confirmed these fears. Babies in the womb and very young children have been found to be more vulnerable than previously thought.

Alarmed by the flood of new evidence, researchers at the Center for Children's Health and the Environment at Mount Sinai Hospital in New York took the unusual step of placing a full page advertisement in the *New York Times*, warning parents about dangers to their unborn or very young children.

'*Johnny can't read, sit still or stop hitting the neighbour's kid*', the advertisement begins. '*Why? Toxic chemicals can cause learning . . . and behavioural disabilities*'. You can read the full advertisement and the science behind it at www.childenvironment.org. The research examines a range of neurotoxins.

Dumbing down our children

Exposure levels to some neurotoxins once considered safe have now been shown to be hazardous.

Although the estimated safe blood level of lead has been downgraded three times since 1960, a study in 2003 found that blood lead levels *below the existing safe limit* damaged children's intelligence. Damage was proportionally greater at low levels than at high levels. Researchers concluded that there is probably *no safe level* of exposure.

These findings mean that 10 per cent of US children may be at risk of learning disabilities from lead exposure, rather than the 2 per cent previously estimated. Exposure to lead has also been associated with attention deficits, aggression and delinquency.

Lead is not the only suspect. Pesticides often contaminate our air, water, soil, food and breast milk. Animal studies show that on a critical day of early development, hyperactivity and brain abnormalities can be caused by *a single small exposure* to chlor-pyrifos, a widely used organophosphate pesticide.

These studies resulted in restrictions on the production and sale of chlorpyrifos in the US but you can still buy chlorpyrifos-based products such as cockroach baits or ant poison in any Australian supermarket, and similar-acting organophosphate pesticides can be used in, for example, hydrobaths for dogs.

> 'We moved into my mum's house for the weekend while the house was sprayed with pesticides. Within half a day of getting home, my baby suddenly became unsettled. Looking back I am sure that it really triggered all of her problems.'
>
> —*Mother of a failsafe two-year-old*

When University of Arizona researchers examined two groups of Mexican children, similar except for pesticide exposure, the pesticide exposed group showed less stamina and poorer coordination, memory and drawing ability. They stood around in a social situation, wouldn't join in and couldn't organise themselves into a neighbourhood game of street cricket.

Watching them in the television documentary *Playing with Poison*, I was reminded of the behaviour of my kids and many others I have observed in playgroups and schools.

What parents can do

In the short term, the most effective way to manage the symptoms of learning or behaviour disorders is to avoid food chemicals.

For children with severe symptoms, doing the diet also means avoiding exposure to environmental chemicals such as volatile organic compounds found in perfumed products, household cleaners, pesticides, paints and solvents. A study of nearly fifty autistic children found their symptoms appeared to be 'fully reversible' with diet accompanied by avoidance of volatile organic compounds (see box below).

Most children are not so sensitive. Avoidance of food chemicals is usually enough to produce a dramatic improvement.

A RESEARCHER SAYS

'The children in the program (universal diet and clean room) returned to normal . . . a broad spectrum of severe and chronic autistic symptoms appear to be . . . caused by chronic exposure to volatile organic compounds.'

Slimak K, 'Reduction of autistic traits following dietary intervention and elimination of exposure to environmental substances' (see p. 247).

A MOTHER SAYS

'My son suffers from food-induced autism. All his autistic symptoms, including rocking, flapping and face blindness, are related to food and environmental chemicals.'

Mother of a failsafe seven-year-old

In the long term

Couples in their childbearing years can take steps to protect their children, particularly around the time of conception, pregnancy and early childhood. It will benefit everyone if we follow the recommendations from the Center for Children's Health and the Environment: reduce your use of pesticides inside and outside the home, and eat a wise diet.

Our conclusion

'You can't stay on a diet forever,' snapped one doctor, in the days when we were still searching for our magic answer. But why not? It's better than endlessly taking medications to deal with all the symptoms of food intolerance.

When we finally got the diet right by taking salicylates *very* seriously we found that it works at least as well as medication.

There are no side effects and it works twenty-four hours a day with no rebound. It is good to be in control of your own destiny, not depending on a drug to do it for you. Ten years since we did our elimination diet, we are all still failsafe, although we no longer need to be on the strictest version of the diet.

Arran understands that his marks and his health are related to what he eats. He is hoping for As in his final exams and is confident of his ability to cater failsafely for himself in a flat at university.

Howard has become more rather than less failsafe over the years and surprised me by hosting an additive-free afternoon tea when he left his last job. He thinks ADHD should be viewed more positively.

'The issue of food is far more important. If you remove the bad temper and learning disabilities caused by food, what you're left with is creativity, lateral thinking and a sense of humour,' he says. He believes that schools and organisations should encourage flexibility so as to utilise the strengths of ADHD children and adults.

Rebecca is now twenty. As well as full-time ballet, she has studied Physics and Maths part-time. Life is not easy for her. She works hard, needs plenty of sleep and has to be on her guard against inadvertently going over her dietary limits. But she has a supportive boyfriend, concentrates on what she wants to achieve and knows how to look after herself. She has gained immensely in fitness, grace, confidence and life skills and can look stunning on stage. When I watched her dance a principal role in *Swan Lake*, I wished the physiotherapist who said 'Your daughter will never do ballet' could be in the audience.

Soon after that production, however, Rebecca's coordination, energy levels, attitude and academic performance started to decline slowly and almost imperceptibly. It took us months to realise that an unlisted food additive was involved. By that time Rebecca's ballet skills, confidence and maths results had plummeted and she was tired and depressed. We were outraged to discover that the culprit was undeclared BHA (320) in a leading brand of butter blend. 'This is serious stuff,' said her ballet teacher. 'If Rebecca was employed, she would have lost her job over this.'

It took a full week for Rebecca to return to her usual happy, energetic self, but in the meantime she had lost nearly six months of her life. We were appalled that it had taken so long for us to realise a food additive was the problem. 'It's like frogs in boiling water,' said one failsafer. Frogs put into a pot of boiling water will hop out, but frogs in a pot of room temperature water heated very slowly will stay there until they die, because they don't notice a gradual change.

Bright colours or bright kids?

How do food manufacturers get away with it? There is not nearly enough monitoring of food additive use and penalties regarding breaches of food labelling regulations – rarely applied – are not enough to encourage manufacturers to take food additives seriously.

It is wrong that so many families must struggle to keep their children on a restricted diet. Since there are safe alternatives, these additives shouldn't be in our foods. Authorities say 'only a few are affected' but *all* children deserve protection. As one father said, 'What do we want – bright colours or bright kids?'

Know your options

We have a friend whose son is the same age as Rebecca. Our children attended ADHD clinics in the same year. Unlike us, they took the medication path. 'It worked like magic when he took it,' the father told us. 'But he refused to take it in high school.' I have heard this story so many times.

With falling marks and increasingly bad attitude, the son finally dropped out of school. He has no qualifications, no job and no prospects. 'He's angry and he hates me, he blames me for his problems.' Seeing our happy family and successful daughter, the father was nearly in tears. 'I wish they had told us about diet,' he said. 'We weren't happy about medication, but we didn't know there was another option.'

part
two

The Failsafe Diet

9 Which foods affect your child's behaviour?

Children's behaviour can be affected by any of a range of fifty food additives, three natural chemicals and several whole foods. Everyone is different. Some children react to only one food chemical, others react to them all. How are you to find out which ones affect *your* child?

There are no laboratory tests to tell you reliably which food chemicals cause behaviour problems. The way to remove the guesswork is to do the elimination diet with challenges.

Before you start the diet, write down your child's scores on the list below. When you have achieved five good days in a row, you will be able to see how much your child has improved.

What's your food intolerance score?

Mark how much each symptom bothers you, where 0 is not at all and 3 is very much

SYMPTOM	SCORE			
Impaired memory and concentration				
Vague or forgetful	0	1	2	3
Unable to concentrate	0	1	2	3
Won't persevere	0	1	2	3
Unmotivated	0	1	2	3
Disorganised	0	1	2	3
Easily distracted	0	1	2	3
Difficulty reading and writing	0	1	2	3

Speech

Loud voice (no volume control)	0	1	2	3
Speech hard to understand	0	1	2	3
Speech delay	0	1	2	3
Repetitive or silly noises	0	1	2	3
Talks too much (empty chatter)	0	1	2	3

Coordination

Poor handwriting	0	1	2	3
Poor coordination	0	1	2	3
Frequent accidents	0	1	2	3

Sleep

Difficulty falling asleep	0	1	2	3
Restless legs	0	1	2	3
Persistent night waking	0	1	2	3
Insomnia	0	1	2	3
Nightmares/night terrors	0	1	2	3

Mood

Mood swings	0	1	2	3
Premenstrual tension	0	1	2	3
Grizzly or unhappy	0	1	2	3
Cries easily or often	0	1	2	3
Irritable	0	1	2	3
Uncooperative	0	1	2	3

Anxiety

Panic attacks	0	1	2	3
Depression	0	1	2	3
Suicidal thoughts, actions	0	1	2	3

Oppositional defiance

Loses temper	0	1	2	3
Argumentative	0	1	2	3
Refuses requests	0	1	2	3
Defies rules	0	1	2	3
Deliberately annoys others	0	1	2	3
Blames others for own mistakes	0	1	2	3
Touchy, easily annoyed	0	1	2	3
Angry, resentful	0	1	2	3

Other behaviour

Inattentive, easily bored, unmotivated	0	1	2	3
Restless, fidgety or overactive	0	1	2	3
Head banging	0	1	2	3
Fights with siblings	0	1	2	3
Difficulty making friends	0	1	2	3
Destructive, aggressive	0	1	2	3
Unreasonable	0	1	2	3
Demanding, never satisfied	0	1	2	3
Disruptive	0	1	2	3
Discipline is ineffective	0	1	2	3

Airways

Asthma	0	1	2	3
Stuffy or runny nose	0	1	2	3
Frequent nose bleeds	0	1	2	3
Chronic throat-clearing	0	1	2	3
Sinusitis	0	1	2	3
Frequent ear infections	0	1	2	3
Frequent tonsillitis	0	1	2	3
Frequent colds and flu	0	1	2	3

Skin

Eczema	0	1	2	3
Urticaria (hives)	0	1	2	3
Other skin rashes	0	1	2	3
Angioedema (swollen lips, eyes, tongue)	0	1	2	3
Geographic tongue (looks like map)	0	1	2	3
Pruritis (itching)	0	1	2	3
Allergic shiners (dark circles under eyes)	0	1	2	3
Pallor (pale skin)	0	1	2	3
Flushing	0	1	2	3
Sweating	0	1	2	3
Body odour	0	1	2	3

Digestive system

Recurrent mouth ulcers	0	1	2	3
Indigestion	0	1	2	3
Nausea	0	1	2	3
Bad breath	0	1	2	3
Vomiting	0	1	2	3
Diarrhoea	0	1	2	3
Stomach ache	0	1	2	3

Bloating	0	1	2	3
Reflux	0	1	2	3
Colic in babies	0	1	2	3
Sluggish bowel syndrome (sticky poos)	0	1	2	3
Soiling (sneaky poos)	0	1	2	3

Bladder

Bedwetting	0	1	2	3
Daytime incontinence	0	1	2	3
Urinary urgency	0	1	2	3
Recurrent inflammation (cystitis)	0	1	2	3

Skeletal

Growing pains	0	1	2	3
Arthritis	0	1	2	3

Eyes

Nystagmus (involuntary movement)	0	1	2	3
Blurred vision	0	1	2	3

Muscles

Low muscle tone	0	1	2	3
Myalgia (muscle pain)	0	1	2	3
Tics (involuntary movement)	0	1	2	3
Stutter	0	1	2	3
Tremor	0	1	2	3
Palpitations	0	1	2	3
Tachycardia (fast heart beat)	0	1	2	3
Angina-type pain	0	1	2	3

Central nervous system

Headaches or migraines	0	1	2	3
Unexplained tiredness	0	1	2	3
Feeling 'hung-over'	0	1	2	3
Confusion	0	1	2	3
Dizziness	0	1	2	3
Agitation	0	1	2	3
Tinnitus (noises in ear)	0	1	2	3
Paraesthesia (pins and needles)	0	1	2	3
Dysaesthesia (numbness)	0	1	2	3
Epileptic seizures	0	1	2	3

Total

10 How to start the Elimination Diet

A step-by-step guide

1. **Check with your doctor** that there is not some other cause for your child's behaviour, for example, children with significant hearing loss or young children with painful dental decay can sometimes appear to have ADHD. If symptoms include asthma or depression, it is important to keep in touch with your health professional.

2. Ask your doctor to refer you to **a dietitian with experience** in supervising the Royal Prince Alfred Hospital elimination diet. If your doctor doesn't know, you can find an experienced dietitian by contacting the Food Intolerance Network (see p. 251) or ask the dietitians' department at your local hospital, community health centre or private dietitians in the *Yellow Pages*.

3. **If weight loss is a problem** especially for children, weigh your child and record the weight once a week. If a skinny child loses weight, ask your dietitian about caloric supplements such as Polycose or stop the diet.

4. **Decide how many foods** you will exclude. This is the hard part. If you don't exclude enough food chemicals, the diet won't work. If you exclude everything from the start, the diet might be unnecessarily difficult.

   - For suspected or diagnosed ADHD, the best place to start is FAILSAFE (free of additives, low in salicylates, amines and flavour enhancers). This is the diet outlined on pp. 186–200.
   - If you have any reason at all to suspect *dairy foods* – have seen a reaction, history of milk allergy, another family member reacts to milk, your child had lactose intolerance

as a baby, frequent ear infections, grommets, would live on milk if you let him/her, drinks litres of milk a day, or hates milk – avoid all dairy products, see p. 193.

- For severe problems you might need to avoid *wheat* or *gluten* as well. A family history of irritable bowel or especially a family member with coeliac disease is an indication of possible problems, see p. 237.
- For severe symptoms including autism and chronic fatigue syndrome, you may need to avoid environmental chemicals, see p. 200.

5. **Read the failsafe diet lists**, p. 186 and shopping list, p. 201.

6. **Check product updates** on the website (see p. 251) or join the newsletter mailing list in case manufacturers have changed ingredients. This happens frequently.

7. **Establish a failsafe house** by eating or giving away all the unsuitable food in your kitchen. It is best if at least one other family member does the diet, and the whole family must appear to do this diet at home. Children who are expected to stick to this diet while others at home eat tempting foods will very reasonably sneak food or money.

8. **Negotiate incentives with your child** – 'what's this worth to you?'. A daily reward with a bonus after three weeks is better than one big bribe. Ask for the support of your partner and anyone else in the household.

9. **Mark D-day** – diet day – on your calendar, preferably on a Monday. You might want to wait until a special occasion, birthday party or school camp is out of the way.

10. Using the recipes, **draw up a week's menu plan**, including snacks, which you feel is workable for your family. It doesn't have to include a lot of variety. In the first three weeks, you just want to get rid of food chemicals and cravings.

11. **Go shopping**. Take a list of the ingredients you need for your recipes and the shopping list on p. 201 for other ideas. The first failsafe shop will be time consuming while you read labels, after that it will be quicker and cheaper than usual.

AVOID THESE ADDITIVES	
Artificial colours 102, 104, 107, 110, 122–129, 132, 133, 142, 143, 151, 155 **Natural colour** 160b annatto (*160a is safe*) **Preservatives** 200–203 sorbates 210–213 benzoates 220–228 sulphites 249–252 nitrates, nitrites 280–283 propionates	**Antioxidants** 310–312 gallates 319–321 TBHQ, BHA, BHT *300–309 are safe* **Flavour enhancers** 620–625 Glutamates (and HVP) 627 Disodium guanylate 631 Disodium inosinate 635 Ribonucleotides **Flavours** unless in approved products (see p. 232)

12. **Try out some recipes** before you get to D-day. For children, cook and freeze some meals and treats such as failsafe mince (p. 218), cakes and biscuits. Have magic cordial (p. 215), pear jam (p. 226) and icypoles (p. 216) ready.

13. **Rate symptoms** on the food intolerance score sheet on p. 155 so that you have a baseline from which to measure your progress.

14. On D-day, **start the diet**.

15. **Join the mailing list** so you can get newsletter updates about product changes, recipes and inspiration. You might also like to join a failsafe email discussion group so you can hear from others who are also doing the diet, or failsafe products in your area, see p. 251.

16. **Keep a diary** of everything that goes in the mouth or on the skin (foods, toothpaste, medications). Record any behaviour, learning and health problems during the diet. It is easier to see effects when looking back. You might like to draw up a checklist of the behaviours which you would

most like to see change on the diet (for example, won't go to bed, argues with brother, refuses to do set chores, refuses to do homework, low reading ability) and rate him or her every day on those. Note any positive behaviours, such as 'fed dog without being asked', 'went to bed without any arguing'. After the diet, keep your diary in a safe place. In future you may want evidence of how food additives affect your child.

17. **Expect withdrawal symptoms** within the first two weeks, often on days four and five. These can include feeling tearful, strong food cravings, irritability and the same symptoms you had before you started the diet. Have an antidote handy, see p. 183. You can minimise withdrawal symptoms by reducing additives over a few weeks before the diet and don't binge on fruit and takeaways – the way we did – the weekend before starting.

18. **Read the checklist of common mistakes** (p. 231) many times. If there is no improvement after two weeks, ask your dietitian, network contact (p. 251) or email group for help. Some children improve within days, others improve slowly and you won't be convinced until the middle of the third week.

19. **Give your child extra love, hugs and time**. Follow the diet yourself, to set a good example. Children cannot be punished into sticking to this diet.

20. **Rate your progress** after three to six weeks (for behaviour, three weeks is usually enough; asthma, skin rashes and chronic fatigue may take longer).

21. You are ready to **start challenges** (p. 163) when you have five good days in a row after three to six weeks. If symptoms include asthma or depression, it is important to discuss challenges with your dietitian, doctor or counsellor. If there is no improvement after six weeks, do the challenges anyway. Some people are best able to notice effects through challenges.

22. As your child becomes more amenable to discipline, **establish a behaviour management program** in your household, see p. 184.

23. When you have learned which foods affect you and established a new food routine, go back to your dietitian and **have your nutrition checked** if you are avoiding salicylates, dairy foods or gluten.

24. Food chemical sensitivity varies depending on the total load to which we are exposed. Environmental chemicals, stress, lack of sleep, illness and hormones can all contribute. **Avoid unnecessary chemicals** (p. 200) and allow time for exercise, sleep and relaxation.

25. Most children eat a fairly high-sugar, high-fat diet when being weaned off processed foods. As your child's tastes settle down, reduce the intake of fats and sugars, and **eat more failsafe vegetables**.

Challenges

After three to six weeks of elimination diet (p. 186), you must test whether you are sensitive to salicylates and amines, otherwise you may be restricting healthy foods unnecessarily. If you are avoiding dairy foods, wheat or gluten, the same applies. Exceptionally sensitive people and young babies need not challenge because reactions to small amounts of salicylate or amine containing foods will be obvious.

Challenges can be carried out with foods or capsules. Teaching hospitals generally use capsule challenges, which give quick and obvious results. Food challenges are not as strong but as I've mentioned before, supervision is highly recommended for people with depression and asthma. Discuss this with your dietitian. Remember – results of food challenges can be confusing unless the rules are followed.

The rules of challenge
- **Five good days** in a row before the first challenge.
- **Three good days** in a row before subsequent challenges.
- **Stick strictly** to the elimination diet during challenges. Start again (three good days) if you make a mistake.
- **Do one challenge at a time** or you won't know which food chemical caused the reaction.

- **Eat only specified foods.** Do not eat foods like oranges and tomatoes which contain more than one food chemical (salicylates and amines).
- **Record any symptoms.** Set short daily homework to test poor concentration, handwriting.
- **Eat enough challenge foods**, at least the minimum amount every day. If you start slowly, you may get confusing results.
- **If there is no change, continue until there is a reaction.** Three days for additives except 282, a full seven days otherwise but ten days or more may be needed.
- **If there is a change but you are not sure for any reason**, stop. Wait for three good days and start the challenge again.
- **Stop when you see a reaction.** You can then use an antidote, p. 183.
- **No mini challenges.** Do not conclude that 'he reacts to orange juice but he's OK with apricots'. Every food which contains salicylates – including apricots – will contribute to problems.

First challenge

Unless you are absolutely sure your child reacts to food colouring, it is best to start with the colour challenge because it is the easiest and will convince skeptics to continue with the diet. After that you can do the challenges in any order you like.

TYPES OF FOOD REACTIONS
1. Starts within a few minutes or hours and lasts a few hours.
2. Starts within five to eight hours and lasts for twenty-four hours.
3. Builds up slowly and peaks on day three, then resolves slowly over a week or up to a month.

Colours and MSG are usually a Type 1 reaction, preservatives and salicylates a Type 2 and amines a Type 3, but everyone is different. Expect anything. Children who take a month to completely recover can be extremely difficult to work with because they improve slowly and can appear to have recovered but may flare up again when asked to do something they don't like.

> **Q.** I did the colour challenge with my son on Monday, Tuesday and Wednesday. He passed. But today he's gone berserk.
> **A.** Your son is having a delayed reaction. It could take him a week or even a month to recover.

IF YOU PASS THE CHALLENGE

In theory, you should be able to add back into your diet any group of food chemicals that don't cause a reaction. However, so many people make mistakes when doing this – such as thinking 'I don't react to salicylates so I can eat broccoli again' although broccoli contains both salicylates and amines – it is better to finish all your challenges before reintroducing the food chemicals you can tolerate.

Colour challenge

Five drops of green food colouring in water or magic cordial (p. 215) three times a day for one day followed by the same procedure with ten drops of red, ten drops of yellow.

Salicylate challenge

Eat at least six serves every day for seven to ten days of the following foods (stop when you see a reaction): One serve equals approximately one cup of mango, asparagus, carrot, pumpkin, capsicum, corn, cucumber, zucchini, Granny Smith apple, apricots, guavas, peaches, nectarines, cherries, strawberries, rockmelons or watermelons. Use also 1 teaspoon cinnamon or curry-type spices (turmeric, cardamom, coriander, cumin, garam marsala, ginger, paprika, pepper) in powder form, not paste, 1 tablespoon honey, 150 ml of preservative-free apple juice, 1 cup peppermint tea. Use moderate salicylate options in recipes, see p. 210. None of the very high salicylate foods (tomatoes, oranges, sultanas, pineapple, grapes) are suitable for the challenge because they all contain amines as well. It is important to give the highest dose of salicylates you can, right from the start.

'I found the salicylate challenge really difficult. Even though salicylates have the worst effect on my children, it took me over a year to work that out because they are delayed responders and the reactions are irrational fears and social withdrawal – not what I had expected.'
—*Reader, Northern Territory*

Amine challenge

Eat two to three ripe bananas and 60–120 g dark chocolate (half for small children) until there is an obvious reaction or for at least seven days. Amine reactions are usually delayed up to several days or more. For dark chocolate use Nestlé Dark Chocolate Choc Bits, Old Gold, Jamaica, or cooking chocolate.

For children who don't like dark chocolate – although most do after three weeks on the elimination diet! – you can cook the choc bits into chocolate cake or banana muffins, or freeze the bananas and process them into banana ice-cream topped with melted chocolate. Eat also as much as you want of: canned tuna, salmon, sardines, frozen fish, seafood except prawns, pork chops and roast pork (but not bacon and ham). In my experience, and research supports this, amines can be associated with aggression and conduct problems in some children. Consider keeping children with a potential to react like this at home for the amine challenge (and preferably all challenges). Use an antidote as soon as you have noticed a reaction.

IF YOU REACT TO BOTH SALICYLATES AND AMINES . . .

Once you are convinced there is a reaction, you can use an antidote, p. 183.

- People who react to both salicylates and amines can stop challenges now as they will probably react to additives as well, unless they are asthmatic.
- It is useful for asthmatics to identify which additives are associated with their asthma.
- If you have passed salicylates or amines, it is worth doing the rest of the challenges. Some people react only to one or two additives, yet if they eat them every day, the result is the same as for a person who reacts to everything.

Sulphites (220–228)

Sulphites are the additive most likely to affect asthmatics, but they are also associated with the complete range of food intolerance symptoms including behaviour. Some people are very sensitive to even tiny amounts. Most foods which contain sulphites (e.g. wine, dried fruit and vegetables and sausages) also contain salicylates or amines so it is best to do those challenges first. If you don't react to salicylates, you can challenge sulphites by trying dried apricots (seven halves per day) or pickled onions. You can try Deb Instant Mashed Potato – one serve every day for three days – although it does contain other additives as well. If asthmatic, discuss this with your health professional first.

Benzoates (210–213)

Drink 1 litre of preserved lemonade (211) a day for three days.

MSG (621 and natural glutamates)

Use four tablespoons of soy sauce mixed into a meal, e.g. fried rice, every day for three days. Vegetable haters who will eat green peas might challenge peas (small amounts of natural glutamates) early. For a **green pea challenge**, eat green peas twice a day every day for three days. If no reaction, you can add peas back into the diet. People who fail the MSG challenge can often manage green peas.

Nitrates (249–252)

Use four slices of ham, bacon or corned beef per day. Not for amine reactors.

Antioxidant challenge

- **gallates (310–312)**
- **TBHQ, BHA, BHT (319–321)**

Eat 3 tablespoons of Western Star Spreadable butter (BHA 320) per day for three days; or frozen french fries with listed TBHQ 319 or BHA 320; or see antioxidant factsheet on my website.

Dairy and wheat challenges
These should be done at some stage if you are avoiding these (one to three cups of milk every day for ten days) and wheat (one cup of plain uncoloured cooked pasta plus twelve water crackers every day for seven days).

Wholegrain wheat
Many people find they can manage refined white flour products such as bread and pasta but wholegrain wheat products affect them. This has been implicated in everything from behaviour to irritable bowel to psoriasis. Eat at least four wholegrain biscuits such as VitaBrits or Weet-Bix per day as well as wholegrain flour, pasta and wholemeal failsafe bread for three days or more.

Bread preservative (282)
This is worth challenging because shopping is easier if you pass. Although the label may list preservative, sometimes the dose is very small so it is safest to challenge with four crumpets, four English toasted muffins, or four slices of preserved bread during summer (when doses are highest) every day for a week.

Annatto colour (160b)
This should be challenged especially if you don't react to dairy products because it is in so many foods. Eat one tub of coloured yoghurt every day for three days.

Flavour enhancer 635, also called ribonucleotides
If you don't react to salicylates, MSG or preservatives, eat one packet of Maggi Instant Chicken Flavoured Noodles or one packet of CCs Corn Chips every day for three days, have antihistamines handy and do it near a hospital or doctors' surgery. This new additive has been associated with behaviour problems but some people can develop an unbearably itchy rash or swelling of the lips, throat and tongue.

Sorbates (200–203)
Use 100 g of preserved cottage cheese and 1 tablespoon of margarine containing additive 202.

Sugar
This challenge is optional. It is for people who are convinced their children react to sugar. In nearly all cases, this will be due to salicylates or additives. However, there are a very few extremely sensitive people who do react to white sugar. You need to test this with a challenge. Eat ten sugar cubes and observe reactions. If no reaction, double the amount.

Other challenges
You can choose to challenge anything you want, from favourite foods to herbal or nutritional supplements. Just follow the rules. My children chose Mars bars – every day for three days – and failed.

For more details see the RPAH booklet from your dietitian.

After challenges – developing tolerance
Some people can develop a tolerance to salicylates by avoiding them for six months – and some families have spent this long by the time they get through their challenges. Reintroduce one moderate serve (carrots, corn or pumpkin for salicylates, bananas for amines) every second day for two weeks. If no reaction, increase to one serve every day for two weeks. If still OK, increase the dose to one cup every second day for two weeks and so on. Go back to the last level if you start reacting.

> 'I am at the stage now where I have reintroduced amines into my diet about twice a week, with the exception of my premenstrual week. I am prone to being over confident and blowing my reintroduction from time to time but I have pretty much worked out the timing and culprits.'
>
> —*Reader, New South Wales*

11 Managing the diet

Frequently asked questions

Q. We feel there is a definite diet relationship between our ten-year-old son's behaviour and food but cannot precisely put our finger on it. We have noticed that chocolate and grapes make him more moody.

A. If you have ever noticed an effect of foods such as chocolate and fruit especially grapes or orange juice, it is likely your child is affected by salicylates or amines. Failsafe challenges will help you to find out exactly what affects your son.

Q. I am taking many herbal remedies. I know they aren't failsafe but they don't seem to cause severe reactions.

A. Herbal remedies contain salicylates. Salicylates rarely cause obvious reactions but if they are a problem, you won't recover fully until you avoid them *all*. You can test your herbal remedies in a challenge.

Q. We are into day four of our salicylate challenge. How do we know if we are grumpy because of salicylates or because we have good reasons to be grumpy?

A. You could stop the challenge, wait for three good days in a row, then start again. If your symptoms all go away, then return on the next challenge, you can be sure they are related to foods.

Q. I'm having trouble getting the medication right for my depression, anxiety and ADHD. It's a bit of a juggling act as the dexamphetamine can trigger the anxiety problem. Could diet help?

A. A medical journal describes a thirty-year-old university graduate with a history of social phobia, anxiety, panic attacks,

ADD without H (hyperactivity) and obsessive–compulsive disorder since childhood. He grew up in a stable and caring family but his symptoms worsened in his late teens and he experienced a depressive episode in his early twenties. Medication did not control his symptoms and sometimes made them worse. On a four week elimination diet, his mood and other symptoms improved significantly. On the first capsule challenge (salicylates) his symptoms worsened considerably and further challenges were abandoned. After one year on the diet he had remained symptom-free. The Mood Disorders Unit at the Prince of Wales Hospital, Randwick, Sydney, is carrying out further research.

Q. My son took a few days to react to salicylates, so they can't be too bad.

A. A day three response to salicylates doesn't mean that you aren't sensitive. It can mean you are a delayed responder, see p. 164. Some delayed responders are very sensitive and can take a week or even up to a month to recover completely. They are the most difficult children of all to work with.

Q. We are doing failsafe about 90 per cent and feel much better but I'm still having a problem sleeping.

A. The golden rule with the elimination diet is: for best results, stick to the diet 100 per cent. Doing 90 per cent diet doesn't give you 90 per cent results. You'll know you've got the diet right when your sleeping problems go away.

Q. My ten-year-old son has passive ADD. We've been doing the elimination diet for six weeks but I haven't seen any improvement.

A. Have you read the checklist of common mistakes on p. 231? Failure to improve is often due to mistakes. Otherwise, it is worth doing challenges (see p. 163). Some people only notice changes during challenges, particularly with inattention.

Q. Our pediatrician recommended an iron elixir supplement. I was wondering if my daughter can take this while on the elimination diet? It contains glucose liquid, ethanol and saccharin sodium.

A. Pharmaceutical product labels don't declare all additives. Check the CMI (consumer medication information sheet), available on the leaflet in the pack, from your pharmacist or at www.myDr.com.au. It shows that your brand of iron supplement also contains 'apricot superarome' or strong apricot flavour, which is not failsafe. All strong fruit flavours are very high in salicylates, see p. 183 for failsafe supplements.

Q. I give my thirteen-year-old son $5 for lunch and tell him to buy something failsafe but he won't stick to it.

A. Your son needs more help than this. It is extremely difficult to buy failsafe food, even in school tuckshops. You need to find out if there are any suitable options at his school. If not, send a packed lunch.

Q. What about vitamin and mineral supplements to improve children's behaviour?

A. The recommended failsafe supplements on p. 183 contain a mixture of about twenty vitamins and minerals in close to the recommended daily allowances, similar to the supplements given to prisoners in the Aylesbury study (p. 248), which, along with fatty acids, resulted in a reduction of antisocial behaviour. There is evidence that fatty acid supplements such as fish oils can help some children. You can trial supplements according to the rules of challenge, see p. 163. Many contain salicylates or amines which may cancel the benefits. Some studies have demonstrated some benefits of megavitamins although it is not yet clear which supplements are effective and some children have had to take up to thirty-two capsules per day.

Q. How safe is soy?

A. Some children do react behaviourally to soy. There is some concern that soy infant formulas contain the highest levels of phytoestrogens, similar to the hormone oestrogen, of any food. Non-allergenic alternatives to cow's milk formula, such as Pepti Junior, Alfare and Neocate, are available.

Q. Are there any natural calm-me-down products which are failsafe ?
A. If your problem is due to a food intolerance reaction, see antidotes on p. 183. Anything else taken by mouth is generally not failsafe. Brain scans of long-term meditation practitioners suggest that meditation is more effective at producing happiness than antidepressants. Other natural alternatives which can have a calming effect include exercise such as walking, bicycling, dancing, gym classes, yoga or fifteen minutes daily swinging in a hammock. Half an hour of stroking your pet can double natural substances associated with a happy, relaxed frame of mind or try laughter therapy with your favourite comedy videos.

Q. I'm pregnant. What can I do to prevent ADHD in my baby?
A. Staying failsafe during your pregnancy will not prevent food intolerance in the same way that avoiding allergens such as peanuts and dairy foods during the last six weeks may help allergic families. It is more important to avoid neurotoxins: alcohol, tobacco and illicit drugs; lead in old paint and drinking water (from pipes or solder); large fish such as shark, swordfish, tuna and king mackerel which are sources of mercury; vaccinations containing the mercury-based preservative thimerosal (thiomersal); occupational exposure to industrial solvents including toluene, xylene, styrene and trichloroethylene and the products that contain them, for example, paints and glues. Postpone house renovations and avoid pesticide use inside and outside your home. Further reading (p. 252). Use non-toxic house cleaners (p. 200). About 50 per cent of very preterm babies suffer neurological deficits. If your baby is born preterm, ask your doctor to avoid corticosteroids preserved with sulphites (p. 249).

Q. Every year my failsafe son develops behaviour problems during the school swimming program.
A. Some sensitive children do react behaviourally in chlorinated pools. When pool chlorine comes into contact with sweat or urine, it can form high levels of chloramines which can affect asthmatics and presumably behavioural amine responders.

Q. Can we do the diet while my son is on ADHD medication?
A. Many families do, although it is more difficult. If you start the diet while using medication, watch for signs of medication overdose – headaches, tearful, zombie-like behaviour – as the diet kicks in. Some families start the diet during holidays when they are not using medication.

Q. How safe is ADHD medication?
A. There is no such thing as a totally safe drug. As drugs go, stimulant medications such as methylphenidate and dexamphetamine are regarded as very safe. The most often reported side-effects are appetite suppression, stomach ache and insomnia, although there have also been some reports of growth suppression, psychotic symptoms and a few alleged deaths, see www.RitalinDeath.com. There is no evidence that methylphenidate is effective in the long term and there is evidence that methylphenidate causes liver cancer in mice, see p. 249.

Q. What about antidepressants?
A. The use of antidepressants for ADHD children is increasing rapidly. Some people say that the drugs are a lifesaver and others that the drugs have made their lives worse. British psychiatrist Dr David Healy led a committee which officially recommended the new SSRI (selective serotonin reuptake inhibitor) antidepressants for children in 1997 but changed his mind when he noticed his in-tray 'filling with files on teenagers committing suicide within a week or two of commencing [the medication]'. The suicides are thought to be associated with akathisia, a drug-induced feeling of inner restlessness or

agitation. The risk is highest when just starting or stopping the drugs. Patients who find they are unable to stop taking their medication because of severe 'discontinuation symptoms' are advised to taper the dose, see www.QuitPaxil.org, depression factsheet on my website and p. 250.

Q. Help! Where do I start?
A. The hardest part about doing the diet is making the decision to do it. If you are going to do it, do it properly. You might as well get the best results possible. Children, teachers, relatives and friends are surprisingly cooperative once they start seeing improvements. See step-by-step instructions for doing the diet on p. 159.

Q. I'm too busy to read labels.
A. I agree. Parents shouldn't have to go to these ridiculous lengths to protect their children. It makes a lot more sense to minimise the use of additives in the foods that children eat.

Q. I saw on the internet that cranberry juice is low in salicylates.
A. Don't believe everything you read on the internet. There are many so-called low salicylate lists which are incorrect. All fruit juices are either high or very high in salicylates except pear juice which is moderate.

Q. How do I know this isn't normal three-year-old behaviour?
A. Try the behaviour management program called *1–2–3 Magic*, see p. 253. If it doesn't work, look at food.

Q. Are you saying that all ADHD children should try diet?
A. I agree with the independent scientists from the Center for Science in the Public Interest who conducted an extensive review of the research and concluded that parents should try dietary management before medication for ADHD children.

Q. My doctor said, 'just do the diet a little bit'.
A. Some families find that just cutting down on processed food and highly flavoured foods such as tomato sauce, fruit juice, cordial, chocolate, Vegemite and honey is enough. But they are not the ones whose children's behaviour is so bad they need to see a doctor. Doing the diet 'a little bit' is a good way to make sure it doesn't work. The elimination diet has been carefully developed over many years to give best results. Stick to it strictly. If your doctor won't support you, the Food Intolerance Network can help you to find one who will.

Q. I tried the diet and it didn't work.
A. Some of the reasons the diet can fail include: • lack of support for the mother; your doctor saying: 'Well, you can try it if you want. It won't do you any harm' is not good enough; parents don't take it seriously • mistakes, see Checklist of Common Mistakes on p. 231 • too many transgressions (such as fruit, tomato sauce, soft drink) per week • failure to avoid dairy foods or wheat when necessary • too many salicylates creeping back into the diet. Mothers who have tried the diet with no success often find on a second try, with more knowledge, that it works well.

Q. What about Vitamin C?
A. Although fruits are restricted, this diet is not deficient in Vitamin C so long as permitted vegetables are eaten. See p. 183 for failsafe supplements. Ask your dietitian to check nutrition.

Q. But fruit is so healthy!
A. Not for the child who is sensitive to salicylates. It took me six years to accept that a glass of orange juice was worse for my daughter than a slice of chocolate cake.

Q. My child won't eat cereal, bread, meat, fruit or vegetables, except potato chips. His diet is so restricted I don't want to take anything more out.
A. In my experience children will eat more, and better, when

provoking foods, often including milk, are removed. Establish a routine. Children eat better if they come hungry to family meals at set times. A 'grazing' pattern of snacking throughout the day whenever hungry will destroy the appetite if snacks are high in sugar or fat. Move towards crackers, vegetable soup and raw vegetables at snack time.

Q. Don't you think the children are deprived, eating such a restricted diet?
A. I lived with the rural people in Nepal for seven months, eating nothing but rice and lentils twice a day, every day, with very occasional vegetables, fruit, yak meat or curd cheese. This is what the Nepalese villagers eat all their lives. The children I met were happy, well coordinated, respectful, cooperative and eager to learn. I agree that the diet can be a problem socially, but if anyone is deprived it is the children who are eating food chemicals which make them restless and disagreeable.

Q. My children won't drink water.
A. Children won't drink water if they have a choice and tap water tastes terrible. Remove cordial, juice and soft drinks from your house and buy bottled water or a water filter. See Product Updates on my website for recommendations.

Q. Since my five-year-old son started on the failsafe diet, I have only seen him improve. However, as he sees his father every second weekend (and can eat what he chooses) he cannot reach his full potential. He often comes home very unsettled, and gets into trouble at school a few days later. Once he's back to failsafe foods, he starts to calm down, only to end up at dad's place again.
A. Some couples include a clause about diet in their parenting agreement. Contact the Food Intolerance Network (p. 251) for more information.

Q. Why didn't my doctor tell me about the diet?
A. Pressure from the pharmaceutical industry is immense.

Doctors are the main targets. Most do not realise how they have been pressured, see p. 241.

Q. How can I get a difficult child to stick to this diet?
A. Failsafe your house by eating or giving away unsuitable foods. **Do the diet with your child**, 'do as I do, not do as I say'. **Bribe, reward and praise**, see p. 108. **You must be able to say no to your child**, as in 'no, you can't have that food right now, but how would you like something else?'. The video *1–2–3 Magic* is fun to watch and it works. **Avoid television advertising** by turning off the television and watching videos instead or tape your favourite shows and fast forward through the ads. **Join an email discussion group** for suggestions and support.

Q. Can you recommend some failsafe rewards?
A. For younger children 'a dip in the jug' which contains small toys and novelties such as party poppers; computer, television or video time; a game or outing with mum; permitted treats, like a carob frog or an iced cake. A preschooler may need three or four small rewards a day for sticking to the diet plus lots of praise and encouragement. 'You're being so good. I know it's hard. Here's a treat for you' helps. A schoolchild probably needs a reward for avoiding the temptations at school and another for after-school care. If they confess to transgressions, thank them for telling you and try to offer substitutes for tempting situations. 'I'd like you to avoid that. What would help you? A special cake?'

Q. I hate cooking.
A. So do I. I choose very simple meals and have a weekly plan, see p. 210. My husband and I share the load; he does the supermarket shopping and cooks two days a week. I do the rest.

Q. Any hints about eating out?
A. Find a restaurant which will make a failsafe meal, e.g. failsafe fried rice, and eat there often; phone the chef beforehand and order a failsafe meal such as grilled steak or steamed

white fresh fish, steamed white rice (no flavours) and steamed green beans; drink soda water; eat before you go and have a decaf coffee.

Q. What's the safest takeaway food ?

A. Jacket baked potato from a potato cart, take your own Philadelphia cream cheese and chives or other topping; satay sticks (if no artificial colour) with steamed rice; fried rice consisting only of rice, shallots and egg at a Chinese café; grilled fish, take your own fresh buttered preservative-free bread rolls with lettuce and make fish burgers.

Q. I have a question about a food not on the list.

A. If the food isn't on the list, apply the taste test. Assume all fruit except pears contain some salicylates, the stronger the flavour, the more salicylates. If you like it, you can't have it. For meats, the stronger the flavour, the higher the amines. You can do a careful challenge, sticking to the rules, p. 164. Don't just eat it once and assume it is OK.

Q. How do we know which added flavours are failsafe?

A. Flavours are trade secrets but you can work out that fruit flavours are not failsafe because of salicylates, and flavours in tasty foods are likely to contain natural flavour enhancers. There are many reports of reactions to flavours, probably vanillin, in chocolate. Approach any product containing flavours with caution. Just because a small dose is OK, don't assume you can eat large quantities. As with other additives, effects are cumulative. During your elimination diet, avoid commercial products containing flavours unless they are included in the shopping list and even then, be careful.

Q. Can I lose weight on the failsafe diet?

A. People who are used to eating processed foods often lose weight without even trying. If that doesn't work, see the Failsafe weight loss factsheet on the website.

Failsafe remedies and supplements

Avoid unnecessary medications

Because medications usually contain colours, flavours or preservatives they have side effects which will confuse the results of your diet. Check ingredients and side effects on the Consumer Medication Information (CMI) sheet which comes with your medication, or on www.myDr.com.au.

- Avoid children's syrups (colours, preservatives, salicylates in flavours).
- Avoid over the counter cold remedies, cough medicines and decongestants except those listed below, or if you have passed your benzoate challenge, Bisolvon white tablets (not elixir) which break down thickened mucus.
- Avoid all vitamin and mineral supplements except those listed on p. 183.
- Avoid herbal and homeopathic remedies (which can contain salicylates).

For essential medications

- Use white tablets where possible (e.g. paracetamol, antihistamines), crushed and sprinkled into golden syrup or pear jam for children. The dose per kilogram is on the pack. Do not exceed recommended dose.
- Empty contents of coloured capsules (e.g. antibiotics) into water or golden syrup or ice-cream.
- Antibiotics are no longer recommended for ear infections as less than 3 per cent of children with ear infections will go on to develop complications which require antibiotics. Treat only for pain, doctors say.
- Wash hard coloured coatings off pills by rubbing gently under the tap.

Most people will get well from most illnesses – like colds and flu – without medications (always consult your doctor when necessary)

Plenty of rest, good food and plenty of water to drink are time-honoured ways of helping your body to recover. Use your allowance of moderate-salicylate fruit or vegetables containing Vitamin C and Vitamin A, especially pawpaws, mangoes, carrots and golden or red delicious apples, p. 189.

Some natural alternatives (always consult your doctor when necessary)

• **Colds, flu, cough:** any hot liquid is good for colds because it makes nasal mucus runnier which gets rid of viruses quicker; try chicken soup, hot lemon drink, p. 182 and drink plenty of warm water; breathe hot water vapours to loosen mucous (head over a basin of very hot water, make a tent with a towel); have hot baths • **sore throat:** gargle hot salt water • **to soothe a ticklish throat:** suck slowly on a hard sweet like Darrell Lea butterscotch or Werther's original butter candy (not completely failsafe because of flavour) • **stuffed up nose:** sniff up warm  salt water (one teaspoon in two cups cool boiled water) or Narium Nasal Mist spray from your pharmacy • **fever:** rest, drink plenty of liquids. The latest medical thinking is that fever is the body's way to heal itself and should run its course • **high fever:** cool the body with tepid water, use plain white paracetamol tablets when necessary • **ear infections:** the latest thinking is avoid antibiotics, treat for pain • **sores, pimples:** scrub with soap and water • **infected wounds:** hot compresses • **itching**, burning, irritations of the skin: for relief, cold compresses, network members recommend zinc creams (e.g. nappy rash creams) for itchy rashes including eczema, psoriasis and ringworm (tinea) • **minor burns:** hold in cold water for ten minutes • **cold sores:** hold ice on blister for one hour at first sign

• **diarrhoea:** drink plenty of liquids. When the person is vomiting or feels too sick to eat, give 'sips and chips' – sips of rehydration drink (1 litre water, 2 tablespoons sugar, $\frac{1}{4}$ teaspoon salt, $\frac{1}{4}$ teaspoon bicarbonate of soda, or unflavoured Gastrolyte) and water, chips of ice. Progress to clear soups (chicken, meat, bean), icypoles, plain boiled rice. Slowly introduce crackers, bananas, stewed apple, pawpaw, potato, progress to chicken, meat, beans, lentils, eggs, no fatty foods. If wheat has ever been a problem, avoid it during diarrhoeal illness. An old backpacker's trick of twenty-four hours with nothing but boiled water and cool boiled rice works well • **constipation:** drink lots of water, eat more fibre in pears, celery, cabbage, other vegetables, rhubarb (moderate in salicylates), rolled oats, All Bran if wheat is OK otherwise rice bran and psyllium husks sprinkled over cereal, rolled oats, rice bran. Distinguish between true constipation (hard, dry stools, 'rabbit pellets' due to lack of fibre and fluids) and 'sticky poos' – bowels 'set like concrete' due to food intolerance. Faeces are sticky and hard to clean up. For 'sticky poos', sprinkle a mixture of rice bran and psyllium husks over cereal when needed but also identify and avoid food chemicals which cause the problem (salicylates, additives, amines). See constipation factsheet on website • **food intolerance symptoms** (temper outbursts, restless legs, growing pains, stomach aches, itchy rash, headaches, difficulty falling asleep): see antidote p. 183.

Hot lemon drink
A soothing drink for colds and flu.

1 mug water
1–2 tbsp magic cordial base (use the strong option with 1 tsp citric acid, p. 215)
1 pinch plain white ascorbic acid or calcium ascorbate (Vitamin C) powder
whisky (optional for adults)

Heat water in microwave. Add magic cordial base and Vitamin C. Stir well.

Antidote for food reactions

Half a teaspoon of bicarbonate of soda in a glass of water, half a cup of bicarbonate of soda in a bath or a Caltrate (calcium carbonate) tablet may ease food intolerance symptoms for a few hours. For young children, half a tablet can be dissolved in water and added to drinks or food. These calcium supplements are available in any pharmacy.

Multivitamin and mineral supplements

Available from pharmacies, www.greataussiefood.com.au or www.pharmacydirect.com.au: • Macro Multi M from Whitehall • Amcal One-A-Day. The dose for children is half the adult dose. **Calcium:** • Caltrate 600 mg plain white tablets (not coloured or fizzy) available at any pharmacy in Australia • Healtheries Calcium supplements 600 mg plain white (not coloured) in health food stores in New Zealand • plain white calcium carbonate powder can sometimes be ordered from pharmacies, the recommended limit per day is 2000 mg. **Vitamin C:** plain white non-chewable tablets or powder (ascorbic acid or calcium ascorbate), such as Bioglan Cal C. Note that one teaspoon of powder contains 5000 mg of Vitamin C compared to the recommended daily allowance of 60 mg, so you only need a tiny amount. Multivitamin supplements above contain Vitamin C and extra daily doses are not recommended except during illness because salicylates and Vitamin C compete for excretion in the kidneys. Large doses of Vitamin C can lead to salicylate toxicity at normally non-toxic doses. **Iron:** • FGF Iron from Abbotts • F.A.B. Co from Medical Research. **Energy:** Polycose from Abbotts, Polycal from Nutricia, Maxijoule from SHS, Polyjoule from Sharpe. These are glucose polymers for increasing caloric intake in people who are losing weight without wanting to, available from pharmacies, ask your dietitian for more information. **Nutritional supplements** (not dairy free): • Ensure from Abbotts, lactose free but contains milk proteins • Sustagen from Mead-Johnson.

Supplements to avoid

• Megavitamins can set up rebound deficiencies • all chewable or fizzy supplements contain flavours which are not failsafe • bioflavonoids and other natural sources of vitamins (e.g. rosehips) contain salicylates • pharmaceuticals are permitted to contain unlisted additives. When labelled 'no preservatives, artificial flavours, yeast, sugar, dairy foods, gluten' etc, they may contain artificial colours and salicylates in natural flavours • vitamin supplements from naturopaths or chiropractors are likely to contain natural sources of vitamins which are high in salicylates.

Tips for ADHD management

Be failsafe. Do the elimination diet strictly to find out which food chemicals affect your child.

Stay calm. Use the counting/time out technique recommended in *1–2–3 Magic*. It will forestall arguments and double the effectiveness of the diet. Avoid hitting which can teach aggression.

Be positive. Children who experience constant criticism and punishment need to feel loved and accepted at home. Schedule regular time for you and your child to enjoy time together such as playing a board game or reading a story, if only for 15 minutes. Avoid put downs. Compliments, praise and success help self-esteem.

Reduce rules. Stick to a few clear, important rules and be firm. Positive commands like 'do this' are better than threats and negatives like 'don't do that'. Make eye contact and give simple commands or written lists rather than yelling from another room. Try rewarding good behaviour with hugs, stars, tokens and rewards such as time with a parent.

Be helpful. Be patient, kind, tolerant and understanding. Criticism isn't helpful. Avoid unnecessary confrontations. Childproof your house. Be prepared to laugh.

Be organised. Use the 3 R's – *routine, repetition, regularity* – for meals, bedtime, homework. Use a kitchen timer constantly: 'the timer says it's time for bed.'

Reduce noise and clutter. Keep toys tidy and manageable. They should be safe, relatively unbreakable and out of sight when not in use. Limit television.

Know when to stop. They never will. It's up to you.

Emphasise strengths and avoid weaknesses. Avoid situations and groups, including schools, which set your child up to fail. Encourage strengths.

Exercise is important. Find an exercise which will suit your ADHD child, from karate, ballet or bicycling to horse-riding, sailing, bushwalking or scuba diving.

> 'Choose "good", helpful addictions such as exercise: Many adults with ADD have an addictive or compulsive personality such that they are always hooked on something. Try to make this something positive.'
>
> 'Exercise is positively one of the best treatments for ADD. It helps work off excess energy and aggression . . . soothes and calms the body . . .'
>
> '50 Tips for ADD Adults' from *Driven to Distraction* by Edward M Hallowell MD and John Ratey MD.

Never give up. It is essential to get diet right first, but diet alone will not always fix a learning delay. Failsafers have reported success with a range of programs (see p. 253), and techniques which were ineffective before diet may be worth a try.

12 Foods to eat, foods to avoid

Food additives

EAT	AVOID
NATURAL COLOURS	**NATURAL COLOURS**
160a betacarotene	160b annatto
101 riboflavin yellow	**ARTIFICIAL COLOURS**
120 cochineal*	102 tartrazine yellow
150 caramel brown	104 quinoline yellow
170 calcium carbonate white	107 yellow 2G
171 titanium dioxide white	110 sunset yellow
172 iron oxides yellow, red,	122 azorubine red
black	123 amaranth red
	124 ponceau red
ADDITIVES UNLIKELY TO	127 erythrosine red
CAUSE REACTIONS	129 allura red
anti-caking agents	132 indigotine blue
bleaches	133 brilliant blue
emulsifiers	142 food green
mineral salts	143 fast green
propellants	151 brilliant black
food acids	155 chocolate brown
sweeteners	
thickening agents	**PRESERVATIVES**
vegetable gums	200–203 sorbic acid, sorbates
vitamins	210–213 benzoic acid,
	benzoates
	220–228 sulphur dioxide,
	sulphites
	249–252 nitrates, nitrites
	280–283 propionic acid,
	propionates

EAT	AVOID
ANTIOXIDANTS in oils 300–304 ascorbates 306–309 tocopherols	**ANTIOXIDANTS in oils** 310–312, 319–320 Gallates, TBHQ, BHA, BHT
	FLAVOUR ENHANCERS 620–625 Glutamates 627 Disodium guanylate 631 Disodium inosinate 635 Ribonucleotides
FLAVOURS vanilla, vanillin: limit 2 drops/day	**FLAVOURS** Added flavours except vanilla (see p. 232)
	ARTIFICIAL SWEETENERS 951 Aspartame

Eat from the left-hand column during your elimination diet. *Cochineal is made from an insect and there have been a few reports of true allergic reactions (occupational asthma, anaphylaxis) in people who work with it. Natural plant-based colours are likely to be moderate in salicylates, exceptions (higher and lower) are listed. As trade secrets, flavours don't have to be identified. Fruit, herb or spicy flavours will contain salicylates, tasty flavours will contain some form of natural glutamates, see p. 231. See my website for updates.

Vegetables

EAT	AVOID S = salicylates A = amines G = glutamates		
LOW	MODERATE	HIGH	VERY HIGH
beans, green	asparagus **S**	alfalfa **S**	broadbean **SA**
brussels	beetroot **S**	artichoke **S**	cauliflower **SA**
sprouts	carrots **S**	capsicum **S**	eggplant **SA**
cabbage	Chinese	chili **S**	gherkin **SA**
(green, red)	greens **S**	chicory **S**	olive **SA**
celery	lettuce (except	corn **S**	
chives	iceberg) **S**	cucumber **S**	broccoli **SAG**
choko	marrow **S**	endive **S**	champignon
dried beans	parsnip **S**	onion **S**	**SAG**
dried peas	potato	radish **S**	mushroom **SAG**
garlic	(new, red) **S**	water	spinach **SAG**
leeks	pumpkin **S**	chestnut	rocket **SAG**
lentils	snow peas	(yambean) **S**	tomato **SAG**
lettuce, iceberg	(and sprouts) **S**	watercress **S**	
potato (large,	sweet potato **S**	zucchini **S**	
white, peeled)	turnip **S**		
shallots			
shoots,	green peas **G**		
bamboo			
sprouts, mung			
swedes			

Eat from the low column during your elimination diet. Since most food chemicals are in the skin or just underneath, peel vegetables thickly. Throw away the outer leaves of lettuce. Note that all dried beans – kidney, butter, borlotti, navy, garbanzo, etc – are failsafe except broadbeans. Potatoes should be large, white or dirty, brown. *Avoid* vegetables in the moderate, high and very high columns, especially tomatoes and tomato products, vegetable juices, vegetable stocks and pastes, canned soups, canned baked beans in sauce, pickled vegetables (SAG); flavoured bean mix (S); sulphites in dried packet soups, dehydrated peas, instant mashed potato; hot chips (fries) and potato gems (also antioxidant in oils); baby food in cans and jars.

Fruit

EAT	AVOID S = salicylates A = amines G = glutamates		
LOW	MODERATE	HIGH	VERY HIGH
pears, peeled, ripe, juicy, soft canned in syrup, or baby puree	apples (golden or red delicious) **S** custard apple **S** loquat **S** mango **S** pears (unripe, unpeeled, canned in natural juice, nashi) **S** persimmon **S** rhubarb **S** banana **A** pawpaw, yellow **A** pawpaw, red **SA**	apples except delicious **S** berries except raspberries **S** currants (black, red) **S** melons (watermelon, rockmelon, honeydew) **S** stone fruit (apricot, cherry, nectarine, peach) **S** guava **S** lychee **S** pomegranate **S** rambutan **S** figs **SA** lemons **SA** sugar banana **SA**	citrus except lemons (oranges, mandarins, grapefruit, pomelo, tangelo) **SA** avocadoes **SA** dates **SA** kiwi fruit **SA** passionfruit **SA** pineapple **SA** raspberries **SA** grapes **SAG** plums **SAG** prunes **SAG** raisins **SAG** sultanas **SAG**

Eat from the low column. For salicylates, ripe is better. For amines, ripe is worse. Cooking does *not* reduce salicylates. *Avoid* fruits in the moderate, high and very high columns; any other fruits, fruit juice, cordials, dried fruits, fruit flavourings and toppings even when all natural; salty plums (SAG, colours and sulphites). Berries high in salicylates include blackberries, blueberries, boysenberries, cranberries, loganberries, mulberries and strawberries. Note that raspberries are rated *very high* in both salicylates and amines. Note that lemons are the only citrus rated *high* in salicylates and amines. Sugar bananas are the short, fat bananas also known as ladyfingers. Don't panic, the recipes will show you how to live without fruit (see p. 212).

Cereals, grains, flours

EAT	AVOID S = salicylates A = amines G = glutamates
LOW	HIGH
amaranth	Avoid all corn products except cornflour. Avoid
arrowroot	cornflakes, cornflake crumbs, popcorn, corn chips,
barley	tacos, cornmeal, wholegrain cornflour or maize
buckwheat	flour, polenta, cereals with corn (e.g. Nutrigrain) **S**
cornflour,	
refined	breakfast cereals with fruit, nuts, coconut (**SA**),
cous cous	honey (**S**), cocoa (**A**)
malt	
millet	basmati, jasmine, wild rice, flavoured rice **S**
potato flour	commercial baby rice cereals **SA**
quinoa	
rice	canned spaghetti, coloured or flavoured noodles,
rolled oats	pasta **SAG**
rye	
sago	breads with corn, dried fruit, seeds except poppy,
semolina	breads with preservatives, mould inhibitors, flour
soy flour	treatment agent 223, whey, vinegar preservatives
spelt	202, 280–283 in bread, pita bread, rolls, muffins,
tapioca	crumpets, pizza base, breadcrumbs **SA**
wheat	

Plain rice cereals, rice cakes and noodles, plain rolled oats, plain wheat cereals, plain uncoloured pasta and noodles, plain and poppyseed preservative-free bread and rolls, plain water crackers, crispbreads, crackers, plain biscuits, plain shortbread are OK, see shopping list. *Avoid* any bakery product containing unsuitable additives or ingredients such as fruit, spices especially cinnamon, chocolate, honey, corn, seeds except poppyseeds, or unsuitable oil, e.g. Christmas cakes and carrot cakes. Gluten free flours such as potato, tapioca and cornflour may contain sulphite residues which may affect extra sensitive people. Some people are affected by wholegrain wheat in bread and breakfast cereals such as Weet-Bix.

Meat and seafood

EAT	AVOID S = salicylates A = amines G = glutamates	
LOW	HIGH	VERY HIGH
beef	aged beef A	anchovies A
veal	bacon, ham A	fish roe, caviar A
lamb	chicken skin, liver A	offal (liver, kidneys) A
rabbit	frozen fish A	pâté (from liver) A
failsafe	meat juice in gravy,	*processed fish*
sausages	stews, stocks A	dried, pickled,
(p. 217)	pork A	salted, canned A
chicken (no		
skin)		
fresh white fish	*non-white seafood*	*smoked products*
fresh crab	prawns A	(meat, fish, chicken) A
freshlobster	salmon A	self-basting turkey G
fresh oysters	sardines A	fish sauces,
fresh mussels	tuna A	marinades SAG
calamari		fish pastes SAG
sea scallops		gravy SAG
		spiced meats
		(devon, pressed
		chicken, meat pies,
		sausage rolls, salami,
		sausages, marinated
		meats, seasoned
		chicken) SAG

Eat from the low column during your elimination diet. Amines increase with age. Buy meat fresh and cook that day or use within one month. Buy fish within twelve hours of catch and cook that day or freeze and use within two weeks. Freeze leftovers (e.g. roasts). Cooking increases amines (browning, grilling, charring, long slow cooking). Microwaving or pressure cooking is safer. *Avoid* processed meats and fish (nitrates in meats; amines in fish; salicylates and MSG in seasonings; amines, colours in fish fingers, crab sticks).

Dairy foods

EAT	AVOID S = salicylates A = amines G = glutamates	
LOW **dairy products, cow or goat** *pure butter*, salted, unsalted, ghee	HIGH dairy blend with unlisted antioxidants 319, 320 ribonucleotides 635	VERY HIGH flavoured butters S
cream, fresh, sour, reduced, thickened		artificial creams
milk, plain, unflavoured, fresh, full-cream, low fat, skim, buttermilk, UHT, condensed, powdered, evaporated		flavoured milk, colours S
yoghurt, vanilla or natural, no annatto or artificial colour		
ice-cream, vanilla, no colour		
fresh cheeses (white – cream, ricotta, farm, mascarpone, cottage, no preservatives, flavours)		

If dairy is permitted, *avoid* artificial colours and annatto 160b in flavoured milks, yoghurt, ice-cream, custard and custard powder. Avoid fruit flavours (S). Vanilla is limited to two drops per day, approach vanilla flavoured yoghurts, soymilk and especially soy ice-creams with caution. Some commercial custards and dairy desserts like crème caramel may be failsafe if colour and preservative-free. Extra sensitive amine responders will not manage sour cream or sharp natural yoghurt. Avoid cheese sticks (preservatives) and all yellow or aged cheeses.

Eggs, non-dairy

EAT	AVOID S = salicylates A = amines G = glutamates	
LOW	HIGH	VERY HIGH
eggs		
fresh eggs		
frozen egg white mix		
dry pavlova mix (no preservative)		
soy products		
soymilks	soymilks with raw sugar (**S**), coldpressed oil (**S**), or unlisted anti-oxidants, see p. 240.	soy sauce, miso tempeh, tamari **AG**
soy yoghurt, no annatto 160b		
tofu, firm or smooth		
vanilla soy ice-cream		
others		
oatmilk	as above	
ricemilk		
Nuttelex dairy-free margarine		

Egg substitutes such as Orgran are failsafe. See also shopping list on p. 205 and recipes on website.

Drinks

DRINK	AVOID S = salicylates A = amines G = glutamates		

LOW
water, spring
  water
soda water
 	
magic cordial,
  p. 215
 	
*lemonade,
  bottled, no
  preservatives
tonic water,
  bottled, no
  preservatives
 	
plain milk (cow,
  goat, sheep),
  malted milk
  powder
carob powder
	MODERATE
	commercial
	  pear juice
	  (contains
	  peel) **S**
		HIGH
		most fruit
		  juices **S**
			VERY HIGH
			orange juice **SA**
			tomato
			  juice **SAG**
			vegetable
			  juice **SAG**
			
			cordials, soft
			  drinks, fruit
			  flavoured
			  drinks and
			  mineral
			  waters **S**
			cola (Coke,
			  Pepsi etc) **SA**
			
			chocolate
			  milk **A**
			other flavoured
			  milk **S**
			cocoa **A**
			chocolate
			  flavoured
			  drinks (Milo,
			  Quik etc) **A**

Choose from the low column during your elimination diet. Water is the best drink. If you don't like the taste, try a filter. Avoid sports drinks and any other drink with colours, flavours, preservatives. Failsafe lemonade (p. 216) is strictly limited to 150 ml per week (less than one glass) because of SA in the lemon juice flavour. With carob powder, be careful, many people complain about reactions to a darker, more bitter variety. See next table for tea, coffee and alcohol.

Tea, coffee, alcohol

DRINK	AVOID S = salicylates A = amines G = glutamates		
LOW **tea and coffee**	MODERATE	HIGH	VERY HIGH
decaffeinated coffee	coffee, coffee substitutes **S** decaf tea **S** herbal tea **S**		tea **S** peppermint tea **S**
alcohol gin vodka whisky			sake **A** beer **SA** cider **SA** brandy **SAG** liqueur **SAG** port **SAG** rum **SAG** sherry **SAG** wine **SAG**

Choose from the low column during your elimination diet. You might need to limit decaf to two cups per day. Wine also contains sulphites unless labelled preservative-free. Beer may contain unlisted sulphites.

Oils, nuts, snacks

EAT			AVOID S = salicylates A = amines G = glutamates			
LOW	MODERATE		HIGH		VERY HIGH	
Oils						
canola, soy,	almond	S	coconut oil	SA		
safflower, or	corn oil	S	copha	SA		
sunflower oil	peanut oil	S	olive oil	SA		
cottonseed			sesame oil	SA		
			walnut oil	SA		
Margarine			flaxseed	S		
from oils above			linseed	S		
Snacks						
cashews (raw)	tacos	S	brazil nuts	SA	almonds	SA
plain potato	corn chips	S	cashews,			
crisps, no			roasted	SA	fruit	
antioxidants			coconut	SA	flavours	SA
pretzels			hazelnuts	SA	honey	
			macadamia	SA	flavours	S
			peanuts	SA	muesli bars	SA
			pecans	SA	spicy	
			pinenuts	SA	flavours	SAG
			pistachio	SA	cheese	
			sesame		flavours	AG
			seeds	SA		
			sunflower			
			seeds	SA		
			walnuts	SA		

Choose from the low column during your elimination diet. Refining reduces salicylates. Avoid coldpressed oils (**S**) except for soy. Avoid antioxidants 310–312 and 319–321 in oils, margarines and products containing oils. Note that any vegetable oil which forms less than 5 per cent of the final product (including bread, butter blends, soymilk, biscuits and frozen french fries) may contain unlisted antioxidants, so stick to recommended brands in the shopping list or phone manufacturers to check. Avoid margarines and spreads with sorbates, flavour enhancers, artificial colours or annatto 160b (160a is failsafe). Avoid commercial salad dressings and mayonnaise. Avoid snack food with colours, flavours, flavour enhancers, preservatives and antioxidants. Raw cashews are limited to ten per day. Poppyseeds are failsafe. Avoid flavoured chips. Hot chips (fries) usually contain antioxidants and sulphites. See snack suggestions p. 213.

Flavourings

EAT	AVOID S = salicylates A = amines G = glutamates		
LOW	MODERATE	HIGH	VERY HIGH
salt (sea, rock)			flavoured
			salts **SAG**
chives		fresh herbs **S**	HVP, HPP,
garlic		dried herbs **S**	TVP **AG**
shallots		spices **S**	meat
parsley			extracts **AG**
poppyseeds			soy paste **AG**
			soy sauce **AG**
saffron			
			tandoori **SA**
citric acid	malt vinegar **A**		vinegar except
			malt **SA**
vanilla			
(2 drops/day)			gravies,
			homemade
			or premix **SAG**
			pastes (fish,
			meat and
			tomato) **SAG**
			sauces **SAG**
			meat
			marinades
			SAG
			tomato sauce,
			puree **SAG**
			stock cubes
			SAG
			yeast extracts
			like Vegemite
			SAG

Avoid flavoured salts like garlic, ham seasoning, etc. Avoid HVP (hydolysed vegetable protein), HPP (hydrolysed plant protein), TVP (textured vegetable protein). Avoid all fresh and dried herbs (including herbal medicines) and spices including allspice, aniseed, bayleaf, cardamom, carraway, cayenne, chili, cinnamon, cloves, coriander, cummin, curry, dill, five spice, garam marsala, ginger, mace, mint, mixed herbs, mustard, nutmeg, oregano, paprika, pepper, pimiento, rosemary, sage, tarragon, turmeric. Use a small amount of parsley for colour only.

Sweets, spreads, cooking ingredients

EAT	AVOID S = salicylates A = amines G = glutamates	
LOW	MODERATE	VERY HIGH
sugars		
sugar (white, brown, icing or caster)	raw sugar S molasses S	honey S
golden syrup	treacle S	liquorice S
maple syrup		mint-flavoured
malt extract		sweets S
		peppermints S
sweets, see below		chewing gum S
	chocolate (white) A	fruit flavoured
spreads		sweets S
caramel topping,		chocolate (brown) A
p. 203		cocoa A
pear jam, ketchup,		
p. 226		jams, jellies SA
cashew paste, raw,		lemon butter SA
		peanut butter SA
baking aids		cashew paste
baking powder		roasted SA
bicarbonate of soda		Nutella SA
(500)		Yeast extracts,
citric acid (330)		Vegemite, Marmite,
cream of tartar (334)		Promite SAG
gelatine (remove		
sulphur dioxide by		
boiling)		
bakers yeast		
Jamsetta		

Avoid maple flavoured syrup (preservatives). Sweets must be from permitted ingredients (avoid colours, preservatives, added flavour except vanilla), see p. 231: carob, caramels, toffees, butterscotch, white marshmallows, milk-based sweets, asthmatics be careful of sulphites in glucose syrup and gelatine based sweets. Raw cashew nut paste limited to two teaspoons per day. Jamsetta is for jam-making: sugar, citric acid, pectin. Avoid fruit-flavoured sweets and ices. Make home-cooking from permitted ingredients (biscuits, cakes, muffins, scones, pancakes, pikelets). Avoid commercial products with colours, preservatives, added flavours), see shopping list p. 201.

Pharmaceuticals

ALLOWED	AVOID
medications essential prescription medications (antibiotics, antihistamines, asthma medications etc) white tablets capsules (powdered contents) antacid tablets and powders (no colours or flavours) pain relief: paracetamol, (acetaminophen), codeine (Panadol, Panadeine), no colours or flavours local anaesthetic (no preservative)	medications which are not essential coloured tablets, capsules syrups, solutions, liquids with colours, flavours, preservatives; colour-free children's syrups with flavours, preservatives; cough syrups, lozenges salicylates in: aspirin preparations, non-steroidal anti-inflammatory drugs, eucalyptus oil, menthol, oil of wintergreen (Vicks Vaporub, Deep Heat etc), p. 180.

supplements, see p. 183
permitted vitamins (no PABA, colours, flavours);
  calcium supplements (no colours, flavours);
  iron supplements (no colours, flavours)
	liquid, flavoured, chewable, or megadose vitamins, supplements p. 235.
	herbal remedies
	essential oils, aromatherapy, incense

Prescribed medications are not necessarily failsafe, but if they are essential you must put up with the consequences. For some coloured tablets, you can wash off the coloured coating. Open coloured capsules, empty powdered contents on to a saucer and mix with syrup, see p. 180. Use salt or soda bicarbonate as a toothpaste substitute. Many people become more sensitive to strong smells for a few months when starting an elimination diet.

Toiletries, cleaners and other chemicals

ALLOWED	AVOID
toiletries	
toothpaste (no colour, flavour, p. 208)	colours, flavours, mouthwashes
	strongly perfumed products
soaps, shampoos, conditioners, moisturisers (light or unscented)	perfumes
	after shave lotion
deodorants (roll-on or stick)	aerosol deodorants or hairspray
sunscreen without PABA	sunscreen with PABA
laundry detergents, soap powders (unscented, no enzymes, p. 209)	fabric conditioners, washing and ironing sprays
other chemicals (for the extra sensitive)	
white or natural coloured playdough	coloured playdough
low-chlorine pools	swimming pool chlorine
low-residue paints	paints and other renovation products
bicarbonate of soda, vinegar, dishwashing detergent	other household cleaners
steam cleaning	carpet and upholstery cleaning products
second-hand cars, computers, furniture	new cars, computers, furniture or leave to 'gas off'
hard floors	new carpets
fly swats, traps, sticky baits, borax	pesticides in home
screens, cover up against mosquitoes	personal insect repellents
home-made pesticide, see below	pesticides (garden)
low scent trees, plants and flowers	strong smelling plants e.g. herbs and trees e.g. pine, eucalypt, especially cut as in Christmas trees, woodburning stoves, strong fragrant flowers

Mosquitoes are attracted to dark coloured clothing, wear light coloured long sleeves and pants. Home-made pesticide for your garden: 3 teaspoons of dishwashing liquid and 3 teaspoons of vegetable oil in 2 litres warm water.

13 Shopping list

Read ingredient labels. Ingredients change constantly. For more details and updates see my website.

Dairy-free, wheat-free and gluten-free suggestions at end of list.

Very sensitive people will react to some of the foods on this list, see p. 231.

VEGETABLES

Potatoes (large white or dirty brown), swedes

Brussels sprouts, cabbage, red cabbage

Green beans (fresh, dried if no preservative, frozen)

Celery, parsley, iceberg lettuce

Chokoes

Leeks, garlic, shallots, chives

Canned or dried lentils and beans, e.g. kidney or butter beans (not broad beans)

Mung bean sprouts, bamboo shoots

FROZEN VEGETABLES

Green beans, Brussels sprouts, diced swede, celery cuts, lima beans, butter beans

CANNED VEGETABLES

Green beans, lima beans, soy beans, red kidney beans, butter beans, borlotti beans, chick peas, three bean mix, four bean mix, bean sprouts (Trident), bamboo shoots (Changs)

DRIED VEGETABLES

Split peas (yellow or green), chick peas, besan flour, lentils (red, brown, green), borlotti beans, soy beans, canellini beans, lima beans, haricot beans, black eye beans, red kidney beans

FRUIT

Pears, peeled, ripe, soft and juicy

Pears canned in light syrup *not juice*

Baby pear purée (Heinz, Gerber)

Limit 2 whole pears/day but this is too much for the very sensitive.

PASTA, NOODLES, FLOUR, RICE

Wheat flour (bleached, unbleached, wholemeal, plain, self-raising), wheaten cornflour

Pasta, spaghetti, durum wheat, barley, rye (no colour, flavour, fillings)

Noodles, uncoloured Asian-style instant (no flavour sachet, Trident, Changs)

Cous cous

Rice noodles (e.g. Fantastic)

Rice, white, brown or gold but not flavoured (basmati, jasmine)

Barley, flour, unpearled, pearl, flakes

Wheat, barley, oat or rice bran

Wheatgerm

Semolina

BREAD

No preservative 280–283, no whey powder, no vinegar, no fruit, no honey, no sulphites (223), no antioxidants (319–320). Plain or poppyseed (no sesame seeds), Brumby's plain breads – loaves, rolls, French bread; Bakers Delight, Country Life Bakery, Demeter, Mountain bread, Moores, Naturis, Dallas, Jakks. Flat bread: Fielders Pocket, Sunray Pita, Long Life Pita, Lavash, Bagels (Sara Lee, Jakks), Brumby's iced finger buns (order with white fondant icing, no cinnamon or topping). Other brands, read labels and be suspicious. You can't always trust labels. Laucke's breadmaker premix.

BREAKFAST CEREALS

Wheat cereals Many brands such as Kellogg's All-Bran, Ready Wheats, Puffed Wheat, Special K. Check ingredient labels, some people do not tolerate wholegrain wheat products.

Oat cereals Plain, Crunchy Oat Bran, Oat Bran, Uncle Tobys Crunchy Oat Flakes, Bubbles, Rolled Oats, regular and quick cook

Rice cereal Kellogg's Rice Bubbles, Rice Pops, Sanitarium Ricies, Uncle Tobys Rice Crispies

Wheat pancakes Many brands are failsafe, e.g. White Wings Shaker Pancakes, White Wings Panjacks

SWEETENERS, TOPPINGS, SPREADS

White sugar, caster sugar, pure icing sugar, brown sugar (not raw sugar), golden syrup, maple syrup (pure, e.g. Camp, Norganic), Malt extract, e.g. Saunders, rice syrup, rice malt syrup, glucose syrup, pear jam, home-made with Jamsetta, or Birgit's pear jam (see p. 226), caramel dessert topping – Windsor Farm, Nestlé Caramel Top 'n' Fill

HEALTHFOOD SECTION

Some people react to carob
Carob powder (not from Turkey), carob buttons, no added flavour, cashew nuts (raw, limited), cashew nut paste (raw, *not* lightly roasted)

CAKES, MUFFINS, BISCUITS

May contain egg and milk
Sara Lee All-purpose Pound Cake, self-saucing sponge (Big Sister Butterscotch, Big Sister Golden), Defiance Instant Success Multi Purpose Baking Mix, Defiance Hot Cake Mix, White Wings Biscuit Base, Betty Crocker Bisquick

PASTRY

May contain milk, soy, egg
Pampas Puff Pastry, Pampas Filo Pastry, Greens Pastry Mix, Spring Roll Pastry (TYJ, Trangs, Pampas)

BISCUITS

Note that biscuits containing vegetable oil may also contain antioxidants 319–321. The reaction is dose related – the more you eat, the more likely you are to react. The oil in Arnott's biscuits no longer contains these potentially harmful antioxidants. Avoid plain sweet biscuits which contain 'flavours'.
Arnott's Original Water Crackers, wholemeal Sao, Sao, Salada, Saltine, Vita-Weat, rice cakes (plain or with buckwheat, check for antioxidants in any which contain vegetable oil); shortbreads (e.g. Glengarry) made from flour, butter and sugar, Milk Arrowroot, Milk Coffee, Scotch Finger

MEAT

Use the day you buy or freeze and eat within 4 weeks.

Beef, e.g. preservative-free mince, steak, chops, roast beef, lamb, e.g. chops, leg of lamb, lamb steak, veal, sausages, especially made with fresh meat, rice flour, sea salt, shallots and/or garlic

CHICKEN

It is not enough to avoid the skin and stuffing on a seasoned, stuffed chicken.

Whole fresh, frozen or rotisserie chicken (no skin, definitely no seasoning, stuffing, or self-basting), chicken fillets, thighs, pieces (no skin, no marinade)

FISH

Cook within 12 hours of capture or freeze and use within 2 weeks.

Fresh (not frozen or canned) white fish (e.g. snapper, barramundi, whiting, not salmon, tuna), crab, lobster, oysters, calamari, scallops but no prawns

EGGS

Fresh eggs, preferably free range, frozen egg white mix (Good Food, Just White, yolk free), Pavlova mix if additive-free (Greens Ezi-pav, Pavlova Magic)

EGG REPLACER

Egglike (Country Harvest), Orgran Egg Replacer, Nutricia

DAIRY FOODS IF DAIRY IS PERMITTED

Thickeners in yoghurt, ice-cream and thickened cream may contain small amounts of gluten.

Milk Fresh, plain, full cream, skim, buttermilk, UHT, sweetened condensed, powdered, evaporated, and reduced lactose (Balance)

Yoghurt *No preservatives, no 160b, no artificial sweetener 951. Avoid all yoghurts if diet is not working.* Plain (*beware of very sharp taste for the extra sensitive, limited for amine responders*), Vaalia natural (*is good for Lactobacillus GG*), vanilla (*beware of flavour if eaten frequently*), Ski, Nestlé Activ LCI, Yoplait Petit Miam Vanilla Surprise Tubes fromage frais, not yoghurt.

Fresh white cheeses like Philadelphia cream cheese, Ricotta (Perfection cheeses, Avanti, Paesanella, Norco, La Deliziosa, United Dairies, No Frills), cottage cheese (no preservative – Jalna, Avanti)

Ice-cream Peters Original Vanilla, Norco Natural, Pauls, No Frills, Homebrand, MasterMaid, Farmland, Woolworths Traditional, Sara Lee (vanilla, and honeycomb and butterscotch)

Rice-cream Vanilla rice cream/creamed rice dessert (Jacaranda)

Cream Fresh, light, regular, rich, sour, canned, thickened, UHT

Butter and margarine Pure butter (cream, water, salt) and ghee are failsafe. Nuttelex milk-free margarine is failsafe. Avoid all softened butter or dairy blends (BHA 320 sometimes unlisted, flavour enhancers, see my website); avoid margarines with colours (except betacarotene 160a), sorbate 200–202, antioxidants TBHQ 319, BHA 320. Eta 5-Star margarine, MeadowLea (not lite) and MeadowLea Logicol (not lite) are failsafe now, but check website or manufacturer. Ingredients change.

Non-dairy Nuttelex margarine, soymilk (calcium fortified, unflavoured, avoid cold-pressed oils, raw sugar, evaporated cane juice, antioxidants 319–321): e.g. SoyLife, Sanitarium So Good (longlife, not fresh which contains linseed oil). If gluten free avoid malt. Soy yoghurt (avoid colour 160b): So Natural vanilla, Soygurt. Soy cream cheese (King Land). Soy custard. Tofu, e.g. King Land Silken Tofu. Vanilla soy ice-cream, e.g. Soylati, Charioto, Fruccio limited because of flavours. Rice milk, (preferably calcium fortified), Oatmilk.

OILS

Canola oil, safflower, sunflower or soy oil, not cold pressed (except for soy), no antioxidants (310–312, 319–321). In Australia, nearly all brands are failsafe, e.g. Dick Smith, Becel, Crisco, Eta, MeadowLea, Sunola, Sunbeam. In New Zealand, only Ideal sunflower oil or cold-pressed soy oils.

DRINKS

Water, filtered water, soda water (commercial or home made), spring water, plain mineral water, tonic water (unpreserved, e.g. Schweppes Tonic Water)

Milk, malted milk, soymilk

Decaffeinated coffee (instant, e.g. Nescafe or ground, e.g. Lavazzo)

Soyaccino (Sanitarium)

Carob powder *not from Turkey*

Unpreserved lemonade (bottled not canned Schweppes, 150 ml/week)

Home-made magic cordial (buy citric acid)

Home-made pear 'juice' – dilute syrup or fresh pears with water or soda water. Not suitable for the very sensitive

Gin, vodka, whisky

HOME COOKING

Salt (sea salt or rock salt), salt substitutes, e.g. Greens Lo salt, baking powder (Wards is gluten free), bicarbonate of soda, citric acid, cream of tartar, tartaric acid, gelatine (boil before use to remove sulphites), vanilla essence (natural or artificial – limited, some people will react to either), baker's yeast, fresh or dried, poppyseeds (not other seeds), chives; garlic – powder, granules, flakes (not paste or in oil because of the antioxidants not listed on the label); parsley (sprinkle only – can affect the very sensitive), saffron powder or threads (not artificially coloured powder)

SNACKS

Colvan Plain Chips, Kettle Plain Chips, Planters Classic Kettle cooked plain salted, pretzels (e.g. Parkers), raw cashew nuts (limit 10 per day), plain pappadums (e.g. Pataks)

FROZEN

McCains Healthy Choice oven bake french fries. Beware of unlisted antioxidants in the oils in other brands – you need to phone the consumer hotline.

SWEETS AND TREATS (NOT FOR THE ELIMINATION DIET)

Be careful of any product that contains 'flavours'. Regard these as treats and do not eat them every day.

Ice-cream cones (read labels, no colours, preservatives. Some contain unlisted antioxidants 310–321 in vegetable oil; contact manufacturers). Pauls Dessert Whip (some people will react to flavour), Peters Microfreeze Vanilla Malt Thickshake (ditto), malted milk powder (Nestlé, Horlicks), flavoured milk drinks – Classic vanilla malt, Good One carob (both limited), custard (Pauls, Ideal Dairy Natural Vanilla, Soy Life)

Peters Lemonade icypoles are now not permitted, the recipe has changed.

Marshmallows (Pascalls Vanilla, limit 4/day)

Caramels (e.g. Allen's Jersey Caramels, limited)

Butterscotch (no colours or artificial flavours so unlimited, e.g. Darrell Lea)

Toffee and butter candy (e.g. Allen's McIntosh Butter Candy, not caramels)

Honeycomb sweets (by Darrell Lea and www.sweettreats.com.au)

Milk-based lollies such as Allen's Milk Shake lollies and Moo Choos, but beware of the cumulative effects of artificial flavours and milk

home-made plain toffees, caramels, butterscotch, caramel fudge

Only for the less sensitive (I do not recommend these)

White jelly beans (limit 4/day, Darrell Lea are the only preservative-free white jelly beans, but many people react to the lemon juice, beware)

Kellogg's Rice Bubble Treats (1/day, definitely not for everyone!)

WHEAT FREE

Wheat and preservative-free rye bread, e.g. Country Life Rye bread, rye crisps, e.g. Ryvita, Kavli, rye flour, use also gluten-free brands

GLUTEN FREE

Note that many gluten-free flours (potato, tapioca, arrowroot, cornflour) contain residual sulphites

which can affect some people. Rice flour is sulphite free.

Rice, brown or white (not jasmine, basmati, wild), rice bran, rice flour, rice noodles, vermicelli, rice pasta, (e.g. Orgran rice-soya garlic and parsley pasta), puffed rice cereals e.g. Happy Human Puffed Rice, Nutra life, rolled rice flakes, Orgran rice crumbs

millet (hulled, unhulled, flour, flakes, meal, puffed)

buckwheat (raw, roasted, cracked, flour), buckwheat pasta, buckwheat puffs, buckwheat pancake mix (Orgran)

amaranth puffed breakfast cereal and quinoa flour

sago and tapioca flour and balls, arrowroot flour

potato flour or starch, fresh potato gnocchi (Guzzi's)

cornflour (maize not wheaten, e.g. White Wings)

soy flour, rolled soy flakes, grits, pasta

psyllium hulls, besan (chick pea) flour, sorghum

xanthan gum and guar gum

BAKING MIX OR FLOUR

Gluten free, wheat free multi-purpose baking mix (many including Freedom Foods, Country Harvest, F.G. Roberts)

GF Bread *Check these and other brands for milk, soy, preservative, vinegar, honey, fruit, seeds.* Rice bread or GF bread mix, check labels. Landsell Cottage, R & R Bakery products, many others, see product updates on website. In NZ, Dovedale GF yeast-free rice bread.

GF Biscuits Rice cakes, thick, plain, with millet, with buckwheat, Carob Rice Cakes (Freedom Foods, Naturally Good), Rice Cookies (Orgran)

GF Pastry *May contain milk, soy, egg.* Pizza and pastry mix (Orgran), rice paper, a gluten-free pastry substitute in Chinese shops

TOILETRIES AND MEDICATIONS

Toothpaste, unflavoured, uncoloured (Soul Pattinsons Plain at www.soulpattinson.com.au or at any of their stores or www.greataussiefood.com.au)

Soap, uncoloured, low-perfume (e.g. Sunlight,

Simple, Imperial Leather, no bubble bath)

Shampoo/conditioner (Pears Natural or Dermaveen from pharmacies)

Deodorant: low-perfume roll-on deodorant.

Washing powder, no perfume, no enzymes, e.g. Planet Ark, Lux, Omo-sensitive, Amway

Toilet paper, plain, uncoloured, unperfumed

Multivitamins and other supplements, permitted brands only see p. 183

MAIL ORDER FAILSAFE FOODS

Magic cordial and a wide range of additive-free cordials are available from www.granmas1908cordials.com.au

Commercially made Lachlan's Lollipops, honeycomb sweets and Christmas candy canes are extremely popular, from failsafer Samantha Tinsley in Brisbane, www.sweettreats.com.au or see Product Updates on website.

For overseas and country failsafers, the following failsafe products are available by mail order from www.greataussiefood.com.au: Soul Pattinson Plain Toothpaste, Caltrate plain white calcium supplements, Macro M multivitamins, CSR Golden Syrup, Pavlova Magic, Sakata Plain Rice Crackers, Kettle Plain Crisps, Pascalls Vanilla Marshmallows, decaf coffee, Egg-like Egg replacer, Arnott's Sao, Vita-Weat, Glengarry Shortbreads, Milk Coffee and Milk Arrowroot, Allen's Milk Shakes.

See website under Product Updates for gluten-free breads, and many butchers selling failsafe sausages.

CAFÉS

Additive/gluten free, some failsafe: The Peasant Feast, Newtown, Sydney (phone 02 9516 5998 two days ahead for failsafe); Silly Yaks Bakery Café, Melbourne www.sillyyaks.com.au.

Always read labels: ingredients change! Many failsafers have been caught out by changes in soymilk and margarine, especially.

14 Failsafe recipes

Failsafe eating is easy for a motivated adult. It is more of a challenge with a difficult child. The suggestions in the box below are only an example.

A SAMPLE DAY

Breakfast: Rice Bubbles or rolled oats with milk · fresh or canned pear · toast (preservative free) with margarine and pear jam.

Lunch: 1 or 2 sandwiches (preservative-free bread): cold home-cooked roast chicken or cream cheese with lettuce, celery, mung sprouts.

Dinner: Grilled or panfried lamb, beef, chicken or fish with mashed potato, green beans and Brussels sprouts · or pasta with chicken and cream cheese topping · or failsafe burgers · or failsafe sausages · or home-made chicken schnitzel and chips · ice-cream with canned pears.

Snacks: Pear · buttered crackers or rice cakes · yoghurt · raw cashew nuts · hard boiled eggs · home made or commercial plain sweet biscuits.

Drinks: Decaf coffee, milk, soymilk, ricemilk, water or permitted alcoholic drinks (adults only).

Each family has to find their own way. This section will give you ideas about how to adapt your present meals using failsafe ingredients. There are some basic recipes here and more in the *Failsafe Cookbook*.

Some failsafe substitutes

alcohol	gin, vodka, whisky
baked beans	canned butter beans
biscuits	shortbreads, commercial biscuits (p. 203), home-made (p. 225)
bread	preservative free (p. 202), rice cakes, low-fat crackers

breadcrumbs	rice crumbs or home-made breadcrumbs
brown sugar	light brown sugar, not dark, and coloured with molasses
burgers	home-made (p. 219)
butter	pure butter, dairy blend, margarine (see p. 205)
cakes	home-made (p. 224) or commercial no additives (p. 203)
cheese	white cheeses (p. 205), soycheese with 160a not 160b
chicken nuggets	home-made (p. 219) or see the *Failsafe Cookbook*
chocolate	use carob instead of chocolate, cocoa, Milo
cooking oil	see p. 226
cordial	see p. 215
croissants	no colours, preservatives, antioxidants, whey powder
crumb mix	see breadcrumbs
dried fruit	soft, ripe pears dried in a home dehydrator (limited)
fish fingers	home-made (p. 215)
'flavours'	enjoy the flavour of fresh, natural, high quality ingredients
fries	home-made (p. 220), failsafe potato crisps (p. 206)
ginger	in gingerbread, brown sugar, see the *Failsafe Cookbook*
gluten free	see p. 207
icypoles	home-made, (p. 216)
jam	see p. 226, or see website
juice	water, home-made icypoles (p. 216), magic cordial (p. 215)
honey	golden syrup, maple syrup, rice malt
KFC	HFC, see the *Failsafe Cookbook*, or p. 219
lemon juice	citric lemon juice (p. 228)
margarine	see p. 227
milk	if dairy free, soymilk, ricemilk, oatmilk
noodles	uncoloured noodles, no flavour sachet
pasta topping	see p. 222
peanut butter	home-made cashew paste, see the *Failsafe Cookbook*
pizza	home-made (p. 221)
salt	use for flavour; failsafe eating is naturally low in salt
soft drinks	see p. 215
soy sauce	golden syrup
tomato sauce	pear ketchup, pear puree, mayonnaise, leek sauce (p. 227)

toothpaste	plain, unflavoured toothpaste (p. 208) or salt
sweets	toffees, caramels, others (p. 207 and p. 225)
Vegemite	plain buttered toast
vitamins	permitted supplements (p. 183)

Breakfasts are easy

You can choose from the following: cereal – rolled oats with brown sugar, commercial cereals such as Rice Bubbles (see shopping list p. 202) • eggs, chops • toast with butter, golden syrup or home-made pear jam • pancakes, home-made or commercial (shopping list p. 202) with butter or margarine and pure maple syrup • fruit: pear, fresh or canned in syrup • yoghurt: mild natural or vanilla, no annatto (160b) • dairy free: soy, rice or oat milk • gluten-free: puffed rice, puffed amaranth, boiled rice, rice cakes, gluten free toast, soymilk with no malt • drinks: decaf coffee, hot carob, milk, water.

Lunches and snacks

'Breakfast is easy, dinner is easy, it's the lunches and snacks I find hard on this diet.' —*Failsafe parent*

SANDWICH SUGGESTIONS

Use preservative-free bread and rolls or rice cakes with failsafe butter or margarine (p. 205) • home-cooked fresh or frozen roast chicken, lamb and beef with salt, lettuce, chopped shallots, mung bean sprouts, parsley or celery • rissoles, sausages, sliced hard-boiled egg • butter beans • cream cheese, soy cream cheese, preservative-free cottage cheese • egg, hard-boiled and mixed with a little warm milk and salt • cashew paste (make your own from raw cashews, oil, salt, see *Failsafe Cookbook*) • pear jam (p. 226) • rice malt • golden syrup.

PRESCHOOL ALTERNATIVES TO A PLATE OF FRUIT

Fresh peeled pear • Golden or Red Delicious apple when permitted • buttered failsafe crackers (for example, Saladas) • pear purée icypole • home made biscuits • for baking days or birthday parties, make a special iced birthday cake at home, cut it into slices, wrap each piece in cling film and put in a freezer bag with your child's name on it. Keep a few slices in the preschool freezer.

LUNCHBOX SUGGESTIONS
Sandwich (p. 212) • slice of
failsafe quiche, pizza, cold
sausage (p. 217) or rissole
(meat leftovers should be
frozen) • home-made pie
or small sausage rolls,
p. 214 (some tuckshops
will reheat them for you)

• vanilla yoghurt or soy yoghurt • stick of celery • hard-boiled egg • cashew nuts, raw (limit 10 per day) • small container with chopped canned pear • home-made treats like lunchbox muffins (p. 224), cookies (p. 225), cake (p. 224), Sarah Lee vanilla pound cake or plain sweet biscuits like shortbreads, see shopping list (p. 203) • failsafe pretzels or chips (p. 206) • white iced finger buns from Brumby's hot bread shops; you might need to order these the day before – they can be frozen in separate bags and used, cut in half, or sliced and buttered in school lunchboxes • water, Soyaccino, magic cordial or soy shake in a water bottle with a small amount of water frozen in the bottom.

SNACK SUGGESTIONS
As for lunchboxes, also: fresh peeled pear or canned pear (limit 2 whole pears per day) • buttered rice cakes, permitted rice crackers, or wheat-based crackers like Saladas with failsafe margarine or with spreads like cashew paste, cream cheese, golden syrup or pear jam • home-made fresh bread rolls with butter (p. 205) or garlic butter • preservative-free toast, celery sticks with cream cheese • plate of raw salad vegetables (p. 201) with dip (*Failsafe Cookbook*) • icypoles (p. 216), jelly cups, sago or custard cups, scones, pikelets and pancakes (*Failsafe Cookbook*) • some additive-free commercial croissants • toasted sandwiches or steak sandwich • home-made potato wedges

• vegetable soup • egg on toast • plate of pasta with butter and salt or frozen mince topping (p. 218) • anything from the breakfast, lunch section or dinner sections • Peters Dixie Cup ice-creams, sweets, home-made or limited commercial • Kellogg's Rice Bubble Treats (LCMs) limited to less than 1 per week – none for some children, see p. 232.

A school looking for an additive-free pie found most contained artificial colours or annatto (160b) in the crust. All contained either MSG or hydrolysed vegetable protein (HVP) which is a natural form of MSG. All contained BHA (320) in fats or vegetable oils, including one pie which claimed to be additive free.

Pies and sausage rolls

You can make your own sausage rolls from mince (flavoured with shallots, garlic, salt), form into sausage shape and place on the middle of a half sheet of Pampas pastry. Roll over, prick top. Cut to required lengths. Bake 20 minutes or until cooked. Use an automatic pie-maker to make pies with failsafe mince or other fillings. See tomato sauce alternatives (p. 227), but after a while you won't miss it.

Q. What's in a hot dog?
A. When we checked, Watsonia frankfurts and saveloys contained sodium metabisulphite (223) and sodium nitrite (250). The colour in the skins weren't listed but turned out to be annatto (160b) and cochineal (120). The roll will probably contain calcium propionate (282).

FINGER FOODS FOR BABIES AND TODDLERS
In an allergic family, delay introduction of eggs, dairy foods, nuts and seafood at least until 12 months: your dietitian can advise you.

Rusks: bake fingers of bread or rye bread in a slow oven for 2 hours or until very hard – good for teething • pureed baby pears or stewed pear • bananas (moderate in amines, if tolerated) • fingers of steamed cooked potato, swede, celery, pumpkin, sweet potato and carrots when permitted • failsafe vegetables – steamed and mashed, formed into a finger shape or different shapes, rolled in rice crumbs (p. 208), bake in a moderate oven for 10–15 minutes or until crispy on the outside • chicken fingers – finger shaped patties of minced chicken, made up with cornflour, oats if permitted and a pinch of salt, bake for 20 minutes or panfried in a little failsafe oil for a real treat • fish fingers – flaked white fish fillets, mixed with mashed potato and dipped in cornflour, egg, rice crumbs • over 12 months, strips of egg • home baked biscuits (reduced sugar is a good idea) • mini sausage rolls (p. 214) • home-made icypoles.

Drinks

Magic cordial
Water, preferably filtered, is the best drink but this is a useful substitute for juice and sweetened beverages.

1 cup sugar
1 cup water
$^1/_2$–1 tsp citric acid

Place water and sugar in a 2 cup jug and heat in microwave for 2 minutes. Stir until sugar is dissolved. Add citric acid. Store in refrigerator. Dilute to taste with water or soda water, about 1:4.

Variations: hot 'lemon' drink, as above, but serve hot and stir in a pinch of white Vitamin C powder before serving • **Whisky Sour** – add to whisky and soda water.

Other failsafe drinks
Water · spring water · soda water · preservative-free tonic (e.g. Schweppes) · home-made milkshakes – from milk, soymilk or ricemilk, flavoured with carob, decaf or caramel topping (p. 203), permitted ice-cream · preservative-free lemonade (e.g. bottled not canned Schweppes, limited to one small glass a week because it contains salicylates and amines in lemon juice).

Icypoles and icecups

You will need your own icypole moulds or plastic cups. Adjust dilutions to suit individual tastes. More water makes the icypole harder, more sugar makes it softer. You can use: plain water • magic cordial, diluted • pear syrup diluted with equal quantities of water (limit 2 whole pears or equivalent per day) • baby pear purée, or canned pears, blended without syrup • yoghurt or home-made iced decaf with extra sugar.

Peters Lemonade icypoles were previously permitted once a week. The recipe has changed. There are now no failsafe commercial icypoles.

Main meals

Vegetable soup

1 packet (375 g) red lentils
4 cups water or home-made
   chicken stock (p. 229)
1 tbsp failsafe oil (p. 226)
1 cup celery, chopped
1 cup leeks or shallots, sliced
2 potatoes, peeled and cubed or
   one potato, one swede
3 cups sliced cabbage
6 Brussels sprouts, halved
1 cup each frozen green beans
   and peas (moderate, use only
   when you have passed your
   pea challenge, p. 167)
extra water

Rinse lentils well. Cover lentils with water or stock and bring to the boil. In a separate saucepan, sauté celery and leeks and add to lentils. Prepare and add remaining vegetables. Add extra water until vegetables are just covered. Reduce heat and simmer gently until cooked, about 40 minutes. Blend or mash. Serves 8.

Commercial soups usually contain MSG and may contain sulphites in the vegetables. Dry packet soups can contain high levels of sulphites in the dried vegetables.

Meat (beef, lamb, veal)

SAUSAGES

Commercial sausages always contain sodium metabisulphite (223) unless labelled preservative free. You can ask your butcher to make failsafe sausages for you, see following. A growing number of butchers are selling frozen failsafe sausages (see my website). Check ingredients, however. Sausages labelled 'preservative and gluten free' are not failsafe because they usually contain herbs and spices and may contain MSG.

A recipe for your butcher
For 10 kg sausages

650 g brown rice flour
(2 kg for 30 kg)
3 leeks (10 leeks for
30 kg)
1 clove garlic
(3 for 30 kg)
¹/₂ cup sea salt
(1¹/₂ cups for 30 kg)
make up to 10 kg with fresh minced beef or chicken

Failsafe mince

Because this recipe does not disguise the flavour of the meat with MSG and strongly flavoured sauces, the mince needs to be fresh and of good quality. If you can't find good mince, ask your butcher to prepare minced topside steak for you. Ask your butcher: 'Does this mince contain preservatives? I really need to know.'

500 g preservative-free low fat
beef or lamb mince
2 shallots or 1 leek, finely
chopped
1 clove or more garlic, crushed
1 tbsp failsafe oil (p. 226)
sea salt to taste
1 tsp chopped parsley
2 tbsp cornflour dissolved
in 2 cups of water or
home-made chicken stock
(p. 229)

In a heavy-based frypan or large saucepan stirfry chopped shallots and garlic in failsafe oil, remove from heat. Add mince to pan, stir until cooked. Drain fat if necessary. Add shallots, garlic, parsley, sea salt and cornflour mixture, stir until thickened. Serve on mashed potato, pasta, noodles, rice, cous cous, toast, pizza and in jaffles and pies. Suitable to make a double batch and freeze in small containers if used within four weeks.

Burgers

'Make mince patties with egg, garlic, finely chopped leek, salt, sprinkle of citric acid. Serve on rolls or toast with lettuce, sprouts, sometimes an extra fried egg. Non-failsafe family members can add whatever they like – beetroot, tomato, sauce, etc – which means everyone is happy.' —*Reader, Sydney*

> Browning meat, charring, or grilling will increase its amine content. It is best to aim for medium rare. Extremely sensitive amine responders may need to steam or microwave their meat. Delicious tasting meat juices and gravy made from meat juices are high in amines, see p. 227. Marinades must be made of failsafe ingredients. Any commercial marinade, sauce or gravy is very high in salicylates, amines and MSG.

Chicken schnitzel

Kids love crumbed food which can ease the pain of avoiding takeaways. You can also use this method for fish, crumbed cutlets and veal schnitzel. These are good hot or cold and can be used in lunchboxes.

500 g chicken breasts, cut into thin slices
flour or gluten-free flour
$1/2$ tsp salt
1 egg, beaten
home-made bread crumbs or rice crumbs
failsafe oil (p. 226) for frying

Cut chicken into thin slices or nugget shapes. Season flour with salt, then coat chicken slices. Dip into beaten egg and cover with crumbs. Fry gently in shallow oil until golden brown on both sides. Drain on paper towels. Garnish with parsley and serve with mashed potato, vegetables and citric lemon juice (p. 228).

> Commercial breadcrumbs all contain preservative (282) and some contain HVP (MSG).

Andra's quick chicken and noodles

1 tbsp failsafe oil (p. 226)
1 cup each failsafe vegetables
    (e.g. leek, cabbage, green
    beans, carrots if permitted)
1 chicken breast fillet, cut into
    strips
extra oil
4 cups water
1 cup home-made chicken stock
    (p. 229) or water
2 packets (250 g each) of
    instant noodles, rice or wheat,
    Fantastic rice noodles (p. 202)
1 tsp salt

Heat oil in a very large pot, sauté vegetables. Remove from pan. Add extra oil and sauté chicken strips until light brown. Add vegetables to pan and add liquid. Arrange noodles over vegetables, add salt and put lid on pot. Cook for 6–8 minutes, stirring occasionally. For very sensitive amine responders, you can omit chicken stock, remove chicken after sautéeing and add at the end, reheating for a few minutes.

TWO-MINUTE NOODLES
Choose colour-free noodles such as Fantastic and avoid flavour sachets which are high in MSG. See topping suggestions (p. 222).

Oven fries

large white potatoes, peeled
    thickly
failsafe oil or spray (p. 226)
sea salt

Cut potatoes into thick chip shapes and microwave until still nearly soft. Coat in failsafe oil by putting them in a plastic bag with the oil and gently rolling around, or spray with oil. Spread in a single layer on an oven tray. Bake for 20–25 minutes at 180°C. Serve sprinkled with salt. Oiled, unbaked chips can be frozen for later use.

Commercial hot chips and fries may have been dipped in sulphites. They are almost always cooked in oil containing at least one potentially harmful antioxidant. They may also contain colours like 160b.

Mum's mash: getting vegetables into children
Start with mashed potato with butter, milk and salt. Very slowly, add small but increasing amounts of swedes, Brussels sprouts and chokos. You can also hide vegetables in mince dishes.

SALADS
For failsafe salad vegetables you will have to make do with celery, iceberg lettuce, mung bean sprouts, red or green cabbage, raw swede sticks, raw choko sticks, cold cooked green beans, dried beans such as kidney or butter beans. With these, you can do a tossed salad, coleslaw, plate of failsafe vegetables or a bean and pasta salad with cooked green beans. See p. 227 for dressings. If you fail your salicylate challenge you will probably have an allowance of moderate vegetables including asparagus, beetroot, carrot, Chinese greens, lettuce other than iceberg, snow peas and snow pea sprouts if tolerated.

PIZZA
You can make your own failsafe pizzas especially if you have a breadmaker for the dough. Some failsafe toppings: **garlic meat topping:** make the failsafe mince on p. 218 with extra garlic • **cheese:** spread pizza base thickly with preservative-free cream cheese. If you do not react to amines and dairy, you can sprinkle over grated mozzarella cheese • **vegetarian:** process 2 tins of partially drained red kidney beans with garlic to form a smooth paste • **chicken topping:** spread base with thick layer of cream cheese, sprinkle over chopped cooked chicken (p. 204 or leftover roast), sliced canned pear, and a sprinkle of finely chopped parsley.

Commercial garlic bread can contain calcium propionate (282) in the bread, colours (102, 110 or 160b), preservatives (200, 202) and antioxidants (319, 320, 321) in the garlic margarine. Make your own, see the *Failsafe Cookbook*.

PASTA

Serve any type of pasta – from twists to spaghetti – with failsafe toppings ranging from butter, garlic and salt, to garlic failsafe mince to the recipe below.

Chicken and cream cheese sauce

$^1/_2$ cup water
1 tsp parsley, finely chopped
1 tbsp shallots, finely chopped
sea salt to taste
2 tbsp cream cheese or soy cream cheese
200 g chopped, cooked chicken

Add parsley and shallots to water. Microwave on high for one minute. Stir in cream cheese. Stir in chicken. Pour over pasta. Serve with green beans. Serves 2.

Fresh garlic is safest. Garlic salt might contain MSG; also, if crushed garlic contains vegetable oil it will probably contain unlabelled antioxidants like BHA (320).

Other main meal suggestions: panfried or grilled fish, chicken, chops or steak; roast chicken, beef or lamb (no gravy, see alternatives p. 227); omelettes, quiche, potato and egg or cream oven bakes; and lasagne – see recipes and more suggestions in the *Failsafe Cookbook*.

Something sweet

People who are avoiding additives but not salicylates and amines can eat fresh fruit (except grapes) but not dried fruit like apricots and coconut which contain sulphur dioxide. There are recipes for desserts from family dinners with pancakes, pear crumble to cheesecakes, pavlovas and special occasion desserts in the *Failsafe Cookbook*.

ICE-CREAM

There are a number of failsafe commercial cow's milk dairy vanilla ice-creams, see p. 205, although you have to avoid yellow colour either artificial or annatto 160b. In my experience, ice-cream is the food dairy-free children miss most. This recipe is dairy free, sulphite free and can be soy free.

Non-dairy frozen dessert

600 ml soymilk or ricemilk
$^3/_4$ cup sugar
1 egg
4 tbsp water
30 g failsafe margarine (p. 227)
$^1/_2$ cup of arrowroot
2 tsp carob powder (cocoa if
    amines are OK)

Heat milk in a large saucepan on the stove. While milk is heating, beat sugar, egg, water, margarine, arrowroot and carob in a bowl. When milk reaches simmering point pour in the egg mixture and continue to beat over the heat until mixture boils and thickens. Remove from heat. Allow to cool a little then pour into icecup containers.

Commercial ice-cream toppings contain preservatives and colours. Use pure maple syrup or caramel topping (p. 203).

Lemon citric sago cups

This is my son's choice of dessert, to be served with ice-cream, of course.

$^1/_2$ cup sago
600 ml water for soaking
$^1/_2$ tsp salt to taste
2 tbsp water
$^1/_4$ tsp citric acid
$^1/_4$ tsp ascorbic acid or
    calcium ascorbate powder
    (Vitamin C)
4 tbsp golden syrup
4 tbsp sugar

Soak sago for one hour or more in water until soft. Add salt to taste. Boil until transparent. Add extra water, citric acid, ascorbic acid, golden syrup and sugar. Pour into moulds or cups to set.

Margie's lunchbox muffins

1¹/₂ cups self-raising flour
¹/₂ cup sugar or brown sugar
1 egg, lightly beaten
³/₄ cup milk or soymilk
¹/₄ cup failsafe oil (p. 226)
¹/₂ cup chopped pears (optional)

Sift flour into a bowl and add remaining ingredients, stirring with a fork until mixed. Lightly grease a 12 cup muffin pan with failsafe margarine or brush with failsafe oil and use an ice-cream scoop or spoon to three-quarter fill cups. Bake at 180°C for 15–20 minutes. For a treat, ice with white icing or add flavour-free carob buttons. These are equally good with gluten-free flour.

Basic plain cake

250 g self-raising flour or
    gluten-free flour (p. 207)
¹/₄ tsp salt
125 g failsafe butter or
    margarine (p. 205)
125 g sugar
2 eggs, well beaten
¹/₂ cup milk
¹/₄ tsp vanilla

Grease a cake tin. Preheat oven to 180°C. Sift flour and salt. Cream butter and sugar. Add beaten eggs gradually. Add flour and salt alternately with milk and vanilla. Put in tin and bake 40–45 minutes. Ice with white icing.

Variation: cup cakes – use paper patty cases. Recipe makes 24. Bake for 12–15 minutes. Ice with white icing. These make a good plate to take to a party or a school fete.

Basic biscuits

125 g failsafe butter or
    margarine (p. 205)
$^1/_2$ cup sugar (caster or icing)
1 egg
1 cup self-raising flour
1 cup plain flour

Preheat oven to 180°C. Cream the butter and sugar, add egg, mix thoroughly. Add sifted flours and mix. Knead until smooth on a floured surface. Roll and cut into desired shapes, place on a greased tray and bake for 15–20 minutes. Slice alternative: press into tray, bake for 30 minutes, ice with white icing and cut into squares.

Sweet treats

It is possible to make a wide range of failsafe caramels, butterscotch, honeycomb, fudge, toffees, marshmallows and milk-based sweets (see the *Failsafe Cookbook*), but nearly all commercial confectionery contains unsuitable colours, flavours, preservatives or antioxidants in margarines. Sulphited glucose syrup in sweets like jelly beans and gelatine in sweets like marshmallows are a potential problem for asthmatics. When making your own, you can boil the gelatine to drive off sulphur dioxide, but glucose syrup may contain well over the legal limit of sulphites and is best avoided during the elimination diet.

Lollipops

1 cup sugar
$^2/_3$ cup water
wooden sticks

Heat sugar and water in heavy-based saucepan over low heat and stir with wooden spoon until sugar dissolves. Bring to the boil and simmer without stirring until a drop snaps in cold water. Arrange rows of small sticks on oiled trays. Drop one teaspoon of toffee on to pointed end of each stick. Allow to set firmly. For a treat, put these lollipops in a small cellophane bag sealed with a fancy sticker.

Miscellaneous

Birgit's pear jam

Pears must be soft and ripe, or your jam will contain some salicylates. Jam-making generally requires roughly equal quantities of sugar and fruit.

1 kg ripe pears, peeled and cut into small pieces (should be about 750 g)
or 2 large tins of soft pears, drained
750 g sugar
1 x 50 g packet of Jamsetta (pectin and sugar mix, available in supermarkets)
1 tsp whisky (optional)

Purée pears. Put in a large saucepan and heat gently. Add sugar, Jamsetta and whisky, stirring with a wooden spoon until sugar is dissolved then bring to the boil and boil rapidly for five minutes, stirring occasionally. Allow to cool. Pour into sterilised glass jars or plastic storage containers. Store in refrigerator or freezer.

FAILSAFE OILS
Canola, safflower, sunflower and soy oils are failsafe · cold-pressed oils are not failsafe (too many salicylates) except for soy · avoid antioxidants 310–312 and 319–321. They will be listed on the label of cooking oils if present (but not when in other products, see labelling loophole p. 240 and shopping list p. 205) · in Australia, nearly all domestic cooking oils are failsafe (but not in restaurants) · in New Zealand, nearly all cooking oils contain harmful antioxidants.

FAILSAFE MARGARINE, DAIRY BLEND
Choose margarine made with canola, sunflower, safflower or soy oils · avoid preservatives 200–203 · avoid antioxidants 310–312, 319–321 · avoid colours 102, 110, 160b but 160a is failsafe · milk free if necessary · in Australia, there are several failsafe margarines and one failsafe dairy-free margarine, Nuttelex, which is now available in New Zealand · see shopping list p. 205 and labelling loophole p. 240.

Quick mayonnaise

400 g tin sweetened condensed milk
equal volume of water
4 tsp citric acid (more or less to thicken)
1 tsp sea salt or to taste

Combine all ingredients in a glass screwtop jar and shake well to mix. Store in refrigerator. You can use malt vinegar instead of water with citric acid if you don't react to amines.

GRAVY AND TOMATO SAUCE SUBSTITUTES
Commercial gravies are very high in salicylates and amines and usually contain added MSG. Even home-made gravies are unsuitable because meat juices are high in amines. Use baby pear purée, or alternatives below.

Basic white sauce

2 tbsp failsafe butter or margarine (p. 205)
1½ tbsp flour or gluten-free flour
1 cup or more of milk or milk substitute
sea salt to taste
1–2 tbsp cream cheese (optional)

Put butter in pan and stir until melted, add the flour to the butter, stir until cooked. The flour and butter have to be well cooked before adding liquid. Add liquid and whisk continually until thickened. Then add salt and remove from heat. Stir through cream cheese for a creamier flavour.

Leek sauce

1 large leek, finely sliced
water
1 tsp failsafe butter (p. 205)
1 quantity of white sauce
    (p. 227)

Cover microwave dish with leek slices. Add water until leek slices are just covered. Add butter. Microwave on high for 3 minutes. Make a white sauce and add leek mixture, stir well.

Birgit's pear chutney

Use instead of tomato sauce with sausages, other grilled meats and roast chicken.

1 large tin (825 g) of pears and
    syrup
$^1/_2$ cup brown sugar
2 tsp citric acid
1 tsp salt

Drain and dice pears. Put syrup in a saucepan and simmer until reduced by half. Add pears and remaining ingredients. Simmer about 15 minutes or until mixture thickens. Allow to cool. Store and use from freezer.

Variation: Pear ketchup: purée mixture in blender • Add chopped leeks, shallots and garlic to diced pears • for a thicker sauce, thicken with cornflour, gluten free if necessary.

Citric lemon juice

Real lemon juice contains salicylates and amines. Bottled lemon juice as used in processed foods contains sulphites as well. Use this substitute in any recipe which calls for lemon juice.

4 tbsp warm water
1 tsp sugar
$^3/_4$ tsp citric acid or to taste
$^1/_4$ tsp ascorbic acid
    (Vitamin C) powder,
    optional

Put sugar in warm water, stir to dissolve. Add remaining ingredients and store in refrigerator.

Quick chicken stock

Commercial chicken stock will usually contain MSG, even if added as HVP and not listed. After a roast chicken, you can put the bones and neck in a saucepan with water and simmer for one hour. To reduce amine build up, cook no longer than necessary. Strain, cool and store in refrigerator or freezer, skim off fat.

Some Australian–American terms

biscuits: crackers or cookies
cordial: a drink base similar to Kool-Aid but sold as a liquid
cornflour: corn starch
cold pressed: expeller pressed
fairy floss: cotton candy
fruit and vegetables:
    choko: chayote, vegetable pear
    marrow: squash
    pawpaw: papaya
    rockmelon: cantaloupe
    shallots: green onions
    sultanas: golden raisins
    swedes: rutabaga
grilled: broiled
icypoles: popsicles
icing sugar: confectionery sugar
icing: frosting
lamingtons: cubes of sponge cake, normally covered in chocolate and coconut
lamington tin, baking tray, swiss roll tin: similar in size to the American standard 13′ × 9′ pan
muesli: granola
paracetamol (e.g. Panadol): acetaminophen (e.g. Tylenol)
Rice Bubbles: Rice Krispies
Rissoles: beef or lamb pattie
sports drinks: thirst quenchers
soft drinks: sodas
soda water: club soda
scones: biscuits
sweets, lollies, confectionery: candies

Nuttelex is a dairy-free margarine made from safflower, sunflower and cottonseed oils, water, salt, emsulifiers 322, 471, flavour (vegetable), vitamins A and D, no added colour. It is very well tolerated by most food sensitive people. While visiting the USA I found a similar product, if you can tolerate soy: Shedd's Willow Run dairy-free soybean margarine contains liquid soybean oil and partially hydrogenated soybean oil, water, salt, soybean flour, lecithin, betacarotene, Vitamin A. For distributors, phone toll free 1800 735 3554.

Golden syrup is not available in the USA. Order from www.greataussiefoods.com.au or make your own: combine 1 cup white sugar, 1 cup brown sugar and 1 cup water, boil steadily uncovered for about 20 minutes until temperature is 230°F (if you don't have a candy thermometer, drop a teaspoon of the boiling liquid in cold water – if it dissolves, keep cooking).

Some failsafe food in the USA not available in Australia: natural maple candy; Wild Oats natural vanilla crème sandwich cookies (www.wildoats.com); many brands of uncoloured vanilla ice-creams.

Warning: Since September 2001, residents in the US have been warned to eat only very well cooked eggs because of the risk of Salmonella due to overcrowding. This means no more licking the bowl while making a cake, no soft-boiled eggs, eggs fried sunny-side up, softly scrambled or in omelettes and French toast. Avoid home-made mayonnaise and ice-cream with eggs. Some of these recipes are not suitable for US eggs.

15 Checklist of common mistakes

If the diet isn't working as well as you expected, you need to talk to someone experienced who will check every item for you. If your dietitian won't do it, you are welcome to email me with a list of everything you eat in a typical day (sdengate@ozemail.com.au), but read the list below first. It is common for me to pick up at least five mistakes – just one mistake is enough to spoil the diet.

Not only foods
Prescription or over-the-counter medications, vitamins and supplements containing colours, flavours or preservatives can affect you. Take only permitted vitamins, see p. 183. Look on your CMI (consumer medication information) leaflet or on www.myDr.com.au to find out whether your medication contains additives. Coloured (even pale pink) toothpaste is not permitted.

Cheating
Do not cheat. If you feel there is something you cannot live without, it is sure to be affecting you. The first rule of food intolerance is: *if you like it you can't have it*. Don't think you are getting away with it because you don't see a reaction – *most* effects of food chemicals are hidden. One woman allowed herself a cup of tea (high salicylates) every day thinking her migraines would be due to amines. Wrong. They were related to salicylates.

Mistakes

Mistakes can occur through eating too many salicylates or amines; buying a food which contains an unlisted additive; allowing too many treats; or eating too much of a healthy food which affects you (such as dairy foods or wheat).

Flavours

As soon as you realise that the diet isn't working, **cut out all commercial products containing 'flavour'**, including yoghurts, custard, flavoured soymilk, biscuits, ice-cream, caramels, toffees and other sweets. Even permitted treats such as Nestlé Rice Bubble Treats (LCMs) and Darrell Lea white jelly beans can affect some children. Home cooking is safer but avoid vanilla. Artificial and natural flavours (e.g. natural fruit flavours) and even natural vanilla (limit, 2 drops per day) can cause problems. White marshmallows other than Pascalls (limit 4 per day) contain too much artificial flavour.

Unlabelled or illegal additives

It is not enough to read labels. Ask about all unpackaged and restaurant foods. If you don't trust your butcher, avoid mince (possible sulphites), buy from a big supermarket, or make your own. Quiz the bakery about your bread (p. 202). Avoid bread with vinegar.

Too many salicylates

If you come from a food intolerant family, salicylates are very likely to be a problem. You will never find out how much until you cut them all out. Ignore well-meaning relatives, doctors and even some dietitians who say 'but an apple (or a carrot) a day won't hurt you'. It will. Worrying about nutrition is counter-productive in the first three weeks. Your most urgent need is to get rid of the food chemicals and the cravings. Stick strictly to the low salicylate list. You won't see a reaction to one apple or one carrot – or even a regular intake of high salicylate items such as avocadoes – but you won't get the improvement you want, either. Or, you will see an improvement but after a while the effects will build up and you'll be back where you started. If you are worried about nutrition, take *permitted supplements only*, see p. 183, and eat permitted vegetables.

Pear juice is not failsafe

Pear juice is *not* failsafe because commercial pear juice contains the peel. Pears canned in juice instead of syrup, including handy little containers for lunchboxes, are *not* permitted (there are some in syrup, see Franklins). Pears and equivalent products (fresh, tinned, puréed, jam and ketchup) are limited to 2 per day, less for some people. Pears must be peeled, ripe, soft and juicy. A few people are *extremely* sensitive to salicylates and cannot tolerate *any* pear products or lemon juice-flavoured products (e.g. bottled not canned Schweppes lemonade, normally limited to 150 ml per week). Note that 7Up used to be failsafe but now contains benzoate preservative.

Mint or herbal flavoured toothpaste

Products like McLeans toothpaste are not permitted. If you can't get Soul Pattinson's plain, use salt. One little boy improved beautifully for two weeks on the diet, then slowly started to get worse. By three weeks he was back to pre-diet behaviour. His family had switched to a new non-failsafe toothpaste at the beginning of the third week. (After the elimination diet, you might manage Colgate white regular, rinse well, no sucking on the toothbrush). Herbal toothpastes such as fennel from health food stores are definitely not failsafe. All herbs contain salicylates.

Natural colour annatto (160b)

This colour is now in a very wide range of foods including low fat 'health' foods (to make them look creamy), most vanilla flavoured dairy foods such as yoghurt and ice-cream, as well as cheese slices, frozen ovenbake chips and a wide variety of other processed foods. Since it usually causes next day grumpiness, people don't realise it affects them.

Antioxidants (310–312, 319–321)
These are used to preserve fats and oils and are not always listed on the label. They are likely to be in any product which contains fats or 'vegetable oil' or specific oils like canola or sunflower oil (300–309 are failsafe). The effect is related to dose. **Avoid any commercial product containing any kind of vegetable oil**, vegetable shortening, vegetable fat, beef fat or tallow unless you are absolutely certain there are no antioxidants (see labelling loophole p. 240). Nearly all oils in New Zealand contain these additives. Ask our Auckland contact for alternatives.

Hot chips and potato crisps
Commercial hot chips can contain sulphites and will always contain harmful antioxidants. Make your own. Some crisps are failsafe (Kettle brand and Colvan). Watch out for 160b in ovenbake chips.

Sulphites in gelatine
Gelatine contains sulphur dioxide. You can drive this preservative off by dissolving gelatine in boiling water. Extra sensitive people will need to avoid gelatine (and glucose syrup).

Peters Lemonade Icypoles
The recipe has changed. Avoid.

Commercial cashew paste
Paste must be made from raw cashews only (*not* roasted).

Ingredient changes in commercial products
Beware, manufacturers can change ingredients at any time. Soymilks and margarines are a constant problem. Read the labels carefully. Join the newsletter list to learn about changes and check Product Updates on the website.

Don't combine failsafe with other interventions
Most medications can interfere with the diet, especially in coloured or flavoured syrup form. Likewise, remedies from naturopaths. If they say their herbal remedies and vitamins are

low-salicylates, they have a different definition of salicylates. Echinacea is just one herbal remedy which has been associated with a wide range of reactions from behaviour to asthma. Some diagnostic eye drops cause reactions. Your dentist will probably use the wrong kind of toothpaste (take your own). Plaque disclosing tablets contain artificial colours. Worm your kids before you start the diet. Do not try to combine a candida diet and failsafe. Your efforts are more likely to be successful if you get failsafe 100 per cent right.

Don't believe everything you read on the internet
Cranberry juice is *not* failsafe. There are many so called low salicylate lists which are not correct.

Carob
Many children react to carob buttons which contain 'flavours'. You can buy unflavoured buttons in some health food stores. Some people react to some brands of carob powder, e.g. from Turkey which is more bitter, tastes faintly of cinnamon and can have black flecks in it.

Rotisseried chicken with seasoning or stuffing
It is *not OK* to eat the meat and avoid the seasoning.

Natural fruit flavours
Avoid flavours in vitamins or children's syrup medications, e.g. such as paracetamol, and cold medications and chewable vitamin tablets.

Herbal remedies and supplements
If products contain herbs, they contain salicylates. Avoid. Fish oil supplements contain amines. Avoid. Take only failsafe supplements. You can challenge others later.

Accidental or deliberate mistakes
For example, Vegemite, hot chips, takeaways. This diet will not work unless it is followed strictly. You can try hot chips as a challenge after you have sorted out the salicylates and amines.

'Mistakes' at school

Is your child sneaking food at school? One desperate family tried the diet unsuccessfully three times before they discovered their daughter had been eating food such as coloured snakes at school nearly every day. Some children do better at home for three weeks while doing the diet, which is how police achieved success with juvenile offenders in the Shipley project (p. 243).

Whole grain wheat cereals, biscuits and bread

Some children react badly to wholewheat grains but can tolerate refined wheat flour and products. Limit to two Weet-Bix every second day or if no improvement, avoid. If you are worried about fibre, try rolled oats and Country Life Rye bread or Brumby's Bavarian Rye.

Raw sugar, dark brown sugar

White, soft brown, icing and caster sugars are failsafe. Raw sugar and dark brown sugar coloured with molasses contain salicylates and molasses contains sulphites. Avoid commercial products which contain raw sugar or dried cane syrup (soymilk, cereals). Maple syrup is safer than golden syrup.

Cold-pressed or expeller-pressed oil

These contain salicylates. The only safe cold-pressed oil is soy. Watch for other cold pressed oils in soymilk.

Whey powder (natural calcium propionate)

Whey powder when fermented can contain natural calcium propionate. You can't tell from the label. Avoid whey powder in bread and croissants or don't eat them every day. It is OK in ice-cream and other dairy products.

Too many amines

Amines build up due to ageing and handling. Be careful with storage and handling of meats and fish, see rules on p. 191.

Fermented products
Fermentation produces amines. Failsafe lists show that fermented products like wine, beer, soy sauce, tempeh and miso are not permitted but be careful also of sauerkraut, natural strong yoghurt and yeast-free breads – these are made by a long rising process which encourages fermentation. Note that bakers' yeast is failsafe, candida is not an issue for failsafers, and yeasted bread is more failsafe than yeast-free bread.

Fetta cheese is not failsafe!
My apologies, this is a mistake in *Fed Up*.

For people in the USA
Cornflour means corn starch: refined white starch from corn. This is failsafe. A flour from corn (cornmeal) which is yellow is not failsafe.

You may need to exclude more foods
People with severe symptoms of any kind (health, behaviour, learning) may have to avoid dairy foods, soy and/or wheat or gluten. A relative with coeliac disease or irritable bowel is a warning sign for the latter. One mother had been doing the diet with what she considered success for two years but still received complaints from school. When her sister was diagnosed as a coeliac, she removed gluten from her son's diet and he became a completely different person. Some people also need to exclude foods like eggs.

For people who are gluten free
Malt contains gluten so beware of cereals and soymilks containing malt. Also watch for cornflour in commercial products – assume it is wheaten cornflour, unless otherwise specified, in marshmallows, honeycomb confectionery and baking powder except Ward's. Even toast crumbs in jam can affect very sensitive gluten responders. When eating out avoid gravies, sauces and anything with thickener see the gluten-free chapter in the *Failsafe Cookbook*.

Sulphites in gluten-free flours

Understand that many gluten-free flours contain traces of sulphites which can affect some sensitive people with a range of symptoms from behaviour to asthma to headaches to irritable bowel. If you are not improving, avoid tapioca, arrowroot, potato flours and cornflour and stick to rice, rice cakes, rice flour and buckwheat for a few weeks.

Extra sensitivity

Some extra sensitive people react to cashews, potatoes, rice, gelatine, citric acid; it's not common, but it happens. A few people react to Kettle chips but can manage Colvan chips. Sunflower oil is safer than canola for these people. Many people report that more than one cup of decaf coffee a day is too much. If you are not improving and don't know why, don't eat these foods every day.

Extra salicylate sensitivity

Some (low) salicylate vegetables are lower than others. Vegetables with a salicylate rating of zero are: bamboo shoots, fresh green cabbage, fresh celery, red and brown dried lentils and chickpeas, iceberg lettuce, large white potatoes thickly peeled and swedes. Of the rest chokoes are the lowest, followed by chives, shallots, green peas (although they do contain some glutamates), mung bean sprouts, Brussels sprouts, leeks and red cabbage.

Don't confuse shallots (green onions) with spring onions

Names vary. See illustration, the ones on your right are failsafe.

Challenges

Challenges can be inconclusive if the dose isn't big enough. For salicylates, you should consume at least six serves every day for a week of recommended foods, e.g. 150 ml of apple juice, 1 cup strawberries and other high salicylate-only fruits, 1 packet of Lifesavers etc. For amines, 2–3 large ripe bananas and 60–120 grams of dark chocolate plus other amine containing foods such as canned tuna, chocolate drinks.

Exposure to environmental chemicals

Avoid environmental chemicals such as paints, food dyes in playdough and preschool paints on skin, household cleaners, air fresheners, workplace chemicals, and perfumes in cosmetics, soaps, shampoos, deodorants and washing powders. Avoid garden pesticides and weedkillers, pesticides on pets, or smells of new or newly cleaned soft furnishings and carpets, new mattresses, cars, formaldehydes in pet shops and shopping malls. Some people are more sensitive than others. Do not renovate your house, have your carpet cleaned, buy new furniture or a new car while doing this diet. People with chemical overexposure may be more sensitive to pesticides on vegetables than to salicylates, others are the opposite. Organic vegetables are higher in salicylates.

Exposure to smells

As above, plus the smell of strong spicy foods, vinegar, lawn clippings and strong smelling plants – herb plants, strongly fragrant flowers, eucalypts, e.g. 'peppermint' gum, pine trees particularly if freshly cut as in Christmas trees, or in wood burning stoves as logs or smoke.

Too much stress

For children, this can come from confrontational parenting or teaching styles. Make your failsafe children feel they are loved and you are on their side. Once the diet has kicked in, watch the *1–2–3 Magic* video (p. 253).

Consider also non-food factors

Absent fathers, moving house, a new baby, bullying, criticism, punishment or lack of friends can all have adverse affects on the diet. In particular, I recommend starting the diet after you have moved house. Children on the diet need love, praise, exercise and lots of time with parents.

This checklist is updated regularly on the website, www.fedupwithfoodadditives.info.

It also has hints for those with extreme sensitivity to salicylates and amines.

The 5 per cent labelling loophole

If the amount of an ingredient in a food is less than 5 per cent of the food (such as 4 per cent sunflower oil added to soymilk, crackers, ovenfry chips or one of the vegetable oils used in a blended butter), a food additive such as BHA (320) in that ingredient does not have to be listed on the ingredients label. However, if you eat that additive every day, you may be affected. For this reason, unless the product is on the shopping list, you must phone the manufacturer's hotline and ask which antioxidants are used in the vegetable oil, or see my website. Ascorbates and tocopherols (300–309) are failsafe; gallates (310–312), TBHQ (319), BHA (320) and BHT (321) are not.

Notes and references

The abstracts of many of the articles mentioned below can be found in a medical database which has indexed 14 million articles dating from the 1960s: www.PubMed.com. There is also a huge amount of information available by doing a Google search. For example, www.google.com, search for: ADHD 'famous people' will turn up lists of famous people thought to have had ADHD.

Introduction

p. ix 'drug companies which spend millions': $1 million a day in Australia, $100 million a day in the US – Moynihan R, 'Sweetening the pill', *Sydney Morning Herald Good Weekend*, 31/5/2003, 18–23.

p. ix 'co-sponsored by the food industry': Jacobson FJ and Schardt D, *Diet, ADHD and behaviour: a quarter-century review*, Center for Science in the Public Interest, 1999, Washington DC, p. iii; the 40-page report can be downloaded from www.cspinet.org.

p. ix Isle of Wight study: *Do food additives cause hyperactivity and behaviour problems in a geographically defined population of 3-year-olds?* MAFF Project Code FS3015, reported in 'Additives do cause temper tantrums', *The Food Magazine*, 2002, issue 59, 1–3, see http://ourworld.compuserve.com/homepages/foodcomm/latest2.htm.

p. x 'nearly 60 per cent': a two week study by Southampton University's Professor Jim Stevenson, funded and filmed by ITV. All the pupils of one class – including one of a set of identical twins – at the Dingle School Cheshire ate additive-free foods at school and home for two weeks. Nearly 60 per cent of parents noted an improvement. Professor Stevenson found the additive-free twin's score had improved 15 per cent more than his brother, see http://news.bbc.co.uk/1/hi/health/2984519.stm and www.itv.com/news/1248567.html.

p. x 'Amines may be associated with . . . aggressive behaviours': in my experience, amines often provoke aggression in some children even when salicylates provoke silly or hyperactive behaviour in the same child. This observation seems to be backed up by studies showing that altered functioning of an enzyme which breaks down amines has been associated with impulsive and aggressive behaviour in animals and children with conduct problems: Lawson DC and others, 'Association analysis of Monoamine Oxidase A and attention deficit hyperactivity disorder', *Am J Med Genet* 2003;116 (1 Suppl):84–89.

p. x   'nearly one child in five': Greater Boston Physicians for Social Responsibility, *In Harm's Way: Toxic Threats to Child Development* which can be downloaded from http://psr.igc.org/ihw.htm.

p. xii   'third highest use of . . . ADHD medication': Berbatis CG and others, 'Licit psychostimulant consumption in Australia, 1984–2000: international and jurisdictional comparison', *Med J Aust* 2002;177(10):539–543.

1 Rebecca 0–2

p. 11   Box: informal notes from a presentation by Dr William G Crook to the American Academy of Otolaryngic Allergy, Kansas City, 27/9/1991.

p. 11   'American child-rearing book': Sears W, *Creative Parenting*, Melbourne, Dove Communications, 1982.

p. 12   'Australian researchers': Rowe KS and Rowe KL, 'Synthetic food colouring and behaviour', *Journal of Pediatrics* 1994; 125:691–698.

2 Beyond the terrible twos

p. 27   No child reacts only to food colouring: Buist R, *Food Chemical Sensitivity*, Sydney, Harper and Row, 1987.

p. 29   *1 – 2 – 3 Magic*: www.thomasphelan.com.

p. 34   Pritikin diet: www.pritikin.com; see also Australian website: http://members.ozemail.com.au/~jdukes.

p. 39   Brain-gym: www.braingym.com.

3 School and learning delays

p. 47   American Psychiatric Association, *Diagnostic and Statistical Manual of Mental Disorders*, 4th Edition Text Revision (DSM-IV-TR), Washington DC, APA, 2000.

p. 48   'low level toxic exposures . . . can be passed down': Daly HB, 'Laboratory rat experiments show consumption of Lake Ontario salmon causes behavioral changes', *J Great Lakes Res* 1993; 19(4):784–788.

p. 48   'Experts now think': Colborn and others, *Our stolen future*, London, Abacus, 1997; see also www.ourstolenfuture.org.

p. 54   'Australian book about ADHD': Serfontein G, *The Hidden Handicap*, Sydney, Simon and Schuster, 1990.

p. 57   'salicylate-induced hypoglycemia': Raschke R and others, 'Refractory hypoglycemia secondary to topical salicylate intoxication', *Arch Intern Med* 1991;151(3):591–593.

p. 61   Criteria for Oppositional Defiant Disorder from DSM IV, on many internet sites such as www.behavenet.com/capsules/disorders/odd.htm; management: Rey JM, 'Treating oppositional defiant disorder', *Australian Doctor*, 4/9/1998, s3–7.

p. 61   '*Shipley Project*': Bennett CPW and others, 'The Shipley Project: treating food allergy to prevent criminal behaviour in community settings', *J Nutr Environ Med* 1998;8:77–83; filmed by the BBC as part of *Little Monsters* in which eight chronic juvenile offenders turn into 'little angels' within three weeks of starting the diet.

p. 61   'violent approach can aggravate': adolescents with Conduct Disorder or ODD have brain activation patterns in response to violence that are different from non-aggressive adolescents: Mathews V, 'Violent video games trigger unusual brain activity in aggressive adolescents', presentation to the annual meeting of the Radiological Society of North America, 2/12/2002.

4 Matthew's year

p. 69   'flippers to floppers', in Serfontein, see notes for p. 54.

p. 72   'stories of illiterate adults': '*The Haunted Man*' by Gary Smith, *Reader's Digest*, September 1991.

p. 80   'system of credit points': Barkley RA, *Defiant Children*, New York, Guildford Press, 1987.

p. 81   'poem about . . . nuns': 'Sister Stephanie and the Gang' from *Sister Madge's Book of Nuns* by Doug MacLeod, Adelaide, Omnibus Books, 1986.

p. 86   'Adelaide survey': Brown GM, Calcium Propionate Analysis, Food Laboratories (Aust), shown on *Today Tonight*, Channel 7, Adelaide, South Australia, April 1999.

p. 86   preservative-free bread: see www.brumbys.com.au and www.bakersdelight.com.au.

p. 86   'FSANZ . . . "a small number" of consumers': personal communication in a letter from ANZFA acting managing director, 31/3/2000. Included with the letter was the 'Facts on Foods' information sheet from the Australian Food and Grocery Council which described food intolerance as affecting 5–10% of the population.

p. 91   '50 Tips for ADD Adults': well worth reading, from *Driven to Distraction* by Drs Edward M Hallowell and John J Ratey, New York, Pantheon Books, 1994, pp. 244–254 or on numerous internet sites, www.google.com search: 50 tips ADD adults.

5 Howard the adult

p. 98   Meditation: Lazar SW and others, 'Functional brain mapping of the relaxation response and meditation', *Neuroreport* 2000;11(7):1581–1585.

6 The big answer

p. 106   'State-dependent learning': first mention of methylphenidate in Swanson JM and Kinsbourne M, 'Stimulant-related state-dependent learning in hyperactive children', *Science* 1976; 192(4246):1354–1357.

p. 107   'side effects included . . . growth suppression': Poulton A and Cowell CT, 'Slowing of growth in height and weight on stimulants: a characteristic pattern', *J Paediatr Child Health* 2003;39(3):180–185.

p. 107   'no evidence for the long-term effectiveness of ADHD medication': Schachter HM and others, 'How efficacious and safe is short-acting methylphenidate for the treatment of attention-deficit disorder in children and adolescents?' *CMAJ* 2001;165(11): 1475–1488. Free through www.PubMed.com.

p. 108   'thoroughly researched': studies using RPAH diet · 1978 – Gibson A and Clancy R, 'An Australian exclusion diet', *Med J Aust* 1:290–292 · 1980 – Gibson A and Clancy R, 'Management of chronic idiopathic urticaria by the identification and exclusion of dietary factors', *Clin Allergy* 10:699–704 · 1991 – Baker GJ and others, 'Bronchospasm induced by metabisulphite-containing foods and drugs', *Med J Aust* 2:614–616 · 1984 – Allen D and others,

'Adverse reactions to foods', *Med J Aust* 141(5):S37–42 · 1985 – Swain A and others, 'Salicylates in foods', *J Am Diet Assoc* 85:950–960; Swain A and others, 'Salicylates, oligoantigenic diets and behaviour', *Lancet*, ii:41–42 · 1986 – Loblay R and Swain A, 'Food intolerance' in Wahlqvist ML and Truswell AS (Editors), *Recent Advances in Clinical Nutrition*, London, John Libbey, 169–177 · 1987 – Allen D and others, 'Monosodium L-glutamate-induced asthma', *J Allergy Clin Immunol* 80(4):530–537 · 1996 – Hodge L and others, 'Assessment of food chemical intolerance in adult asthmatic subjects', *Thorax* 51: 805–809; Clarke L and others, 'The dietary management of food allergy and food intolerance in children and adults', *Australian Journal of Nutrition and Dietetics* 53(3):89–94 · 2002 – Dengate S and Ruben A, 'Controlled trial of cumulative behavioural effects of a common bread preservative', *J Paediatr Child Health* 38(4):373–376; Parker G and Watkins T, 'Treatment-resistant depression: when antidepressant drug intolerance may indicate food intolerance', *Aust NZ J Psychiatry* 36(2):263–265.

7 High school

p. 119   Chronic fatigue: Nijs J and others, 'High prevalence of Mycoplasma infections among European chronic fatigue syndrome patients', *FEMS Immunol Med Microbiol* 2002;34(3):209–214; officially recognised – http://www.ivillagehealth.com/news/infdisease/content/0,,412639_579880,00.html.

p. 120   Homeschoolers: a book by prize winning author and former high school teacher David Guterson, *Family matters: why homeschooling makes sense*, New York, Harcourt Brace, Jovanovich, 1992.

p. 121   Self-control: Goleman D, *Emotional Intelligence*, Bloomsbury, 1996.

p. 127   'learning is the one we most desire': Hillary E, 'My story', *National Geographic*, May 2003, 38–40.

p. 128   Nathan Pritikin: see notes for p. 34.

p. 130   'a supermarket chain': www.iceland.co.uk.

p. 136   'it worked for his gluten intolerance': a newly identified probiotic named lactobacillus GG has been found to be extremely beneficial for antibiotic-induced diarrhoea and other gut problems, see *Fed Up with Asthma*, pp. 120–122. Lactobacillus GG is available in Australia in Vaalia yoghurt. Only the natural flavour is failsafe.

8 The end of the story

p. 137   'our national food regulators': then called NFA, National Food Authority, later ANZFA, Australia New Zealand Food Authority and now FSANZ, Food Standards Australia New Zealand.

p. 138   Bread preservative study: Dengate S and Ruben A, 'Controlled trial of cumulative behavioural effects of a common bread preservative', *J Paediatr Child Health* 2002;38(4):373–376.

p. 139   'new Food Standards Code': December 2002, www.food standards.gov.au.

p. 139   'propionic acidemia . . . identified as a distinct disorder': propionic and methylmalonic acidemias both relate to the same defective enzyme and were originally thought to be the same disorder, first reported in 1961; Hsia YE and others, 'Inherited propionyl-Coa carboxylase deficiency in "ketotic hyperglycinemia" ', *J Clin Invest* 1971;50(1): 127–130.

p. 139   Patricia Stallings' story on the Mothers Against Munchausen's Association (MAMA) website: www.msbp.com.

p. 139   'antifreeze in the baby's blood': Shoemaker JD and others, 'Misidentification of propionic acid as ethylene glycol in a patient with methylmalonic acidemia', *J Pediatr* 1992;120(3):417–421.

p. 140   'propionic acidemia in young rats': Brusque AM and others, 'Effect of chemically induced propionic acidemia on neurobehavioral development of rats', *Pharmacol Biochem Behav* 1999;64(3):529–534.

p. 141   'giving the rats ascorbic acid': Pettenuzzo LF and others, 'Ascorbic acid prevents cognitive deficits caused by chronic administration of propionic acid to rats in the water maze', *Pharmacol Biochem Behav* 2002;73(3):623–629.

p. 141   'propionic acid . . . not very thoroughly researched': WHO toxicological evaluation of propionic acid and its salts at http://www.inchem.org/documents/jecfa/jecmono/v05je16.htm.

p. 145   CSPI review of research: report by Jacobson and Schardt, see notes for p. ix.

pp. 145–146   EEGs and diet: Uhlig T and others, 'Topographic mapping of brain electrical activity in children with food-induced attention deficit hyperkinetic disorder', *Eur J Pediatr* 1997; 156:557–561; Kiefer CH and others, 'Schlafveranderungen bei Kindern mit nahrungsmittelinduziertem hyperkinetischen syndrom', as cited in Jacobson and Schardt, see notes for p. ix.

p. 147   Isle of Wight study: see notes for p. ix.

p. 147   'nearly 60 per cent': see notes for p. x.

p. 147   'four additive-free schools': Barnabas School in Drakes Broughton, Worcestershire, *Additive ban improves class behaviour*; Tywardreath School in Cornwall, *Number is up for pupils tuck'*; Seaford College, West Sussex, *School bans sweets to calm pupils*; New End Primary School in Hampstead, *Junk food ban 'calms pupils'* reports at http://news.bbc.co.uk/2/hi/uk news/england/ 2497133.stm, england/1689566.stm, education/946735.stm and education/2404169.stm, respectively.

p. 148   'as long ago as 1980': Swanson JM and Kinsbourne M, 'Food dyes impair performance of hyperactive children on a laboratory learning test, *Science* 1980;207:1485–1487.

p. 148   'Johnny can't read': NY Times advertisement and scientific background paper about chemicals including chlorpyrifos available at www.childenvironment.org.

p. 148   'no safe level of exposure': Canfield RL and others, 'Intellectual impairment in children with blood lead concentrations below 10 microg per deciliter', *New England J Med* 2003; 348(16):1517–1526.

p. 149   Organophosphate and similar pesticides – diazinon, malathion and carbamates including carbaryl: Landrigan P and others, *Raising Healthy Children in a Toxic World*, Rodale Press, 2002.

p. 149   'University of Arizona researchers': Guillette E and others, *An anthropological approach to the evaluation of preschool children exposed to pesticides in Mexico*, as seen in documentary *Playing with Poison* (http://www.bullfrogfilms.com/catalog/play.html) and reported in the paper by Greater Boston Physicians for Social Responsibility, *In Harm's Way: Toxic Threats to Child Development*, which can be downloaded from http://psr.igc.org/ihw.htm.

p. 150   Box: Slimak K, *Reduction of autistic traits following dietary intervention and elimination of exposure to environmental substances* in Proceedings of 2003 International Symposium on Indoor Air Quality and Health Hazards, National Institute of Environmental Health Sciences, USA, and Architectural Institute of Japan, Jan 8–11, 2003, Tokyo, Japan, Vol 2, pp. 206–216, see www.special foods.com.

p. 150   'eat a wise diet': this includes avoiding food additives and eating organic food, see Landrigan (note for p. 148). Organic fruit and vegetables can sometimes be higher in salicylates than their supermarket counterparts.

9 Which foods affect your child's behaviour?

pp. 155–158   Food intolerance symptoms, see notes for p. 108, 'thoroughly researched'.

p. 158   'Bedwetting' and 'Daytime incontinence': Egger J and others, 'Effects of diet treatment on enuresis in children with migraine or hyperkinetic behavior', *Clin Pediatr* (Phila) 1992;31(5):302–307.

p. 158   'Nystagmus': 'a variety of neurologic and neuromuscular disturbances (grand mal, petit mal, psychomotor seizures; La Tourette syndrome; autism; retardation; the behavioural component of Down's syndrome; and oculomotor disturbances) may be induced by [food] chemicals' in Feingold BF, 'Dietary management of nystagmus', *J Neural Transmission* 1979;45:107–115.

p. 158   Rowe and Rowe 1994, see notes for p. 12.

10 Challenges

p. 166   'amines can be associated with aggression': see notes for p. x.

11 Managing the diet

p. 170   '[medication] can trigger the anxiety': Parker G and Watkins T, 'Treatment-resistant depression: when antidepressant drug intolerance may indicate food intolerance', *Aust NZ J Psychiatry* 2002;36(2):263–265.

p. 172   Aylesbury prison study: Gesch CB and others, 'Influence of supplementary vitamins, minerals and essential fatty acids on the antisocial behaviour of young adult prisoners', *Br J Psychiatry* 2002;181:22–28.

p. 172   'benefits of megavitamins': Kaplan B and others, 'Treatment of mood lability and explosive rage with minerals and vitamins: two case studies in children', *J Child Adol Psychopharm* 2002; 12(3):205–219.

p. 172   'How safe is soy?': Randerson J, 'Warning against soya for infants', *New Scientist*, 17/5/2003, 10.

p. 173   'meditation is more effective': Flanagan O, 'The colour of happiness', *New Scientist*, 24/5/2003, 44.

p. 173   'stroking your pet can double natural substances': 'Stroking your pet can double endorphins, dopamine and prolactin, and reduce your blood pressure', *New Scientist*, 19/4/2003, 19.

p. 173   'very preterm babies': researchers studying the effectiveness of medications to prevent neurological deficits in very preterm babies found that sulphite-free corticosteroids were effective, corticosteroids containing sulphites were not. Tests confirmed the neurotoxicity of sulphites. Researchers warned 'injectible dexamethasone should be used with caution during the perinatal period' – Baud O and others, 'Neurotoxic effects of fluorinated glucocorticoid preparations on the developing mouse brain: role of preservatives', *Pediatr Res* 2001; 50(6):706–711; full free text at www.pedresearch.org.

p. 174   'growth suppression': see notes for p. 107.

p. 174   'psychotic symptoms': Cherland E and Fitzpatrick R, 'Psychotic side effects of psychostimulants', *Can J Psychiatry* 1999; 44(8):811–813.

p. 174   'no evidence that . . . effective in the long term': Schachter HM and others, 2001, see notes for p. 107.

p. 174   'causes liver cancer in mice': Jacobson and Schadt, 1999, p. 14, see notes for p. ix.

p. 174   Antidepressants: transcript of BBC *Panorama* program, 'The secrets of Seroxat', first shown on ABC *Four Corners* 28/4/2003 as 'The hazards of the happy pill', see http://news.bbc.co.uk/1/shared/spl/hi/programmes/panorama/transcripts/seroxat.txt.

p. 174   'drugs are a lifesaver and others . . . made their lives worse': Else L, 'Power to the patients!', *New Scientist* 2003;179 (2410):40–44.

p. 174   'teenagers committing suicide': Healy DH, Correspondence between Dr David Healy and the Medicines Control Agency, www.socialaudit.org.au/58000-00.htm, letter to the CAM dated 4/11/1999; Healy D, 'Lines of evidence on the risks of suicide with selective serotonin reuptake inhibitors', *Psychother Psychom* 2003; 72(2):71–79.

p. 174   Akathisia: Hamilton MS and Opler LA, 'Akathisia, suicidality, and fluoxetine', *J Clin Psychiatry* 1992:53(11):410–416.

p. 175   'risk is highest': Cameron D and Jackson A, 'The pill that killed', *Sydney Morning Herald*, 26/05/2001, see http://old.smh.com.au/news/0105/26/review/review3.html, accessed 22/5/2003; Thompson A, 'Paxil maker held liable in murder/ suicide', *Lawyers Weekly USA*, 9/7/2001, see http://www.baumhedlundlaw.com/media/ssri/Paxil_murder.htm.

p. 175   'discontinuation symptoms': see www.QuitPaxil.org.

p. 180   'Antibiotics are no longer recommended for ear infections': Del Mar C and Glasziou P, 'A child with earache', *Aust Fam Phys* 2002;31(2):141–144. See *Fed Up with Asthma*, pp. 74–75.

p. 181   'Most people will get well': Werner D, 'Where there is no doctor', *Oxfam Village Health Care Handbook*, MacMillan, many editions.

p. 181   'fever is the body's way to heal itself': Kluger MJ and others, 'The adaptive value of fever', *Infect Dis Clin North Am* 1996; 10(1):1–20.

p. 185   '50 Tips for ADD adults': see notes for p. 91.

12 Foods to eat, foods to avoid

The food tables are based on the research at RPAH hospital, see notes for p. 108, as well as my own experiences during ten years following, working with and researching the failsafe diet.

14 Failsafe recipes

p. 230   Eggs in the USA: Ackerman J, 'Food: how safe?', *National Geographic* 2002;201(5):2–52.

15 Checklist of common mistakes

p. 236   Shipley project: see notes for p. 61.

Support and further information

The Food Intolerance Network provides:
- failsafe email newsletters
- failsafe email discussion groups (regional and international)
- failsafe support groups
- support phone numbers
- contact details for failsafe friendly dietitians
- local information about failsafe foods such as bread and sausages
- recipes
- information about latest research

Website: www.fedupwithfoodadditives.info.

Contact us: confoodnet@ozemail.com.au (to join the mailing lists or groups or for information about failsafe-friendly health professionals) and sdengate@ozemail.com.au (for questions and feedback). If you don't have a computer, ask your librarian or a friend how to print out the 'Contacts' and 'Product Updates' pages.

Phone contacts: Brisbane, Jan 07 3264 4265 • Canberra, Sheryl 02 6294 1720 • Darwin, Erica 08 8927 0121 • Launceston, Megan 03 6382 2561 • Melbourne, Jenny 03 9740 5645 • Perth, Ingrid 08 9248 2147 • Sydney, Karyn, 02 9546 8257 • **New Zealand** • Auckland, Linda 09 416 9438 • Christchurch, Robin 03 312 8824 • see website for more.

Further information

The Failsafe Cookbook by Sue Dengate, Random House, 2001, contains failsafe recipes and suggestions for every occasion.

Fed Up by Sue Dengate, Random House, 1998, details how food can affect children's health, learning ability and behaviour.

Fed Up with Asthma by Sue Dengate, Random House, 2003, looks at the effects of food chemicals on asthma, additives and salicylates in drugs, how to avoid specific additives, and preventing allergy and intolerance in babies and young children.

The Simplified Elimination Diet and ***Salicylates, Amines and MSG*** are available as a set of two booklets from your dietitian or from the Royal Prince Alfred Hospital Allergy Unit at $7 a set. Ask for an order form or send your money with your name and address and the name and address of your doctor. Booklets will be sent to your doctor. The RPAH's cookbook, ***Friendly Foods*** by Dr Swain and others, Sydney, Murdoch Books, 1991, is available from bookstores or from the RPAH Allergy Unit, Suite 210, 100 Carillon Avenue, Newtown NSW 2042, (allergy@email.cs.nsw.gov.au). The failsafe diet is based on the ongoing research of Dr Anne Swain, Dr Velencia Soutter and Dr Robert Loblay of the Allergy Unit. This group and their publications act as a resource to dietitians around the world.

New Additive Code Breaker by Maurice Hanssen, Lothian, 2002.

Fast Food Nation by Eric Schlosser, Penguin, 2001 – a gripping inside look at methods of fast food manufacture, you'll never want to eat it again.

Hitchhiking through Asperger Syndrome by Lise Pyles, London and Philadelphia, Jessica Kingsley Publishers, 2002. The story of a mother who gave up a well-paid career to homeschool her Asperger's son when all else failed; an inspiring read packed with useful management suggestions.

Raising healthy children in a toxic world by Dr Philip Landrigan and others, Emmaus Pennsylvania, Rodale Press, 2001, a practical book by the Director of the Center for Children's Health and the Environment, see www.childenvironment.org.

The Toxic Playground by Jo Immig, Sydney, Total Environment Centre, 2000, see www.tec.nccnsw.org.au.

1-2-3 Magic is the easiest and most effective behaviour management program. It is available as an expensive and very funny US video or as a much cheaper book, see www.thomas phelan.com or in Australia www.silvereye.com.au.

The Explosive Child by Ross W Greene, New York, Harper Collins, 2001, see www.explosivechild.com.

Websites

Australian Breastfeeding Association: www.breastfeeding. asn.au.

Center for Science in the Public Interest: www.cspinet.org.

Alternatives to harmful chemicals in this game-style website: www.checnet.org.

Chemical sensitivity: www.asehaqld.org.au.

Information about prescription drugs: www.myDr.com.au, www.my.webMD.com.

Movement for young children: www.gymbaroo.com.au.

Homeschooling: http://www.gomilpitas.com/homeschooling/ regional/australia.htm.

Learning programs

Davis Dyslexia Correction Program, www.dyslexia.com, and *The Gift of Dyslexia* by Ronald Davis New York, Berkley Publishing Group, 1997.

Right brained children in a left-brained world by Jeffrey Freed and Laurie Parsons, Simon and Schuster, 1997, also helpful for senior skills such as essay writing, see www.jeffreyfreed.com, available in Australia from www.silvereye.com.au.

Irlen Dyslexia Centres (if different coloured cellophane overlays help your child to read), see http://www.newcastle. edu.au/centre/sed/irlen/.

Learning Connections (Brisbane): www.learningconnections. com.au.

Barbara Pheloung's movement program: www.movetolearn. com.au.

Reading Writing national hotline referral service for adults; 1-300 6 555 06

ADHD Support groups

ACT: Canberra and Queanbeyan ADHD support group, phone 02 6290 1984, www.addact.org.au.

NSW: Sydney, Hyperactivity Attention Deficit Association, 02 411 2186; Central Coast, RAISE Network support group for disabilities, disorders and syndromes, phone 02 4329 5055; Learning Difficulties Coalition, phone 02 9806 9960, www.learningdifficultiescoalition.org.au.

South Australia: Attention Disorders Association of South Australia, 08 8232 0685.

Victoria: Melbourne, ADDVIC, phone 03 9890 2144; Bendigo, phone 03 5442 7897.

Index